Studies in Anglican History

Series Editor
Peter W. Williams, Miami University

Sponsored by the Historical Society
of the Episcopal Church

Books in the Series

The Education of Phillips Brooks
John F. Woolverton

Prayer, Despair, and Drama:
Elizabethan Introspection
Peter Iver Kaufman

Accommodating High Churchmen:
The Clergy of Sussex, 1700–1745
Jeffrey S. Chamberlain

Accommodating High Churchmen

Accommodating High Churchmen

The Clergy of Sussex, 1700–1745

Jeffrey S. Chamberlain

University of Illinois Press
Urbana and Chicago

Publication of this book was supported by a grant from the Historical Society of the Episcopal Church.

This book is printed on acid-free paper.

Library of Congress Cataloging-in-Publication Data
Chamberlain, Jeffrey S. (Scott), 1958–
    Accommodating high churchmen : the clergy of Sussex,
1700–1745 / Jeffrey S. Chamberlain.
        p.   cm. — (Studies in Anglican history)
    Includes bibliographical references and index.
    ISBN 0-252-02308-0 (alk. paper)
    1. Church of England—England—Sussex—Clergy—
History—18th century. 2. High Church movement—
England—Sussex—History—18th century. 3. Sussex
(England)—Church history—18th century. 4. Sussex
(England)—Politics and government. I. Title. II. Series.
BX5110.S87C48   1997
283'.4225'09033—dc20   96-25377
                                                   CIP

Series Editor's Preface

Peter W. Williams

Studies in Anglican History is a series of scholarly monographs sponsored by the Historical Society of the Episcopal Church and published by the University of Illinois Press. It is intended to bring the best of contemporary international scholarship on the history of the entire Anglican Communion, including the Church of England and the Episcopal church in the United States, to a broader readership.

Jeffrey S. Chamberlain, who teaches history at the College of Saint Francis in Joliet, Illinois, takes a fresh look in this volume at the disdain that the "Vicar of Bray"—the archetypal "weathercock" clergyman of eighteenth-century England—has received in the past years as an unprincipled political accommodationist. Through a detailed study of the Church of England clergy of Sussex, Chamberlain argues that these clergy did in fact accommodate themselves to the Hanoverian regime, but hardly in an unprincipled fashion. Rather, with the decline of sectarian dissent and with a growing perception that Whigs could in fact make loyal churchmen, they came to realize that they need not remain loyal to the memory of the Stuarts and traditional high churchmanship in order to preserve the best interests of Anglicanism. Based on extensive original research, Chamberlain's work provides much-needed nuance to the unflattering and unfounded clichés that have colored earlier portraits on the Church of England in the Georgian era.

For my parents

Contents

Acknowledgments

Since my debts for this project are legion, I cannot possibly acknowledge them all. The following people, however, were of very special importance in completing it. I am grateful, first of all, to Stephen Taylor of the University of Reading for his gracious help and sponsorship, for his encouragement, and for his expertise, which has challenged me to hone my arguments. John Walsh of Jesus College, Oxford, was no less encouraging. His personal attention, suggestions, and reassurance meant a great deal. I am indebted for the wisdom and guidance of my advisors and readers while this project was in its dissertation phase. As my advisor at the University of Chicago, Ted Cook was gracious with his time and always right on the money with his critiques. Bill Heyck of Northwestern was a joy to work with: as an outside reader, he did far more than he needed to, and his interest and encouragement frequently sustained me. Gerald Brauer and Mark Kishlansky also read the manuscript and contributed rich insights.

There are many people whose knowledge of Sussex history and archival resources were invaluable to me. At the West Sussex Record Office in Chichester I felt that I was among friends. Archivists Peter Wilkinson and Tim and Allison McCann were interested in my project and they cheerfully assisted me time and time again, even when I asked the most elementary of questions. I am particularly grateful to Tim McCann, who treated me more as a friend than a patron. His assistance was invaluable.

At the East Sussex Record Office I depended upon Christopher Whittick and Judith Brent, both of whom were knowledgeable and helpful. Colin Brent, Judith's husband, is a historian of Lewes and East Sussex, and he graciously read the manuscript and gave me suggestions for revising it. I am also indebted to Joyce Crowe, Honorary Librarian at the Sussex Archaeological Society, and all of the staff there, who went out of their way to assist me in my research.

The staffs of libraries and archives I frequented were invariably competent and helpful. These included the British Library (especially the Manuscript Reading Room and the Rare Books Room), the Public Record Office, Dr. William's Library, the Society for the Propagation of Christian Knowledge, the Minet Library (Lambeth Archives), Christ Church Library (Oxford), and the Bodleian Library at Oxford (especially Duke Humphrey's Library).

I am grateful, too, to all those who gave me ideas and helped with sources. Peter Le Fevre was a goldmine of information. His tips paid off time and time again. John Farrant, Paul Monod, Conrad Russell, Jeremy Gregory, Donald Spaeth, Stuart Handley, Jonathan Barry, and Richard Sharp all made suggestions and gave me the benefit of their knowledge and expertise.

I owe a special debt of gratitude to the friends and family who encouraged and supported me. Cathy Patterson was a friend on whom I leaned when I was discouraged while in England. She was also very helpful in providing me with citations from places I was not able to visit. Kathleen Colquhoun, Tom Holien, and Mark Norris are all Americans I met in England who were doing dissertation research at the same time as I was. We became good friends and colleagues. I also deeply appreciate the many people at All Souls Church in London and St. Pancras Church in Chichester who helped and encouraged me. In the States, many others contributed: Jim and Martha Polizzi, Fred Beuttler, John Woodbridge, Steve Cray, Susan Connolly, Paul Glezen, Bill Thompson, April Chamberlain, Reid Chamberlain, and David Jacobson were all of great help in one way or another. I am grateful, too, to the partners and staff of Piser Weinstein Menorah Chapels for providing me with a special "fellowship" that allowed me to complete my graduate studies and the dissertation.

I am indebted to my editor, Peter Williams, for shepherding the manuscript through its various stages. He was always courteous, helpful, and supportive. I owe a debt of gratitude to my colleagues at the College of St. Francis, who are the best friends one could hope to find. They are warm, generous people, and their interest and encouragement have frequently buoyed me. I have, in addition, been frequently assisted by the staff of the Department of Information Services at the College, who have helped me get the computer to do what I wanted it to do.

Finally, my most heartfelt thanks are reserved for my parents, who have sustained me in many ways through every stage of this project. They counseled me with their wisdom, consoled me when difficulties arose, and feted me in my victories. They have always "been there" for me, and, for this reason, I dedicate this book to them.

Abbreviations

ArchW	Archbishop Wake's Papers, Christ Church, Oxford
BL	British Library, London
ESRO	East Sussex Record Office, Lewes
FRE	Frewen Papers, ESRO
KAO	Kent Archives Office, Maidstone
PRO	Public Record Office, London
SAC	*Sussex Archaeological Collections*
SAS	Sussex Archaeological Society, Lewes
SNQ	*Sussex Notes and Queries*
SP	State Papers
SPCK	Society for the Promotion of Christian Knowledge
VCH	*The Victoria History of the County of Sussex*
WSRO	West Sussex Record Office, Chichester

Accommodating High Churchmen

Something happened to the clergy soon after George I's accession to the throne in 1714. Some sea-change had taken place that had affected their sympathies and allegiances, such that they seemed to change their whole orientation. This change seemed so abrupt that contemporaries did not know what to make of it. Frequently, they assumed that clergymen, despite their rhetoric of principle, were weathercocks whose values and allegiances were as fickle as the wind. This was what the Tory candidates standing for the county of Sussex in 1734 puzzled over. It seemed to them that the parsons of the shire, heretofore solidly High Church and Tory, had sold out en masse to the Whigs. The very ones who had feared Whiggish toleration for Dissenters and lamented the Hanoverian accession because it amounted to an overturning of divine-right hereditary succession of the Crown, were now championing their erstwhile nemeses. They were embracing their hated enemies, much to the amazement and distress of the opposition leaders. The Tories simply could not understand what would prompt such a wholesale shift in allegiance.

Thus John Fuller, the Tory candidate, was confused. Once when he stepped into a coffeehouse on one of his campaign rounds, he found Robert Burnett, the Duke of Newcastle's Whig agent, there. After expressing his desire that the campaign be run amicably, Fuller pondered aloud what had been weighing on his mind. He said that he wondered "that there should be such an alteration amongst the Clergey, that when he stood last he had all of them, and now but very few."[1] It was inconceivable to him that such an abrupt and wholesale change could take place within an entire class of men.

On another occasion, the Whig Thomas Spence was riding along the downs on his way to canvass voters in the eastern part of the county when he came upon a rival agent, a Mr. Middleton. Middleton too commented on the apparent transformation of the clergy, and asked his counterpart for some rationale for it. Spence responded simply that churchmen had come to trust the Pelham and Newcastle interest, and no longer felt their views were detrimental to religion and state.[2] This explanation, of course, did not satisfy the Tories. It was still a mystery to them that the clergy had turned away from their principles and had capitulated so completely to the Whigs and their ideals as to offer the latter unswerving support.

In 1741, the Tories were still baffled and dismayed by the eagerness of the clergy to ingratiate themselves to a Whig administration. In that year Lord Middlesex, the son of the Duke of Dorset, stood for Knight of the Shire in a bi-election. Though he was a reputed rake and infidel, he had the support of the Duke of Newcastle and his formidable patronage machine, and he overwhelmed the opposition. Once again the Tories complained of the lack of scruples amongst the clergy. As Thomas Frewen wrote to his clerical cousin, Thankful Frewen, it was inexcusable for Sussex parsons, who seemed to be fawning over Lord Middlesex, to vote for a man who was for repealing the Test Act. He said "I can scarce refrain from Tears to see our native Land in such bondage, and in so dangerous Hands. I think the clergy who were such strenuous Advocates for him [Lord Middlesex] can scarce be reckon'd friends to that Rubrick they have subscribed, For if repealing the Test Act, be not undermining our church & its very foundation; I desire them to tell me what is?"[3] By this comment, Frewen alleged that the political sympathies of the clergy reflected their piety, or lack of it. The entire church was in danger because Sussex churchmen, once keen to preserve the church from all encroachments, were now either oblivious or indifferent to the hazards within and without. Frewen, just like his Tory friends, could not understand what had happened, but he knew that there had been a radical turnabout in the sympathies of the clergy.

What about that change? Was it as extensive as the Tories felt? If so, what caused it? Was it just political expedience—a bid for an interest in preferment? What was really involved in this shift? These are questions central to this book, and they go to the heart of the Anglican religious establishment in England in the eighteenth century.

Historians have by and large accepted the contemporary assessments that there was a massive redirection of clerical sympathies, and they have sought to explain this shift in different ways. Intellectual historians have seen it primarily from a Whig perspective—as a revolution, not only of politics, but of the whole structure of Anglican religion. Clergymen were carried away by the prevailing intellectual milieu of the Enlightenment and wound up, almost overnight, jettisoning classical Anglican views of doctrine and liturgy. It was a quantum leap to a new world of thinking—away from the superstitious, binding dogma of the late medieval period (which continued in the Reformation and Puritan mental worlds) to a rational, enlightened view; away from religion as sacramental mystery to religion as ethics and morality; away from paternalism and hierarchy in society and state to autonomy and egalitarianism; away from conservatism to progressivism; away from the old world and into the new. Thus the eighteenth-century church has been portrayed as qualitatively different from previous generations.

This new attitude, Gerald Cragg and others have asserted, developed on account of several factors. First, there was a weariness of the wars and fighting prompted by religious intolerance. The century and a half after the Reformation had seen a proliferation of competing theologies and persuasions. So wars of religion became endemic, with each faction attempting through force to impose its religious convictions on the rest of the world. Gradually it became clear that this bitter struggle, never decisive in its outcome, could not continue indefinitely. The Thirty Years' War, in particular, soured men as to the possibility of maintaining religious conformity. The only other possibility was toleration. Thus a new indulgent attitude developed.[4]

Second, the new science brought challenges and opportunities. A fascination with this new knowledge emerged in the learned community—a community that was comprised predominantly of clergymen—and efforts to accommodate it to theology were legion. The preoccupation, then, with this scholarship fostered a heightened appreciation for the physical world and an attenuation of the age-old recourse to the supernatural world for explanations and refuge. Thus eighteenth-century divines were more interested in natural revelation than revealed; more concerned with this world than the next.[5]

Third, there was a dawning sense of nobility in man, an awareness of his ability to grow and advance in all that is good, admirable, and exalted. Whereas once man had been thought to be only a wretched sinner and totally depraved, now he was considered a diamond in the rough—flawed, perhaps, but still a diamond, which, when sculpted and polished, would gleam with brilliant luster. Thus Georgian clergymen concentrated on human potential rather than defects. The Fall in the Garden of Eden represented merely a glitch, a hindrance, in man's moral progress rather than a fatal and irrevocable failure that doomed the human race to bondage in sin and degradation. To the "enlightened" clergy, the disease of sin could be cured, with the help of God, by dint of moral reformation.[6]

All of these factors combined to mold a church in England that was markedly different from what had gone before. This new optimistic outlook resulted, ironically, in a church without zeal. It had lost much of the essence of religion and had become a drowsy establishment. Clergymen were animated only by the affairs of this life—they exalted reason in their sermons; pursued riches, pleasure, and status in their careers; and were heedless of the needs of their parishioners. Parson James Woodforde, the clerical diarist who recorded more about his dining habits than his religion, was seen to be paradigmatic for divines in the Age of Reason.[7] Typical of this perspective is the analysis by Cragg, who summed up the Hanoverian Church by saying that

> In outlook it was neither mystical nor otherworldly. It set exaggerated store by moderation, and the qualities it esteemed most highly were temperance, restraint, and reasonableness. It had little sympathy with the more austere virtues and studiously ignored the claims of self denial. It adapted itself all too readily to the tastes of an age which exalted common sense and pursued material prosperity, yet it stoutly resisted the rampant immorality and the rationalist disbelief of a hardbitten society.[8]

Thus the church had been transformed through quaffing the heady drafts of new and progressive ideas. It was intoxicated with the wonder of the dawn of a new era, and in its euphoria it forgot its ties with the past. It sloughed off the traditional emphasis on theology and metaphysics and forged a moral, ethical, this-worldly church. In the process, it lost much of the vitality and strength it had possessed in earlier ages.[9]

Political historians, too, have perceived a shift, but for them this "new-world perspective" came about not with self-conscious resolution or as part of the age of enlightenment, but as an unintended effect of patronage. When the political establishment turned irrevocably Whig at the time of the Hanoverian accession, the clergy tracked with it out of pure self-interest—they swerved and deviated from their long-sacred principles for the sake of status and pecuniary gain. Far from being driven by high-minded ideals, these men acted out of overweening desire for worldly advancement. And in the process they embraced progressive Whig views, and the church was changed forever. Thus they were little more than trimming sycophants, who at the beck and call of their patrons sacrificed all of their beliefs and ideals with little or no compunction.

Though clergymen were frequently castigated for placing interest above principle by contemporaries, it was the followers of Sir Lewis Namier that created a historiographical school based upon the assumption that interest was the primary motivating factor of Hanoverian clergy. Namier pioneered the method of prosopography (a method utilized in this study), and used it to determine the political makeup of the House of Commons at the time of the accession of George III. Patronage and interest became for him the be-all and end-all of political, and perhaps every other element of, life.[10] Though his analysis yielded tremendous insight into the political life of the Hanoverians, it was unbalanced, at least when applied to other periods and aspects of life. Furthermore, his portrayal of the meaning of patronage to the participants of the system was truncated. Patronage was far more than a means of pursuing self-interest: it expressed friendship, loyalty, and principle, as we shall see.

Nevertheless, historians still seem to attribute clerical motivations to self-interest and preferment more than anything else. Thus the shift that has been observed of the clergy in the early part of the eighteenth-century is thought to have come about through the extension of the Whig patronage network—a network that with remarkable speed smothered High Church and Tory sympathy with its lure of preferment. The only clerical pockets of resistance to Whig hegemony came in regions where Tories still clutched the rights of patronage through ownership of advowsons. But as the resources of Tory patrons dwindled, clerical Toryism and High Churchmanship "withered and died of inanition."[11] Thus when the Hanoverians clipped the Tory roots, the High Church died as well.[12]

There is, however, a more recent school of thought that challenges all of the above. This school argues that there was virtually no change at all. This is the position of J. C. D. Clark, who has argued in his *English Society, 1688–1832,* that the ancien regime was alive and well in the eighteenth century, and that, far from being destroyed by the Enlightenment, or the Glorious Revolution, or Whiggism, the three traditional elements of the old world—patriarchalism, monarchism, and Anglican conservatism—continued to dominate society until the time of the Reform Bill in 1832. Though Clark's work has been seen as a watershed in eighteenth-century scholarship, it remains controversial. At the very least, it has generated new interest and new perspectives on the period. Few have seen fit to wholeheartedly endorse Clark's interpretations,[13] but many have been prompted by his works to reevaluate the nature of the Hanoverian Church and society. In fact, many seem to have been working in this direction anyway.[14]

New studies on the church in the eighteenth century are being made, and new perspectives are emerging.[15] But no consensus has yet been attained. Further, it will be impossible to draw an accurate, comprehensive picture of Hanoverian religion without careful local studies. This is the gap that this book intends to fill.

It is, perhaps, because transition is so notoriously difficult to capture on the canvas of history that this change has hitherto been painted in such stark hues. The decline of the High Church undoubtedly occurred more gradually than most accounts (even contemporary accounts) have allowed. Historians have foreshortened the process in their analyses because they have not been able to demonstrate or document the step-by-step nature of the change. Only in a study that charts the development, or lack of it, of individuals through time can the changing nature of society and religion be adequately explored. It is the extent and direction of the evolution (or decline) of the High Church that will be considered in this book.

The nature of these issues is such that they are most profitably examined from the bottom (i.e., the diocesan and parochial level) up. This is so for several reasons. First of all, if the question concerns how extensive the changes were, local parsons must be included, otherwise the majority of the country's five thousand clergymen will be entirely discounted. If parochial clergymen are neglected, therefore, no reasonable estimate can be made for the scope of change.

Second, it is only on this micro-level that the factors that made a difference can be discerned. The bulk of clergymen lived quiet lives with obscure people in out-of-the-way places. Their relationships with friends, family, parishioners, and patrons, not to mention the practical problems of ministry, shaped their thinking at least as much as did the esoteric political, philosophical, or theological theory they learned at university. Their intellectual lives were not segregated from their workaday worlds. A local study, therefore, is the ideal vehicle for combining intellectual and social history and painting a more complete picture of the sympathies and allegiances of clergymen.

Third, the issues of patronage can be analyzed much more fully on the local level. What did patronage mean to the average parson? Did they all bow to the pressure of their patrons, or did some successfully resist? If a rector or vicar capitulated, did that mean that he appropriated the perspective of his patron lock, stock, and barrel? Or was it more complicated than that? The local context is critical if we are to answer these questions. We can also discern from such a microscopic study whether or not those who were within the orbit of the Whig patronage network managed to procure substantially better preferments than those in the opposition.

Local and county studies are not, of course, new. They have been very popular, especially since Alan Everitt published his landmark *The Community of Kent and the Great Rebellion.*[16] But oddly enough, even the ones that focused on the church and the countywide clerical establishment have failed to grapple with these issues and wrest from the data significant conclusions concerning them. More often than not, they have concentrated either on clerical efficiency, the local administrative structure of the church, or the status and living conditions of parsons—all of which are important, but none of which sheds adequate light on the issues at hand.[17]

Part of the reason for this omission in these studies is due, undoubtedly, to the difficulty of finding adequate sources. Diocesan archives for the period are frequently barren of anything but the most perfunctory administrative records. Very little can be determined about the beliefs and feelings of the clergy from this source. Furthermore, few parsons left significant remains of their thoughts—in fact, it was not unusual for these men to have requested in their wills that their sermons be burned upon their deaths, which when carried out, left a lamentable void of information for the historian. In despair, the researcher sometimes yearns even for just a whiff of the smoke ascending from the ashes.

Despite the paucity of official records and manuscript sermons, there are ways of getting at the issue. The diocese of Chichester provides a marvelous opportunity for glimpsing the complexion of the parochial clergy. First of all, there is a relatively complete register of biographical information for the clergy of the diocese compiled by a late-nineteenth/early-twentieth-century antiquarian (E. H. W. Dunkin) and deposited in the British Library.[18] Then there are five poll books from the first third of the eighteenth century, which by themselves would demonstrate whether there was a significant change in political allegiance of the clergy. Furthermore, for the 1734 election and the 1741 election (the latter of which has no poll book since the opposition surrendered at the last moment) there is copious correspondence between the Duke of Newcastle and his agents for the Whig candidates. These contain manifold references regarding the attitudes and actions of the Sussex clergy and offer many insights into their behavior. Supplementing these sources are the Wake Manuscripts,[19] which contain correspondence from and about Chichester parsons, the SPCK letter abstract books,[20] various family papers, clergy wills,[21] and even State Papers.[22] There is, in addition, a fairly extensive amount of printed material—primary works from clergymen who published their sermons or other writings, and secondary articles on many facets of Sussex history brought together in the *Sussex Archaeological Collections.* From these sources, a composite picture of the clergy of the diocese can be drawn, which demonstrates in a new light the forces that were at work in their lives.

As mentioned above, the method used here is prosopography, or collective biography. A database has been carefully assembled from all of the above sources. This database contains entries for each clergyman of the diocese, and it chronicles each man's background, education, livings, patronage, preferment, chaplainships, voting pattern, friendships, kinship, churchmanship, and so on. These data enable the historian to discern patterns not otherwise visible. More information is available for some clergymen than for others, of course, but a general outline is perceptible nonetheless. With the addition of anecdotal material, a fairly detailed, and sometimes highly entertaining, picture emerges.

There is, in addition, the important question of whether or not Sussex was representative. The answer to this must be yes and no. It was probably representative in the sense that clergy everywhere faced the same issues and had the same sensibilities. It was different in the sense that Chichester had far more ducal influence—particularly that of the Duke of Newcastle—than most dioceses, so the pressures and/or opportunities from patronage were probably greater. But regardless of what differences there might have been, this provincial study will yield critical data that can be applied to a greater understanding of social and religious life under the Hanoverians.[23]

This book aims to demonstrate that the clergy did not act only out of selfish desire for preferment or other worldly gain. Though a shift did occur, it was not unprincipled. The thesis proposed here is that the clerical High Church/Tory alliance was broken not so much as a result of shifting religious sympathies or political ideology, as it was because of other occurrences. First of all, the Dissenters were declining rapidly both in numbers and influence. They simply did not pose the threat that they once did, and so the issues of toleration and conformity became non-issues. Second, the clergy of Sussex seemed content with the piety of their Whig patrons. The Pelhams—the Duke of Newcastle, Henry Pelham, and other local family members—gained the support of the county's incumbents because of their reputation as godly men who were not about to let the church be destroyed. Thus the Whigs managed to overturn the High Church/Tory fears, as it had been exemplified earlier in the century in Sacheverell's preaching, by their apparent sincere devotion to the church and its establishment. Third, as old threats to the church diminished, new threats arose that united churchmen in a new way. The new menace was heterodoxy, which, though it had existed prior to the Toleration Act, grew more and more virulent (at least in the minds of the clergy) until it jeopardized the orthodoxy of the establishment. High and Low Churchmen alike fought this new danger side by side, and, though their temperaments were somewhat different and they had different solutions to the problem, they were able to set aside old divisions and join forces against their common enemy.

High-Church sentiment, then, did not just disappear. It did not decline because its proponents grew old and passed from the scene. It did not diminish because patrons "bought" the loyalties of the clergy. It did not go away because it had been superseded by a new spirit of toleration arising from the Enlightenment. Rather, it lost its differentiating force because the issues upon which it was built receded in importance and relevance. As the dangers passed, High Churchmen did, in fact, lose some of their distinctive features and change their outlooks and behaviors, and therefore the church appeared to be significantly different. But the majority of churchmen were still "high" in the preaching and practice of their religion—strong liturgical and sacramental piety still dominated the scene well into the eighteenth century, and parsons were generally as diligent as in most other eras in the history of Anglicanism.

This book, therefore, maps out a new understanding of clerical life, sensibilities, and allegiances. The revised picture imparts key evidence for the reevaluation of the nature of eighteenth-century English society. Thus, though the focus of this study is circumscribed, its ramifications are not. Much is riding on this and other provincial studies—they integrally affect no less than the characterization of an entire age. As it stands, there is much uncertainty about eighteenth-century life, and the historiography appears to be at a turning point. This study traces new contours and dabs fresh colors onto a sizable section of the canvas erected for the revised portrait of Augustan society.

As one High Churchman wrote in the 1750s, "the Changes and Chances of this mortal Life are Sudden and Sundry."[24] Many shifts did indeed occur in the first half of the eighteenth century, and High Churchmen felt them keenly. But the shifts had been not so much intrinsic as extrinsic. The "changes and chances of this mortal life" brought about conditions that were more agreeable and led to the "accommodation of High Churchmen." But this title is a deliberate double entendre, because it was true *both* that High Churchmen accommodated themselves to the changes of this mortal life—to this new world—*and* that the new world accommodated them.

Notes

1. Robert Burnett to Newcastle, August 1733, BL Add. MS. 32,688, ff. 127–28.

2. Thomas Spence to Newcastle, 5 September 1733, BL Add. MS. 32,688, ff. 261–63.

3. ESRO FRE 1302, Thomas Frewen to Thankful Frewen, 29 December 1741.

4. Cragg maintains, in his *Church in the Age of Reason,* that it was the Thirty Years' War, ending with the Peace of Westphalia in 1648, that was the turning point. The problem with this theory is that the church in England was probably *less* tolerant *after* the Restoration (1660) than it was before the Civil War. It suppressed, sometimes ruthlessly, all expressions of diversity. It was only after the Glorious Revolution of 1688 that toleration was granted to dissenters.

5. Richard S. Westfall, *Science and Religion in Seventeenth-Century England* (New Haven: Yale University Press, 1958); Margaret C. Jacob, *The Newtonians and the English Revolution, 1689–1720* (Ithaca: Cornell University Press, 1976); Barbara J. Shapiro, *Probability and Certainty in Seventeenth-Century England* (Princeton: Princeton University Press, 1983).

6. C. John Sommerville, *Popular Religion in Restoration England* (Gainesville: University of Florida Press, 1977), 89–97; Hampson, *The Enlightenment;* Rosalie Colie, *Light and Enlightenment: A Study of the Cambridge Platonists and the Dutch Arminians* (Cambridge: Cambridge University Press, 1957); Cragg, *Reason and Authority.*

7. Sykes, *Church and State in England,* and *From Sheldon to Secker,* 177–87; Blythe, "Introduction" to *A Country Parson,* 9–13; Tindal-Hart, *Eighteenth-Century Country Parson,* 124–27.

8. Cragg, *Church and the Age of Reason,* 140.

9. Davies observes that the Anglican church under the influence of John Tillotson preached "an unequaled combination of eudaemonism, utilitarianism, and pelagianism, masquerading as Christianity." Further, he notes, "The halo and mandorla, the chiaroscura and the mystery" were "all banished in the light of common day" (*Worship and Theology in England* 3:56–57). See also Curtis, *Anglican Moods of the Eighteenth-Century.* Gregory Scholtz charges eighteenth-century Anglicans with supplanting the Reformation doctrine of justification by faith with that of works, making the "conditionality of salvation" the distinguishing mark (or, perhaps, bane) of Augustan theology. "Anglicanism in the Age of Johnson: The Doctrine of Conditional Salvation," *Eighteenth-Century Studies* 22 (Winter 1988–89): 182–207.

10. Namier, *England in the Age of the American Revolution,* especially 173–210, and *Structure of Politics.*

11. Holmes, *Politics, Religion and Society,* 211–12.

12. For recent expositions of this perspective, see Baskerville, "Political Behaviour of the Cheshire Clergy," ; and Langford, "Convocation and the Tory Clergy, 107–22. Triffitt ("Believing and Belonging") demonstrates the way in which Whigs could use politics to overcome Tories, but his study is more about personal conflicts than about churchmanship, and it is doubtful that his conclusions can be considered normative.

13. Those most sympathetic to Clark's thesis are those who work on the conservative elements of society. Monod's *Jacobitism and the English People,* for example, while not accepting Clark's views wholesale, tends toward the same kind of conclusions. Colley's *In Defiance of Oligarchy,* though written before *English Society* and with much more reserve, also emphasizes the conservative nature of society in the period. Eveline Cruickshanks too has for years pointed to the remarkable persistence of Jacobites and other conservative forces. From the perspective of the administration of the church, there is one more voice for the conservative view, and that is Virgin's *Church in an Age of Negligence.* Virgin argues that "The Church of Joseph Butler, of Warburton, of Gibson and of Hoadly was pretty well continuous with the church of Burnet, of Laud, of Andrewes, and even of Hooker; and it was this church which was destined to come face to face with all the difficulties, and all the problems, unavoidable in any society striving to work its way through a period of profound change and equally profound discontent" (3).

14. Because few have adopted Clark's views wholesale, it seems a bit exaggerated to speak of a "Clarkite Revolution," as Sack does in his recent book. See Sack, *From Jacobite to Conservative,* 36.

15. On the implications of the Glorious Revolution, see Grell et al., eds., *From Persecution to Toleration.* On the Hanoverian Church, see the following: Mather, "Georgian Churchmanship Reconsidered," and *High Church Prophet;* John Walsh, Colin Haydon, and Stephen Taylor, eds., *The Church of England c. 1689–c. 1833: From Toleration to Tractarianism* (Cambridge: Cambridge University Press,

1993). The "Introduction" to this last volume, authored by Walsh and Taylor, is one of the best surveys of Georgian Anglicanism available, though it is quite tentative in many places (reflective of the emerging, but yet inchoate, historiography).

16. Everitt was the first to talk of a county as a unit of community. Fletcher continued in this tradition for the county of Sussex with his *County Community in Peace and War.*

17. A partial listing of these includes the following: Pruett, *Parish Clergy under the Later Stuarts;* Tindal-Hart, *Eighteenth-Century Country Parson,* and *Country Counting House;* Addison, *English Country Parson;* Stieg, *Laud's Laboratory;* McClatchey, *Oxfordshire Clergy;* Arthur Warne, *Church and Society;* Evans, "Anglican Clergy of Northern England"; and Viviane Barrie-Curien, "The Clergy in the Diocese of London in the Eighteenth-Century" in Walsh et al., eds., *Church of England,* 86–105.

18. The Dunkin Collection, BL Add. MSS. 39,326–39,546. MS. 32,326 alone is comprised of twenty-five volumes of biographical information on Sussex clergymen.

19. ArchW, Christ Church, Oxford.

20. Housed in the SPCK headquarters, Marylebone Rd., London.

21. Distributed between the Public Record Office, Chancery Lane, London; the West Sussex Record Office, Chichester; and the East Sussex Record Office, Lewes.

22. In the Public Record Office, Chancery Lane, London.

23. The Sussex pattern is distinctive from the one that emerges from Jan Albers's study of the clergy in Lancashire, largely because the structure of society in Lancashire was so different from Sussex. Nevertheless, there are many similarities too. Albers, "Seeds of Contention."

24. Unknown correspondent to Alexander Catcott, 17 January 1757. Catcott Correspondence, Jeffries Collection, SR 43, Bristol Central Library, Bristol.

The High-Church Ethos and
Its Development

Definitions are crucial in history, and that is especially true for any movement or self-conscious group such as High Churchmen. But defining High Churchmanship has proven extraordinarily difficult.[1] The moment a definition is tried it is found wanting because "High Churchmen" can be found who do not seem to fit the pattern. But despite the pitfalls inherent in the task, this chapter will set out to define High Churchmanship and describe its progress. An understanding of the issues that animated High Churchmen will be vital background to the thesis developed in subsequent chapters. High Churchmanship will be described here in terms of ethos, rather than just specific doctrines or practices, in order to make the definition as comprehensive as possible and to get as close as reasonably possible to the essence of the phenomenon.

In the broadest and most general sense, High Churchmanship was concerned with two overarching principles: loyalty to the church and loyalty to the Crown. These two matters were, in most cases, inextricably linked, such that politics and churchmanship went hand in hand. To be a High Churchman was to be a Tory, and vice versa. So interwoven were the religious and political that it was said that High Churchmen were simply "Tories at prayer."[2]

High Churchmen were, first of all, loyal to the church. This in itself, of course, would not seem to distinguish them from any other Anglican clergymen, except in the form and zeal in which they expressed their loyalty. It meant loyalty to a certain vision of the church, and that vision was episcopal, sacramental, liturgical, and uniform. Most High Churchmen at the turn of the century were so convinced that episcopacy was the correct polity for the church that they considered it ordained of God. Not only was it the apostolic pattern, it was the *jus divinum*—the law of God.[3] Though some High Churchmen in the eighteenth century were reluctant to be quite this doctrinaire about it, they always maintained a high view of episcopacy. Sacramentalism was also a key element in the ethos. Deriving the emphasis from Laud and his interpreters, High Churchmen stressed that grace came through the sacraments, particularly baptism and the Eucharist. The form in which the sacraments were administered was also extremely important. They had to be offered with decorum and high ritual, and the closer they were to the apostolic example, the better.[4] Other aspects of worship also were to be performed with external gestures, such as bowing at the name of Jesus and kneeling at communion, in order to demonstrate internal piety.[5] High Churchmen also were extremely partial to the liturgy found in the Book of Common Prayer. Since they felt that its pattern was ancient and could not be improved upon, they resisted all attempts to revise it. They particularly objected to any changes that would give concessions to Dissenters. They believed, rather, that Anglican liturgy and practice were already moderate and that all worshipers should conform to the set pattern. For this reason, uniformity was a stickling point for High Churchmen. They insisted that people should be compelled to worship properly (according to the church's practice) if they would not do so voluntarily. Leniency was not valued: making concessions to Dissenters might bring them into the fold of the church, but it would also fatally weaken it. By such attitudes and actions High Churchmen demonstrated their fierce loyalty to the church.

They were also fiercely loyal to the Crown. This was the political side of High Churchmanship. By the late seventeenth century, High Churchmen had come to believe that monarchy, just like episcopacy, was *jus divinum*. Obedience to the king was, accordingly, absolutely required of every Christian. The king ruled as God's viceregent, and though he was expected to rule by law, if he did not, one had no right to actively rebel. Passive, rather than active, resistance was the only acceptable means of opposition. Furthermore, the divine right of succession was hereditary. Only the next heir of a king could legitimately claim a right to the throne. Insistence on this point, of course, was what caused the crisis when efforts were made to exclude the Catholic Duke of York from the throne in the late 1670s and early 1680s.

In fact, it was at this time that High Churchmanship clearly emerged. Though there were many precedents in the Caroline period and the Interregnum,[6] most historians agree that the High-Church ethos (and its concomitant partisanship) coalesced during the critical juncture of the "Restoration Crisis."[7] Fears of Catholic conspiracies arose in the wake of the "Popish Plot" of 1678 and 1679, in which several informers whipped up a frenzied report about plans to murder king Charles II and put the Catholic James on the throne.[8] Though largely unfounded, this was enough to whip up opposition to James's succession. The Whigs, led by the Earl of Shaftesbury, initiated a crusade for Exclusion. The campaign to exclude James, though ultimately futile, awakened many Churchmen and Tories to the dangerous designs of the Whigs, and they were recruited in the effort to block exclusion.[9] After all, no less than the constitution of church and state were at stake. Deep down the Tories feared that if the Whigs had their way, they would abolish divine-right rule in favor of a contractual arrangement and would reduce the church to a voluntary establishment. These changes would revolutionize England from top to bottom, and for people to whom the status quo was sacred, this was treason. Whig principles, therefore, threatened the very core of the High Church/Tory ethos, and it was from this time onward that Whigs became the bitter enemies of Tories, and vice versa.[10]

It was at this time that Sir Robert Filmer articulated the doctrines of passive obedience and indefeasible hereditary right—doctrines that formed the blueprint of the High-Church ethos. In his *Patriarcha,* Filmer constructed a rationale for absolute monarchy based primarily upon a recital of biblical history.[11] He asserted that kings were, at the first, the patriarchs of families or clans. As the clans grew, so did the patriarch's power, until he eventually ruled over enough people to constitute a nation, at which time he became a monarch. Thus the king had a natural—and divine— right to rule, just as did the father of a family. Filmer did not believe that subjects should have any influence in the choice of their ruler, nor were they to have the privilege of rebellion. To the argument that people needed some checks on their sovereigns if they were to avoid tyranny, Filmer replied that the fear of tyranny was trumped up, and not likely to be a serious problem: in six hundred years of monarchy in England, there had not been one king "taxed by our Historians for Tyrannical Government." This monarchy, like patriarchy, was not only absolute, it was hereditary—

power was passed from father to son, ad infinitum. This was the God-ordained, "natural" order of government.[12]

Filmer's treatise amounted to a theological rationale for divine-right absolute monarchy, indefeasible hereditary succession, and unconditional obedience of subjects. Though Filmer was not himself a clergyman, he wrote as a religious man and with the blessing of renowned High Churchmen.[13] Filmer's work was more than a theological treatise: it was also a call for political action. It bade all good churchmen to fight for the Tory cause. From this time on, the Tory party was the "church party."

It was during the 1680s, too, that clergymen faced new fears over the threat of Nonconformity. Since Dissenters would not conform, and since they preached liberty of conscience, they could not be trusted to be loyal, obedient subjects. They might rise in rebellion at a time of upheaval or uncertainty—such as the present. Some Latitudinarians—those churchmen who were in favor of a broader church that gave "latitude" to Nonconformists[14]—raised their voices in defense of the Dissenters, but they were drowned out by the angry voices of High Churchmen. The Latitudinarians pleaded for moderation and toleration on several grounds. Edward Pearse, for example, in his *Conformists Plea for the Nonconformists,* maintained that the Dissenters were not unreasonable, contentious persons. For the most part they were, on the contrary, peaceable, sincere, and worthy persons, and they were suffering greatly under the persecution. Since they had not conformed in the space of eighteen years under persecution, perhaps it was time to "widen the Terms" under which some kind of comprehension could take place. He urged "moderation," meaning an easing of restrictions and requirements for communion with the Church of England.[15]

This kind of "moderation" was anathema to most churchmen, for it signaled defeat for them—it smacked of retrenchment and dilution. High Churchmen, therefore, argued that the moderation that Latitudinarians espoused was actually trimming, and it portended anarchy and destruction. As John Evans stated,

> the common Notion of a moderate Minister is this: One who will marry upon occasion without the Ring, Christen without the Cross, Godfathers and Godmothers, in complyance with weak and tender Consciences, Give the Sacrament Kneeling or Sitting or Standing, Bury with an Exhortation of his own, permit a man to convey his Dead into the Grave without any Common Prayer at all; one that will be out of the way, and in the way, as men please, how they will; one that will comply

with the humours and fancies of all Parties, and oblige them by con-
descentions of this nature. And if this be Moderation, the old Vicar of
Bray was the most moderate man that ever breathed.[16]

This kind of moderation would not heal the church; it would ruin it:
"Moderate men . . . are so far from contributing any thing towards the
composing of our present Differences, that they create, keep up and credit
our Divisions, they are false and treacherous friends to that side they profess to be of; for they really weaken the Church of *England,* while they seem
to strengthen her hands."[17]

This is not to say that High Churchmen deprecated moderation. On
the contrary, they gloried in the moderation of the Church of England.
But in their view, the church was *already* moderate. As Timothy Puller
observed, "the entire Constitution of our Church doth exhibit as great
Moderation, and as equal temper, as any Church in the Christian World
doth or ever did since Primitive Times."[18] Any further moderation was
tantamount to dilution and diminution, and with that they could have no
truck. Dissenters must relent or suffer the consequences; there was no
other way. Again, Puller explained why additional moderation or toleration would be destructive: "This would be to expose the dignity of the
Church, and of Constitutions settled by such long prescription, to the
scorn of every bold dissenter, which can have no other effect but to encourage them in their Schism, and heap contempt upon our selves, when
we prostitute Law and authority to such affronts." Dissenters had to admit their obstinacy and their error, or they could never be tolerated or
comprehended. If Dissenters and Latitudinarians had their way, High
Churchmen thought, the church would be awash in indifference and
mediocrity—surely a recipe for disaster.[19]

The practice of occasional conformity further convinced High Churchmen that Nonconformists were insincere and duplicitous. Dissenters had
originated the practice in order to maintain their separation, yet reap the
social and political benefits of Anglican churchmanship. As long as they
could produce a certificate that acknowledged their participation in the
sacrament of communion at least once a year, they were technically members in good standing of the Church of England and could attend university and gain entrance into government office. To High Churchmen, this
was perfidy. Since Dissenters practiced occasional conformity, they could
not consider communion with the Church of England as wrong in and of
itself. "Therefore we conclude," wrote William Sherlock, "that those who

communicate occasionally with the Church of England, do thereby declare that they believe, there is nothing sinful in our Communion; and we thank them for this good opinion."[20]

But if this was the case, why did they still persist in the separation? High Churchmen surmised that it must be because they were "schismaticks" at heart—they separated for the sake of being contentious. As Sherlock stated, "Christ hath but one Church, and one Body, and therefore where there are two Churchs divided from each other by Separate Communions, there is a Schism and Rent in the Body, and whoever Communicates with both these Churches, on one Side or other, Communicates in Schism." Presbyterians, Independents, and all other sectarians separated merely for the sake of promoting schism, and High Churchmen were not about to condone such infamy or allow it to continue.[21]

All parties concerned—High Churchmen, Latitudinarians, and Dissenters—wanted peace in the church and unity. But they differed on how to achieve those goals. Latitudinarians proposed altering the requirements for communion in the Church of England to satisfy Dissenters, and many of the Dissenters themselves would have been happy with such an arrangement. But High Churchmen felt that this proposition entailed treason, since it lowered the standards of the church, and would ultimately reduce it to ruin.[22] "Moderation" was not a virtue when the church was threatened; rather, what was needed was "*Zeal* now that must defend and maintain it, and that very moderation [upon which the church was founded] is a just warrant for such a zeal."[23]

These debates signaled the beginning of the suspicion and antipathy between High and Low Churchmen that reached fever pitch in the generation between the Glorious Revolution and the Hanoverian Accession. And parochial clergymen evinced these attitudes just as fully as did churchmen of national prominence.

The split between clerical factions in the late Restoration, then, arose from fundamental differences over the constitution of church and state. The two groups, High Churchmen and Latitudinarians, differed little on doctrine or even polity.[24] The difference was one of ethos: High Churchmen were confident (at least outwardly) and unyielding; Latitudinarians were diffident, charitable, and to some degree, open-minded. The former were intimidated by loose threads that did not fit neatly into their system; the latter acknowledged that there were remnants and attempted to incorporate them. The former wanted absolute consistency in the fibers of church and society; the latter were satisfied with a patchwork quilt. The former felt that Dissenters should be coerced into conformity; the latter felt that they could be wooed, and if need be, enticed with concessions. The Latitudinarians prized peace above all, and were willing (within limits) to compromise if peace could be achieved. There was give and take in their system. High Churchmen had order (and order based on historical precedent) and conformity as their chief objective, and they were not willing to sacrifice any order for the peace of the church. It should be noted that High Churchmen were not necessarily spiteful or bitter; it was only that they were trained to believe that society could not function except with complete uniformity, and the basis of that uniformity had already been laid down in the Reformation in the articles and canons of the church. And in the political realm, the only thing that would guarantee order and stability was an absolute monarchy. As Robert Filmer argued, "The Best Order, the Greatest Strength, the Most Stability, and easiest Government, are to be found all in Monarchy."[25] High Churchmen could not envision a society that was different or broader than that—mixture spelled disaster, both in the political and ecclesiastical realms.

In the late Restoration period, then, there were fissures in the church separating High and Low Churchmen. After the Glorious Revolution, a wedge was driven into those fissures that sundered the church in two. The debates between High and Low Churchmen in the 1680s were foreboding clouds that appeared in the church and began to cast a shadow on the ecclesiastical landscape. Churchmen continued to speak in glowing terms of their excellent communion, but that belied the pall over the land. After the Glorious Revolution, the clouds let loose their fury, and the ecclesiastical establishment was shaken. The church was split into two camps, and lightning flashed between them as they hurled invective at each other.

James II's accession and his subsequent actions presented a dilemma to High Churchmen and Tories. They were obligated to support him because of their own teaching on indefeasible hereditary right, and they were committed to obeying him (at least passively) because of their doctrine of passive obedience, but he seemed to threaten the entire church establishment by his attempts to promote toleration. In fact, they feared James was trying to uproot the Anglican Church and plant Catholicism as the national institution in its stead. So, ironically, they were bound by their principles to support the man who was trying to destroy everything they held sacred.[26]

Fortunately for High Churchmen, fate (or, from their perspective, providence) stepped in. On 5 November 1688, William of Orange landed at Torbay, on the coast of Cornwall, and began to march towards London. By the end of December James had fled and the Crown was effectively vacant. A Convention Parliament was summarily assembled, and by February the Declaration of Rights was promulgated and William and Mary were jointly offered the Crown.

This was, in some ways, an awkward solution to the dilemma James presented, for William and Mary posed new problems. There were two primary issues that High Churchmen had to cope with after William's accession to the Crown. The first involved the legitimacy of William as king, and the second had to do with the threat to the Church of Dissent and heterodoxy. The former took an immediate toll on High Churchmanship; the latter disturbed the church for years.

The most pressing problem High Churchmen faced upon the crowning of William and Mary was whether or not the new sovereigns could be considered legitimate. The doctrine of indefeasible hereditary right meant that only James or James's offspring, as long as they lived, held title to the throne. Any others were "pretenders." A significant minority of High Churchmen were so committed to these principles that they refused to take the Oath of Allegiance when it was demanded of them in order to maintain their positions in the church and government. These became known as the Non-jurors, because they refused to swear loyalty to William and Mary (and take the oath abjuring allegiance to James II or his heirs).[27]

The Non-jurors established an alternate church, avowing that they now were the only true church, and that the Church of England had ceased to be a true church because it had capitulated and become impure in its alliance with the usurpers, William and Mary. Though the number of ejections nationwide seems large (four hundred), in reality only a small proportion of clergymen—the radical fringe—were expelled.[28] Though over 30 percent of the bishops became Non-jurors, only about 10 percent of the parochial clergy refused the oaths and were deprived.[29] The High Church suffered little in strength because of the exodus of the Non-jurors. Though they espoused a lost cause and were never very powerful, the Non-jurors maintained a separate church tradition for nearly a hundred years. They were very particular in their practices of the liturgy and rites of the church because they respected apostolic tradition so highly.[30]

Non-jurors were Jacobites (those who maintained loyalty to James or James's offspring) by definition, but there were many Jacobites, active and passive, who either by dissembling or by taking advantage of technicalities were able to subscribe to the oath.[31] Since the church had been preaching the doctrine of hereditary right for so long, and since the majority of clergymen—at least, parochial clergymen—could be considered High Churchmen, the church was suspected to be a hotbed of Jacobite activity.[32] The church harbored unknown numbers of Jacobites, and the authorities were always uneasy about the possibilities of pious exercises becoming mixed with treasonous activities. The Society for the Promotion of Christian Knowledge, for example, was suspected of abetting Jacobitism in some of its meetings. In 1718, Archbishop Wake admonished the societies to steer clear of sedition: their purpose was religious, not political, and they were not to use the church as a vehicle for treason. The archbishop warned that if rumors of such conduct continued, the society would lose some of its privileges.[33]

But, as Paul Monod has pointed out, there was a wide range of commitment to Jacobitism. There was a certain sadness about the exclusion of the Stuarts among a great many, but that did not always mean active intrigue.[34] Frequently Jacobite sympathy was expressed with little more than lack of enthusiasm for the Orange, and then Hanoverian, regimes, or grumbling against them. For churchmen, many things could signal disaffection: associations, unwillingness to read certain services of the church, avoidance of the prayer for the royal family, even liturgical preferences could give hints.[35] People were constantly divining the actions of the clergy and speculating on hidden meanings in obscure passages in their preaching in order to ascertain their true sympathies.

Though there was constant anxiety in the new administrations over the loyalty of churchmen and fear that there was large-scale disaffection lurking just below the surface, most clergymen remained loyal. But how was it that these men, most of them High Church to the core, were able to accept the new sovereigns? The majority of High Churchmen simply decided that the doctrine of indefeasible hereditary right was expendable. Pledging loyalty to William and Mary was the lesser of two evils—better to drop one tenet than to allow the church to be subjugated and enslaved by Catholicism. Besides, there was a convenient way out of the dilemma that even Robert Filmer himself might have adopted—the ascription of responsibility to providence.[36] Though it is tempting to label much of the High-Church rhetoric following the Revolution cant and hypocrisy, it is not at all fair to do so. Clergymen honestly believed that their church and their country had been rescued by God's intervention, so that it never came to a question of whether or not to rebel against James. By attributing William's victory and James's defeat (even though there had not been a battle) to

God's providence, High Churchmen solved the problem of loyalty without losing their cherished principles. Divine-right monarchy was as fully espoused *after* William's accession as it was before. There was no need for churchmen to adopt a theory of contract government: England had not chosen William so much as he had been anointed by God, and that anointing was manifested in successful conquest. Indeed, the idea of contractual government was still as loathsome to Anglicans as it had been in Filmer's day.[37] The Revolution had not changed that. The Revolution was not "glorious" because it championed Whig principles; it was "glorious" because the hand of providence had rescued the nation from arbitrary government and the tyranny of Catholicism, and that without any bloodshed.[38]

The second major issue in High Churchmanship was one that more directly affected the well-being of the church. High Churchmen may have reconciled themselves to the fact of the change in the royal succession, but they could not help but feel that the church was in serious danger from the threats of Nonconformity and heterodoxy. As we have already seen, High Churchmen felt that Dissent should be proscribed, but in the wake of the Revolution, more and more efforts were made to undo the protections and safeguards that the church had so carefully put in place. This raised fears in High Churchmen and agitated them until they suspected the presence of a nefarious conspiracy organized by Low Churchmen. In the years between 1688 and 1714, therefore, there were constant and bitter conflicts between High Churchmen and Latitudinarians, and the two groups squared off against each other frequently on an ideologically charged battleground.

The dispute was stirred up by the renewed efforts of some clergymen to close the gap between Dissenters and Anglicans following the Revolution. Edward Stillingfleet, John Tillotson, and Gilbert Burnet et al. (the Latitudinarians), had been trying to negotiate some settlement with Dissenters for years. Now, since the new king was himself Dutch Reformed, they had a golden opportunity. Once more they proposed a Bill of Comprehension that would reduce the requirements of subscription to Anglicanism, so that many Nonconformists would be able to join its communion. They advocated that concessions be made on a number of issues: the acceptance of Presbyterian ordination for clergy, the option of wearing or not wearing the surplice while officiating at services, the elimination of the requirement to kneel at communion and sign the cross in baptism, and the exclusion in subscription of the articles that concerned polity or discipline. They also proposed revoking the Test Act.[39]

But Comprehension was too much to be hoped for. Many Anglicans feared that, once admitted to the church, Presbyterians would seek to abolish episcopacy. The Scottish Presbyterians had, in fact, recently taken that action. Furthermore, if Comprehension passed in England, Dutchmen and Huguenots would be able to slip into the church, and the xenophobic High Churchmen recoiled at this possibility. There was, therefore, a rising crescendo of opposition to the bill, and the attempts to push it through Convocation ultimately ground to a halt.[40]

Toleration was the next best option for Low Churchmen. Accordingly, a committee drew up a Bill of Toleration that passed in Convocation and Parliament, and hence came into law. The Toleration Act did not grant Dissenters the privileges of citizenship, as the Comprehension Act would have, nor did it exempt them from paying tithes to the established church, but it did protect them from prosecution for Nonconformity. Dissenters could now worship separately, construct houses of worship, and establish their own schools, but they were still excluded from universities and governmental posts. The bill also contained provisions for monitoring Dissent, since it required Nonconformists to petition diocesan authorities for licenses in order to meet. It was not unlimited toleration, either, since Roman Catholics and anti-trinitarians were excluded from its provisions.[41]

But this was only the beginning of High-Church fears that the church was under attack. Until 1714, that fear continued to escalate until it verged on paranoia. Immediately after the Toleration Act came into law, there was an attempt to revise the Book of Common Prayer, which engendered controversy and fed the growing anxiety of churchmen. A commission was appointed in 1689 to evaluate the liturgy of the church and to make recommendations for revisions that would then be put before Convocation for ratification. The commission was broad in its composition, covering the whole spectrum of the church, and that, perhaps, was part of the problem. The Latitudinarians, who had failed to get Comprehension passed, saw a second chance—a second-best method of accomplishing the same thing. They wanted to revise the liturgy such that Nonconformist sensibilities would be satisfied: they proposed eliminating the use of the surplice for most occasions, making both the cross in baptism and kneeling at communion optional, reducing the role of godparents in the church, and discarding the Athanasian Creed (since it gave offense on account of its damnatory clauses). But once again, High Churchmen blocked their attempts, and the revisionists merely polished, rather than revamped, the liturgy. High Churchmen were satisfied with the liturgy as it was, and recoiled at the idea of making revisions that would kowtow to the Dissenters.[42]

The Toleration also led to a greater freedom of speech. After its enactment, censorship of the press was allowed to lapse. This opened the door for publication of all manner of heterodox treatises. Soon Socinian, Unitarian, and Deist tracts were pouring from the presses.[43] Comparatively few individuals ever really espoused full-blown deism or trinitarian heresy, but the increasing volume of literature on these subjects fed the already burning fire of anxiety amongst the clergy.

Arthur Bury's *The Naked Gospel* could be said to have precipitated the scare over heterodoxy. Bury was the Rector of Exeter College, Oxford, and when he wrote *The Naked Gospel* he intended it to be considered privately by a meeting of Convocation. But the work was circulated at Oxford, where it raised more than a few eyebrows because of its Socinian tendencies. To add insult to injury, Bury had rebuffed the Bishop of Exeter by refusing to allow him to visit the college. A vote was taken by the chancellor, vice-chancellor and heads of the colleges, and Bury was censured, removed from his post, and his book burned in the square outside the Bodleian library. But Bury was not ejected from the church: he retained a living as the Vicar of Bampton, and even managed to preach once in a while at the University Church.[44]

Bury's work elicited concern in the university and church, but if he had been alone in questioning the deity of Christ, the whole affair might have stopped there. Unfortunately, it soon became clear to apprehensive clergymen that doctrinal errors were becoming a significant problem. Bury had his friends in the church, and it was apparent that they had imbibed his uncertainty about the incarnation. Soon prominent churchmen came under scrutiny and, frequently, indictment. Gilbert Burnet's trinitarianism was questioned, as was Archbishop Tillotson's. Even defenders of the trinity were often accused of leaning toward one trinitarian heresy or another.[45] Since the orthodox formulation of the trinity was so complex and delicately constructed, it was easy to make questionable assertions regarding it, and difficult to make unequivocally orthodox ones.

A further shock to the sensibilities of churchmen came with the publication of unabashedly deist books. In 1695 John Toland published his *Christianity not Mysterious,* which argued that revealed religion was little more than a carbon copy of what could be known about God through nature. John Locke's *Reasonableness of Christianity,* which made similar arguments (though less baldly), was released the same year. Both these works provoked storms of protest and convinced churchmen that the theological locusts were swarming and preparing to devour the ecclesiastical landscape.

Angst flooded the church establishment. In 1697 this fear was articulated in a *Letter to a Convocation Man,* which set the tone for the High Church/Low Church disputes that raged throughout the church in the first decade and a half of the eighteenth century. The *Letter,* which was revised (but probably not written) by Francis Atterbury, amounted to a hue and cry for Convocation to deal with the dangerous and destructive issues of heresy within, and Dissent without, the church. It was, first and foremost, a report on the state of the church. Though there had been many concerns about threats to the church since the Restoration, the *Letter* described a baleful situation. The author made it sound as if the church was a tiny island in the middle of a sea of infidelity and impiety, and the church was being "over-run" in a "deluge" of damnable heresies. Dissent, heterodoxy, deism, atheism, and impiety were all elements of a "universal conspiracy" "to undermine and overthrow the Catholick Faith."[46]

The *Letter,* as well as Atterbury's subsequent *Rights, Powers, and Privileges of an English Convocation* (1700), demanded that the lower house of Convocation—the elected proctors—be granted the power, as part of Parliament, to investigate and proceed against heresy or schism. The lower house of Convocation, in its late seventeenth-century form, was subject to the upper house, or the bishops, who treated it like an advisory council. Since William's accession to the throne, the upper house had been packed with Whig lackeys, which meant to Atterbury that no real prosecution of heterodoxy or heresy would be undertaken by that body. The *Letter* engendered a controversy over the rights and privileges of Convocation, and was the culmination of disputes between Low Churchmen, who were predominantly Erastian, and the High Churchmen and Non-jurors, who lobbied for the rights of the episcopal order on the basis of divine commission. But the flames of the dispute were fanned because of the presence of heresy. High Churchmen felt deep in their souls that the church was in trouble, and they felt that it should be carefully regulated, but Erastian Low Churchmen thwarted their intentions to suppress heterodoxy. The Low Churchmen, who dominated the upper house of Convocation, still believed that latitude and moderation were the order of the day. If Convocation, Parliament, or the king tried to regulate doctrine too carefully or define orthodoxy too narrowly, they would disqualify from service many otherwise fine churchmen. Censorship on the level that the High

Churchmen desired was neither advisable nor feasible. The church would simply have to live with some amount of diversity. So the lower house of Convocation was, for all intents and purposes, muzzled, and the power of clergymen to regulate doctrine was curtailed.[47]

To the High Churchmen, this refusal to act on the dangers facing the church was tantamount to treason. Ultimately they did manage to obtain a censure for Toland's *Christianity not Mysterious,* but they were angered when Parliament also censured works written by those who were attempting to expose the heresy. Surely, the Tories thought, this was indicative of a major lapse of concern over heresy among the upper clergy. In the perspective of the High Churchmen, the Latitudinarians were playing a dangerous game—they either underestimated the seriousness of these challenges to the faith, or, worse, they were deliberately contributing to them. Thus High Churchmen began to feel that the Low Churchmen were part of a massive conspiracy to undermine the church and its doctrine. It is no wonder that a rift developed between the two parties. The Convocation controversy hardened the division between High Church and Low Church and reinforced their respective ties to the Tory and Whig parties.[48]

In 1702, however, High Churchmen gained new hope: King William died and was succeeded by the Tory Queen Anne, the daughter of James II. Anne promised to be a champion of the church, and this raised the spirits of the frustrated Tories. Though they gained momentum and respectability from her, High Churchmen were ultimately doomed to fail in their attempts to protect the church. Anne was not the redemptress they had hoped, for she could not bring herself to proscribe the Whigs for the benefit of the Tories, nor could she countenance losing as much royal prerogative as Atterbury's schemes threatened. Nevertheless, the atmosphere was better for High Churchmen in her reign than in William's. And they did their best to institute their program for the welfare of church and country.

The first step they took to diminish the peril facing the church during Anne's reign was to limit the freedom and influence of Dissenters by attempting to pass a bill in Parliament against occasional conformity. Occasional conformity—where dissenters would gain entrance to universities and government posts by receiving communion once a year in the established church—had been a problem for years. But in the wake of the heightened apprehension over the dangers of Dissent to church and state, High Churchmen became obsessed with outlawing the practice. They made no fewer than three attempts to pass a bill to end occasional conformity between 1702 and 1704; none of these, ultimately, was successful. The ironic thing about the failure of these bills is that they were stopped not by the House of Commons, but by the bishops in the House of Lords. The provisions of these bills stipulated that no government official would be permitted to retain office if, after having taken communion in the Anglican Church, he began to attend a Dissenting congregation. Though supported by the vast majority of the clergy as well as Tory laymen, the bills were killed by the bishops, who had a Low-Church majority. This gave High Churchmen even more reason to believe that there was a conspiracy among Latitudinarians to bring the church to ruin. Frustrated in every way, High Churchmen were livid over the fact that these measures to save the church were obstructed by churchmen.

It was for this reason that the rhetoric attained such a fever pitch. After the failure of the last Occasional Conformity bill, which proponents had "tacked on" to a land tax bill in order to coax it through Parliament, the Whigs once more took the initiative and gained ascendancy. Even an attempt to vote "the church in danger" failed in 1705, and High Churchmen were left with nothing to show for all their efforts—and that even with a Tory Queen. It is no wonder that the rhetoric of clergymen sounded the theme that they were the last tattered regiments of the faithful defending the beleaguered church establishment against the hordes of vicious infidels and traitors.

Henry Sacheverell was the master of such rhetoric. In 1701 he published a venomous book against the Latitudinarians entitled, *The Character of a Low Churchman,* which represented Whiggish churchmen as apathetic and indolent, if not downright seditious. There was no doubt what he thought of the Latitudinarians and Whigs after he preached his notorious sermon, *The Perils of False Brethren, both in Church, and State,* in 1709: there he branded them as turncoats and traitors, betraying both church and state. In his mind the church was all but in ruins, since

Her Holy Communion has been Rent, and Divided by Factious, and Schismatical Imposters; Her Pure Doctrin has been Corrupted, and Defil'd; Her Primitive Worship, and Discipline Profan'd, and Abus'd; Her Sacred Orders Deny'd, and Vilify'd; Her Priests, and Professors (like St. Paul,) Calumniated, Misrepresented and Ridicul'd; Her Altars, and Sacraments Prostituted to Hypocrites, Deists, Socinians and Atheists; and this done . . . not only by Our Profess'd Enemies, but which is worse, by Our Pretended Friends, and FALSE BRETHREN.[49]

The "false brethren," the Whigs and Low Churchmen, understandably took offense at this sermon, and they decided to make an example of Sacheverell. In response to his slander, they brought charges of "crimes and misdemeanors" against him in a dramatic court scene in Parliament in 1710. Sacheverell was impeached, but the terms were so lenient that High Churchmen became convinced that it was a victory for them. The episode backfired, at least temporarily, for the Whigs: the trial stirred up fear that the Whigs might actually be doing just what Sacheverell charged. To their dismay, Low Churchmen found that instead of dealing a death-blow to the opposition, they had actually quickened it by creating a martyr, who, ironically, journeyed around the country on a sort of victory tour after his impeachment.[50]

Thus the Tories displayed one last gasp of strength: they won the majority in Parliament in the next election, and once again pushed for legislation to suppress the Dissenters. They managed to pass two bills to that effect: the Occasional Conformity Act of 1711 and the Schism Act of 1714, which prohibited Dissenters from forming their own academies. Unfortunately for them the former bill was not very effective and the latter came into law on the very day that Queen Anne died, making it virtually a dead letter. Further, the Tory hegemony in Parliament ended abruptly when George I came to the throne, since not only were they proscribed and passed over when government posts were bestowed, but also they failed to carry majorities in any subsequent election.[51]

This was the historical development of the division between High and Low Churchmen. Now it remains to characterize the ethos—or essence—of each. First Low Churchmen: Low Churchmen were not necessarily much different from High Churchmen in their piety, but their ethos was distinct nonetheless. They held their beliefs much less rigidly. Though many Low Churchmen believed in episcopacy, few of them thought that it was the only acceptable way in the sight of God. This allowed them to have some kind of sympathy, or at least "latitude," with the Dissenters. Further, the erosion of a hierarchical world view among them meant that, in their minds, monarchical authority was derived more from practical concerns than divine ordination.

This was one of the key areas isolated by an early eighteenth-century writer in *The Criterion; or, TOUCHSTONE, by Which to judge of the Principles of High and Low-Church,* an unusually dispassionate and objective piece. He argued that government, for Low Churchmen, was a convention. It was necessary and, in that broader sense, ordained of God, but no particular system was decreed by God. Whatever organization would provide better security and welfare for the citizens of a given country was the preferred one for that country. Monarchy may have been an ancient, time-tested method of government, but it was not the only one allowed by God, as High Churchmen believed. Obedience was still important for them, but it was not an absolute, unlimited (or passive) obedience.[52]

The difference applied to the realm of ecclesiastical government too. High Churchmen believed that episcopacy was *jure divino*—by the law of God—and that it was inviolable. Low Churchmen may have esteemed episcopacy very highly, and may even have believed its origin was ancient, but they did not think that it was sacrosanct. Since "there was no design in the Scripture writers to settle the Form of Government," other systems could, in fact, be permitted. This also had implications for the authority of the clergy. High-Church parsons feared that if Low-Church designs were instituted, their authority as pastors would be diminished, and this, they felt, was directly attributable to the erosion of the doctrine of *jure divino* episcopacy. If the sanctity of episcopacy could be reinstated and protected, then their own authority would be more secure.[53]

The Low-Church retreat from the doctrine of divine ordination of church and state could have implications for worship too. To High Churchmen, the liturgy and sacraments were non-negotiables. They acknowledged that the Anglican rites were not necessarily perfect images of the divine pattern, but they were as close as humans were likely to come, and therefore, they were not to be tampered with. The Latitudinarians saw the liturgy as a fluid expression of worship, and they had little compunction about altering it if, in so doing, a greater object could be achieved. Thus many of them proposed making revisions in order that the Dissenters' objections could be assuaged.

Second, Low Churchmen felt that liberty of conscience was more important than control and authority. Whereas High Churchmen could argue that it was better to force individuals into being hypocrites for the sake of societal order, the Whigs felt that "God has the sole Authority over Conscience" and leaders could not, and should not, force submission in areas of conscience. Thus they were able to maintain latitude with regard to Dissenters. They felt that "'tis the natural Right of all Mankind to have the Liberty of Worshipping God in that Way which they think most acceptable to him," and that, therefore, Dissenters should not be unduly disturbed or hindered.[54]

This latitude did have limits, however. Even Latitudinarians were unprepared to tolerate atheism and deism. They had not completely abandoned the idea of a divine order—it was just that in their view the order was much less rigid than what High Churchmen perceived. The fact remains, therefore, that their moderation was much more moderate than the moderation of High Churchmen.[55]

These were the primary areas in which the Latitudinarians had modified the High-Church ethos. In other ways, they were virtually indistinguishable. It is not true that Low Churchmen were "no Church-Men," as High Churchmen charged.[56] On the contrary, most of them were as religious, as pious, as the best of the "True Church Men." Neither were they, on the whole, heterodox. It is true that more Latitudinarians ended up espousing a questionable orthodoxy than High Churchmen, but that is only because there was a freedom and a latitude among Low Churchmen that allowed for more diversity. In reality, the vast majority of them appreciated and adhered to the historic doctrines of the church. The Latitudinarians, too, seemed to have remained sacramental in their worship. They argued just as frequently as did High Churchmen from the precedents of antiquity. The church fathers and other ancient authorities were just as important to them as to their opponents. The difference was, simply, that they read the patristics from another perspective and came up with different conclusions, just as they did with Scripture.

At bottom, it was the world views of High and Low Churchmen that were beginning to diverge. Whereas High Churchmen clung to the age-old perspective of an immutable divine order, Low Churchmen saw the world as progressive and malleable. There may have been a divine order, but it was not nearly as rigid as the High Churchmen perceived. And in this more liberated organization, the individual human came to have more significance—a man's conscience and dignity were more important than where he fit in the system.

High Churchmen were wrong when they insisted that the church was in danger. It was not really the church that was in jeopardy, it was the underlying foundation upon which they built their conception of the church, and indeed the universe, that was threatened. Their ethos had come under attack from Low Churchmen, and the danger of the collapse of that was very real.

But in fact, it did not collapse. Rather, High Churchmen found ways to adapt to the new world order without undermining their world view. This is where the example from Sussex is so important—it demonstrates that High Churchmen could be accommodated, that they could participate in a Whig world without adopting Whig ideas. It is the story of accommodation rather than capitulation.

Notes

1. In his recent survey of High Churchmanship, *High Churchmanship in the Church of England* (1–5 and pass.), Kenneth Hylson-Smith was clearly sensitive to the problems of definition. Despite this his own attempts to characterize the phenomenon are unsatisfactory because he included such a disparate group of people, some of whom had little in common other than that they were Anglican and were pious.

2. Sharp, "New Perspectives," 4; Walsh and Taylor, "Introduction," 34.

3. Though Archbishop William Laud and his friends had espoused a form of *jure divino* episcopacy, the concept was most fully developed by the ejected clergy of the Interregnum, divines such as Henry Hammond. See Packer, *Transformation of Anglicanism*, 105–27. By the Restoration, the idea of *jure divino* episcopacy was firmly entrenched. See Spurr, *Restoration Church of England,* 133–37, 150–52.

4. Sharp, "New Perspectives," 9, 11.

5. See, for instance, the pattern that the Frewens set. Chamberlain, "Portrait of a High Church Clerical Dynasty."

6. The legacy of the Caroline and Interregnum divines is debated, but it can, at least, be said that men such as William Laud, Henry Hammond, Gilbert Sheldon, and so on, articulated beliefs that, in one form or another, would be taken up by late seventeenth-century High Churchmen. Their emphases on the sacraments, on episcopacy, on divine-right monarchy, and on conformity all anticipate High Churchmanship.

7. The term "Restoration Crisis" is being used now by many historians because the convulsions of the time were deeper and broader than just the question of whether or not to exclude James, the Duke of York, from the succession. See, for example, Scott, *Algernon Sidney,* and the discussion between Gary De Krey, Richard Greaves, Tim Harris, James Rosenheim, and Jonathan Scott in *Albion* 25, no. 4 (Winter 1993):565–651.

8. For background on this affair, see Kenyon, *The Popish Plot.*

9. Spurr, *Restoration Church,* 75–82.

10. Jones, *Country and Court,* 197–216; Holmes, *Politics, Religion and Society,* 196; Feiling, *History of the Tory Party,* 175–202; Willman, "Origins of 'Whig' and 'Tory.'" The exact nature of the crisis and the emergence of parties has recently been vigorously debated. See the series of articles in *Albion* 25, no. 4 (Winter 1993).

11. "Absolute monarchy" was not understood as unrestricted or tyrannous autocracy, as it might be today. It meant, rather, authority from the top down, rather than the bottom up. Kings were expected to obey the law, but subjects had no

control over them. In the minds of High Churchmen, God was a far better supervisor of kings than the people anyway, hence, he was expected to be the watchdog over the monarchy, not them.

12. Filmer, *Patriarcha*, 20, 74.

13. Peter Heylin, for example, wrote the preface for the 1680 edition of *Patriarcha*, in which he stressed Filmer's affection for and attachment to the church, and gave his wholehearted endorsement to his construction of monarchy and government.

14. For the origin and early history of Latitudinarianism, see Patrick, *Brief Account*; Spurr, "'Latitudinarianism,'"; and especially Spellman, *Latitudinarians*.

15. Pearse, *Conformists Plea*.

16. Evans, *Moderation Stated*, 40–41. This High-Church portrayal was accepted at face value by many historians. Since Latitudinarians were branded as religious liberals, historians have tended to depict them that way. See, for example, Cragg, *Church in the Age of Reason*; Stromberg, *English Religious Liberalism*; Bredvold, *Intellectual Milieu of John Dryden*; Sykes, *Church and State*, and *From Sheldon to Secker*; Rupp, *Religion in England*; and Abbey and Overton, *English Church in the Eighteenth Century*. Modern revisionists are in the process of dismantling this traditional view. These works stress that Low Churchmen may have been liberal according to High-Church standards, but, contrary to their charges, the Latitudinarians had not given up any fundamental Christian doctrine. They were not, by and large, deists in ecclesiastical garb; they were not theological trimmers; and very few of them tended toward heterodoxy. See Spellman, *Latitudinarians*. Unfortunately, however, some of the revisionists are tending toward the opposite distortion: that Latitudinarianism, as a distinguishable entity, did not exist. See Spurr, "'Latitudinarianism,'" and Taylor, "Church and State in England," 215–16. But, as is demonstrated here and infra, Latitudinarianism was a distinct ethos, and could be distinguished from High Churchmanship well into the eighteenth century. See also Chamberlain, "Limits of Moderation," and Beaver, "Symbol and Boundary," 238–44, for distinctions between High and Low Churchmen.

17. Evans, *Moderation Stated*, 40. Note the Sacheverellian rhetoric in use thirty years before Sacheverell's "The Perils of False Brethren."

18. Puller, *Moderation of the Church of England*, 28.

19. Ibid., 27–31.

20. Sherlock, *Resolution*, 43, 49, 50.

21. Ibid., 49, 50.

22. Henry Roby, future Vicar of Ashburnham, argued that repealing the Test Act would even be detrimental to Dissenters, since it ultimately would weaken the link between church and state. "While the Church and State have divided interests," he asserted, "there will be perpetual convulsions, jealousies, fears and intrigues." BL Add. MS 47,126, ff. 81b–83b.

23. *Distinction, of High-Church and Low-Church*, 49–53.

24. Spellman, *Latitudinarians,* conclusion.

25. Filmer, *Patriarcha,* 53.

26. So much for Filmer's glib dismissal of the dangers of tyranny: "Whereas many out of imaginary Fear pretend the Power of the People to be necessary for the repressing of the Insolencies of Tyrants; wherein they propound a Remedy far worse than the Disease, neither is the Disease indeed so frequent as they would have us think." Unfortunately for Filmer, the "disease" struck less than ten years after he wrote. Filmer, *Patriarcha,* 73, 74. Jones, *Country and Court,* 234–35.

27. Rupp, *Religion in England,* 6–29; Overton, *Non-jurors.*

28. The influence of Non-juring theorists on the High Church party, however, should not be underestimated. See Goldie, "Nonjurors."

29. Wand, *High Church Schism,* 10–11. See also Lathbury, *History of the Non-jurors,* and Overton, *Nonjurors.*

30. This, in itself, implies that there was more to the High-Church ethos than politics. It was not just a political party, but a world view, an ethos, that was at stake with the events of the time. See Sharp, "100 Years of a Lost Cause."

31. For example, *Letter Written to a Gentleman,* 12–13, maintained that one need not renounce James's hereditary right to the throne in order to subscribe to the oaths, only his legal right. And since James was now aligned with a foreign country his legal claim was invalidated. Thus one could safely, though reluctantly, swear the oath. Complete satisfaction and affection to the government was not necessary. This pamphlet is in ESRO FRE 1091.

32. Rupp, *Religion in England,* 54–55; Pruett, *Parish Clergy under the Later Stuarts,* 160–71.

33. Wake wrote, "It is commonly reported that there are many in the Societies who are utterly disaffected to the present Government, & do even deny the Lawful Authority of it. That of these, several make it their Business to meet together about Political Matters, to dispute of, and to determine the Rights of Princes, and to argue against that Settlement which the Highest Authority of this Kingdom hath established . . . this ought by no means to be endured: But that better it were that these Religious Societies should be wholly disolved, then such Libertys be taken." SPCK Abstract Letter Book, CRI 8:5581. See also Rose, "Seminarys of Faction and Rebellion." I am grateful to Dr. Rose for providing me with a typescript of this article before it was published.

34. Monod, *Jacobitism and the English People,* 4–10.

35. John Harris, for example, suspected one of his associates, Dr. Charles Humphreys, his lecturer at St. Mildreds Bread St., London, of disloyalty. Harris reported to the world that Humphreys, "by usual Expressions in his Prayers, and Sermons, had discovered great Disaffection to the Government." But Humphreys was no fool: he was circumspect and chary in his expressions, and was never overtly treasonous. His intentions, however, were clear to Harris and some of the parishioners. When he referred to the "king," he seemed to be talking about James

rather than George; he declined to use certain parts of the liturgy, especially those that spoke of the king's supremacy; and he said things with connotations, but never denotations, that left people with the distinct impression that he objected to the present government. Nevertheless, when he was confronted, he professed loyalty, and the Bishop of London refused to press charges against him. Harris, *True State.*

36. Filmer allowed that kingship could be established by conquest as well as inheritance. The thing Filmer objected to was a conception of contractual government—that the people had the right to choose their own rulers. *Patriarcha*, 25ff.

37. It was, in fact, the year after the Revolution that one of the most famous books on passive obedience and divine-right monarchy was published: Abednego Seller's *History of Passive Obedience Since the Reformation* (Amsterdam, 1689). He lamented that the doctrine of contractual government was being taken seriously by so many, "as if the Doctrine were Apostolical." But the popularity of his book belies the prevalence of the doctrine he wrote to oppose. *The History of Passive Obedience* was an immediate bestseller, and was referred to as the definitive work by churchmen for years.

38. Straka, *Anglican Reaction*, 117–31. Mark Goldie asserts that it was Anglican political theory, in fact, that enabled the Revolution to take place. Goldie emphasizes the rather odd practice of the Anglicans to "disobey unrighteous sovereigns but never to rebel," and he believes that the disobedience of clergymen was based on a two-sphere theory of authority, with each sphere being "coterminous but autonomous." So, Anglicans not only justified the revolution, they precipitated it. Goldie, "Political Thought," 102–36. Spurr demonstrates in "'Virtue, Religion and Government,'" that, in many ways, the Anglican Church was prepared to champion a providential argument through its recourse to providentialism in the Restoration period.

39. Every, *High Church Party*, 25–33.

40. Ibid., 34–40.

41. Watts, *Dissenters*, 259–60.

42. Every, *High Church Party*, 43–60.

43. By the eighteenth century, the term "Socinian" was frequently used interchangeably with "Unitarian," both pejoratives applied to those individuals who espoused a less-than-orthodox Christology that denied the trinity or the divinity of Christ. But technically, Socinianism is the doctrine that Christ was given the title of divinity without the substance. He was a titular God, and not at all equal to the Father. Socinianism also entailed moralism, since it maintained that salvation was accomplished more from following Christ's example than it was from the atonement of Calvary.

44. Redwood, *Reason, Ridicule and Religion*, 156–61.

45. See Sherlock, for example, in his *Vindication of the Doctrine of the Holy and Ever Blessed Trinity and the Incarnation of the Son of God.*

46. Quoted in Every, *High Church Party*, 83.

47. Ibid., 83–104; Goldie, "Nonjurors," 15–30.

48. Bennett, *White Kennett,* 26–53.

49. Sacheverell, *Perils of False Brethren,* 8.

50. For a careful analysis of the entire Sacheverell affair, see Holmes, *Trial of Doctor Sacheverell.*

51. Speck, *Stability and Strife,* 93.

52. *The Criterion; or, TOUCHSTONE,* 5–6.

53. Ibid.

54. Ibid. High Churchmen could, of course, argue for liberty of conscience, and many did. Many also suffered for conscience's sake (e.g., the Nonjurors). However, when it came down to it, High Churchmen could not endorse a system in which liberty of conscience was preeminent, because this would endanger the solidarity and conformity of the church.

55. See, for example, Chamberlain, "Limits of Moderation."

56. *Distinction of High-Church and Low-Church,* 26.

High Churchmanship in Sussex,
1688–1734

It has generally been assumed that High Churchmanship was dominant among the parish clergy in the late seventeenth and early eighteenth centuries.[1] But seldom has that dominance been documented other than by impressionistic studies and anecdotal evidence. This chapter will examine the nature of High Churchmanship in Sussex during the period before 1734 by examining clerical writings, observing disputes and controversies, and noting the electoral behavior of the incumbents. From these sources, a full picture of what it meant to be High Church will be drawn, and the relative strength of High Churchmanship in the county will be ascertained. It may be helpful first, however, to make a few comments about the structure of the county community and its religious establishment.

Structure of the County and Diocese

Sussex is located on the southern coast of England, just to the west of Kent. In the eighteenth century the boundaries of the county were virtually coterminous with those of the Diocese of Chichester. Both the county and diocese were divided administratively and, to some extent, in loyalty and allegiance, between east and west. Each half of the county had a provincial capital—Lewes in the east and Chichester in the west. Though Chichester was the larger, and was, perhaps, more prosperous in the eighteenth century, both were necessary centers of political, civil, and religious administration. Chichester was the diocesan capital, and had been so since the original Saxon cathedral was moved from Selsey (which had been the original center of the diocese) to Chichester in 1075.[2]

The diocese of Chichester was comprised of 292 parishes. The parishes were administered through a complicated and confusing hierarchy, created by centuries of tradition and haphazard augmentation rather than by plan.[3] Though the bishop was the head of the diocese, he did not have jurisdiction over all parishes within his see. Several so-called peculiars—the deaneries of South Malling, Tarring, Pagham, Battle, and Chichester—were exempt from his scrutiny and supervision, mainly because of the manner in which those particular districts were formed.[4] The parishes in these areas were usually administered directly by the Archbishop of Canterbury, since they did not usually have a dean in residence (the exceptions were Chichester and Battle; but Battle had only a single parish in its jurisdiction, so the Rector of Battle was its dean, and he was dean only of the parish of Battle).

The rest of the diocese was broken into two archdeaconries under the bishop—Lewes and Chichester—which were the administrative divisions in which much of the work of the diocese was carried out. Archdeacons held courts, carried out triennial visitations, arbitrated in disputes, and kept ecclesiastical records. In many ways, it can be said that they were little or suffragan bishops, since their responsibilities resembled or paralleled those of the bishop, only in a smaller arena. The archdeacon, then, was essentially the bishop of the archdeaconry.[5]

The cathedral was in many respects the center of the diocese. The bishop's palace was adjacent to it, and, unlike some other dioceses, the Bishop of Chichester was frequently resident in the eighteenth century. There was a wide variety of other offices attached to the cathedral; some of them were important for diocesan administration, and some of them were merely sinecures. The "chapter" was the organization of the cathedral clergy, and it was headed by the Dean of Chichester. The dean supervised the activities of the cathedral and the clergy under him, and, in addition, oversaw the administration of the peculiar of Chichester, which was his jurisdiction rather than the bishop's. Besides the dean, the officers of the chapter included the precentor (or leader of the cathedral choir), the treasurer, and the chancellor.[6]

The chancellor was important within the diocese, since he was the judicial official—he administered the bishop's court. Thus it was his responsibility to see to it that religious and moral offenses were prosecuted efficiently. If he was lax or ailing, the court tended not to be as aggressive.[7]

Under the cathedral officers were the other dignitaries—the canons residentiary and prebendaries. All were assigned stalls in the choir of the cathedral, but only the canons were required to live in the close, or cathedral precincts.[8] Though there had been as many as twelve canons residentiary at one time, by the eighteenth century the number was fixed at four, and the number of other prebendaries was twenty-eight.[9]

There were four types of professional parish clergymen in Sussex, as in the rest of England: rector, vicar, perpetual curate, and curate. Rectors and vicars were beneficed clergy, which means that they were appointed to a post for life and that they were given the tithes of the parish. They had patrons who owned the advowson of the parish, which gave them the right to appoint the parson when the living fell vacant. Beneficed clergymen were, therefore, indebted to the patron who chose them for the post. Often parsons would be granted multiple benefices—approximately 50 percent of the clergy in Sussex had more than one living—but this was only supposed to be permitted because of the poor revenues of these parishes (in reality, of course, the system was much abused and the church came in for a great deal of criticism because of this). The perpetual curate was given a stipend rather than tithes, but he, too, was appointed for life. The curate, however, was little more than a hireling for the beneficed clergy. He was an individual, usually freshly ordained as a deacon, who would, in return for a small stipend of between 12 and 40 pounds paid by the rector or vicar, attend to the "cure of souls" while his superior took care of other business (such as another cure, cathedral duties, or anything else that could keep him from doing it himself). Curates probably suffered the most of all clergymen in the diocese. Their stipends were notoriously low and they had to do the bulk of the work in their parish.[10] Understanding this framework is important for understanding how clerical attitudes and sympathies were formed and changed.

High Churchmanship and the Succession

In chapter 1 it was noted that the interruption of the hereditary succession of the Stuart line did not devastate the High Church. A few of the hardliners became Non-jurors, but the majority merely adjusted themselves to the change in monarchy. This was the pattern in Sussex too, where there were relatively few who became Non-jurors. Though the Bishop of Chichester, John Lake, refused the oaths,[11] only about 4 percent (twelve out of over two hundred) of the parochial clergy followed his example.[12] This amounted to less than half the national average of 10 percent. The clergy of the diocese, therefore, appear to have been fairly accommodating on this matter. Some parsons undoubtedly respected the actions of the Non-jurors, however, and may have sympathized with their plight, since at least two of them were buried in the chancels of churches and one was buried with a pall of six clergymen.[13]

There were some who took the oaths who later revealed that they still nursed Jacobite sympathies, but they appear to have been in the minority. Moreover, the contexts of these revelations were frequently suspect. Clergymen would imbibe a bit too much, and suddenly demonstrate a mettle in defense of the exiled king that went way beyond the loyalties they expressed when sober. Peregrine Periam, the perpetual curate of Midhurst, for example, was apparently emboldened to utter seditious libel while he was tippling. In 1692, he was bound over to the assizes for drinking a health to King James and the prince of Wales and calling William a "Usurper."[14]

Meredith Jones, similarly, was a lionheart for the Pretender when he was "in liquor." In 1718 Jones was curate of the parish of Haslemere, Surrey, which was just across the border from Sussex. One day he was at the Angel Inn in that town, undoubtedly quaffing ale heartily, when he picked a fight with one of his parishioners. Two men gave depositions as to their curate's deportment that day. One of them claimed that the argument started when Jones cast aspersions on the Duke of Marlborough, saying that the general was a "Judas" since he had betrayed his mistress (Queen Anne). The witness then observed that Jones had boasted that he had been at the Battle of Preston fighting for the Pretender, and "that he saw Genl Wills & fired a pistoll, & said he woud dye in the cause." The deponent then asserted that he had suspected Jones of Jacobitism all along because when the curate "prayed for the king the Congregation could not hear him for he alter'd his voice & spoke inwardly." Jones admitted as much while in his drunken condition, and said that "He did not owne him [George] to be king for he had no right to the Crowne." Further he claimed that "he had never taken the oaths to him & never wou'd, but if he was put to it he could swallow an oath as well as another man."[15]

But despite all of this bluster, the episode proves very little about Jones's true loyalties. He may well have said all of these things, but the cocky statements of a man under the influence of liquor may bear little resemblance either to his true sentiments or his willingness to act on them. Furthermore, the witnesses may have had something against their curate and found this a convenient way of getting back at him. Whatever the case, this episode did not keep Jones from obtaining preferment, since he appeared as the Vicar of West Dean the very next year on the presentation of the king.[16] He does not appear to have stirred up any trouble whatsoever from this time on.

There were undoubtedly some Sussex clergymen who lamented the passing of the Stuart line, but their Jacobitism, if it can be called such, was usually sentimental and nostalgic, rather than treasonous. Though they were not really happy with the Protestant Succession, they were not prepared to oppose it. They simply doted on what might have been and bemoaned what was.[17]

But many, if not most, Sussex clergymen were satisfied with the new regime, and argued for the Protestant succession on the basis of God's providence, in conformity with the standard Anglican rationale. They still believed in divine-right monarchy and passive obedience, but they shifted allegiance with alacrity to the new king because he was the new anointed leader of England.

John Shore, Rector of Hamsey, for instance, though he consistently voted Tory and upheld the doctrine of passive obedience, was so happy with the monarchy of William and Mary that he preached ebulliently about their reign in his panegyric for Queen Mary upon her death in 1695. He lamented that there were many who unjustifiably questioned her and her husband's legitimacy, for it was God himself that brought them to the throne in a marvelous display of his power, justice, and mercy: "I look upon all the Enemies of the Government to be . . . men that fight against God, who by a miraculous Revolution has set our present Prince upon the Throne." He marveled that there were so many who grumbled against the succession, since by it God had rescued the English Church and, for that matter, the entire nation from slavery and servitude. Those who were "impatient" with the present government were foolish to "wish for the former Evil again." He compared Englishmen to the Israelites in the wilderness who longed to return to Egypt, and forgot the severity of the bondage there. God had delivered England, just as he had delivered the Israelites, and it was no less a miracle. But Englishmen had short memories just like their ancient counterparts, and they longed for a return to the old days, forgetting the perfidy of James in subverting Anglicanism and imposing arbitrary government. Shore concluded by pleading for complete and hearty obedience to King William, the deliverer.[18]

Peter Heald, Vicar of Cowfold, was also a Tory, and he too counseled obedience to King William. William and Mary were the sovereigns ordained by God to rule over England. How did he know that they were God's appointees?—"because the Powers that are, are ordained of God," pure and simple. The course of the succession did not dictate whether or not citizens owed obedience to the monarch. Passive obedience was still obligatory under God's law. And those who refused to render that obedience would face a fearful reckoning, because "they that resist, resist the Ordinance of God, and shall receive to themselves Damnation."[19]

Edward Wilson, Vicar of Rye, told his parishioners the same thing during Queen Anne's rule in his sermon of 30 January 1712.[20] He advised them "to leave the Government of the World to him that made it, and the Government of the Nation to those he has set at the Helm [evidently, without regard to the succession]." Commoners were not to meddle with their rulers or have any power over them. Absolute obedience was still mandatory, and resistance never an option, even if the government was anti-Christian. After all, he argued, the biblical injunctions for obedience were issued at the very time when an anti-Christian government existed. Order was much more important to Wilson than freedom, and control more desirable than liberty. He echoed Filmer's observation that England was always more in danger of anarchy than arbitrary government, and proved the point by recounting God's deliverance from James by means of King William, which was in his mind clearly a divine, not human, event. This arrangement was in no way a compact between ruler and ruled, as the Whigs claimed. In fact, the episode proved just the opposite to Wilson—it proved that God was directing the course of government, and ought to be left alone to do it, without human interference.[21]

William Bridgen, the future Rector of Folkington and West Dean, was also a staunch Tory, and he used the same line of argumentation with his listeners. Bridgen contended that the monarch was God's anointed, no matter what the circumstances of his or her accession. Kings and queens were still to be absolute rulers—the Acts of Succession had not changed that. Since he took Solomon's dictum—"There is no rising up against the king"—to be prescriptive, Bridgen would countenance no disobedience to the Crown. He berated Whigs for their doctrine of contractual government, for he believed that the people had no power or control over their ruler other than through prayer. Active resistance of any sort would be rewarded with damnation.[22]

Even the Whig, Ezekiel Bristed, Rector of Meeching, avoided preaching contractual government. He too averred that William obtained his right to the throne on account of conquest. Bristed compared William to Constantine, the archetype of Christian rulers. Constantine's legitimacy, he maintained, derived from his piety, which God rewarded in military victory: "as this Emperour thus *Honour'd* God, *in Ministring to his Church,* and Promoting his Religion, so God was pleas'd to honour him with glorious victories and great Prosperity." There was little hint in Bristed's preaching, even though he aligned himself with the Whig party, that government was based on contract. There was, of course, no mention of hereditary right in his sermon, but the idea of government by divine right was very much present. William had earned God's commission to rule because of his piety, which God rewarded with victory over James. Obedience was due him and his successors because of the Providential manner of their appointment.[23]

Clergymen often thought of the accession of George I in the same providential terms. Humphrey Hammond, Rector of East Guildford, for instance, believed that the succession of King George was "wonderfully favour'd by Divine Providence." He was anointed of God to lead England, and his person was "the darling Care of Heaven." Hammond waxed eloquent on the theme of providence guiding the new king: divine winds, he said, "Landed him safe on the wished-for Shore, where he was welcom'd to his Lawful Dominions, by the Loud Acclamations of all that wish'd well to their King and Country; so that if smiling Heavens, prosperous Gales, and a smooth and easy Passage through the terrible Deep, be any lucky Omens and Prognostications of Prosperity and good Success, we have them all conspiring to second our Wishes, and typify our Happiness."[24] Providential theory helped clergymen accept the transitions of government without substantially altering their cherished principle of divine right.[25]

In all of the political sermons preached by the Sussex parish clergy which are extant for these years, there is only one that is unequivocally Whiggish, and that was a sermon by Thomas Blennerhaysett, Rector of Patching, on 30 January 1716, the day on which Tories mourned the "martyrdom" of King Charles I. The title itself left little doubt as to his sympathies: *Legal Obedience, in Opposition to Unlimited.* Blennerhaysett argued, in classical Whig form, that government was a joint venture between the people and ruler.[26] Each had their own responsibility, and each was to be kept in check by the other, and law was to be the arbiter between them. The people were obligated to be subject to their ruler as long as he ruled by law. But if he became arbitrary, it was their privilege—in fact their duty—to cancel their allegiance to him and set up another in his place. In Blennerhaysett's mind, Scripture taught contractual, not absolute government. He made reference to some of the very same passages on obedience as the High Churchmen, but insisted that they were predicated on the behavior of the ruler and on his adherence to government according to the law. Solomon, for example, was very far from demanding adherence to an arbitrary government. He placed just as much emphasis on the responsibility of the ruler as that of the ruled.[27]

These sermons give us a sense of what the Tory/High-Church parsons were thinking. Though the number of extant sermons is, regrettably, quite small, the very fact that the majority of sermons published were High Church is significant. When coupled with the evidence from elections (*infra*), they confirm that the majority of Sussex clergymen were clearly in the Tory camp. Despite their politics and churchmanship, incumbents accepted the leadership of the new king with enthusiasm, or at least good grace. As long as the Church of England was secure they were satisfied.[28] Further, they seldom objected to the Act of Succession that settled the monarchy on the House of Hanover. By 1715 there was only one who was unwilling to take the Oath of Abjuration at George I's accession. That one was Richard Russel, the Vicar of Alfriston and the Rector of Selmeston. Feeling alone and outnumbered because of the very small group of clergy who joined him in refusing the oaths, Russel preached a farewell sermon to his congregation in his own defense, not so much on the rightness of Jacobitism, as on the reasonableness of his decision because of the doubts he entertained about taking the oaths. He admonished those who subscribed even though they had some reservations, and he seemed to think that they amounted to a large group. He was saddened, he said, that several clergymen he knew and respected had seemed resolved to become Non-jurors along with him, but then capitulated and signed the oaths. There were several reasons that such men acquiesced: the persuasion and assurance of others, the sad consequences of not signing, and the lure of preferment. None of these was adequate as far as Russel was concerned. If one subscribed for any reason other than principle, he was a perjurer, and he would face more dire consequences from God than from the government of England: "Whoever therefore is not prepared to suffer, rather than swear falsely, has not, at Present, Christianity enough to be saved, whatever he may attain to hereafter." Russel was prepared, and he suffered. Whatever else he may have been, he was a man of principle and a man of his word.[29]

But Russel stood alone. No other parson in Sussex refused the oaths, not even those whom Russel counted as friends and kindred spirits. Though some may have held similar doubts about the legitimacy of the Hanoverian regime, none were prepared to suffer as Russel did.

From all of this it seems reasonably certain that there was little active Jacobitism among the clergy in Sussex, and whatever loyalty there was to the Stuarts declined rapidly after 1715. There were some rumors of disaffection among the clergy, but these were due as much to personal conflicts as they were to political postures.[30] Some parsons, of course, may have nursed a nostalgic Jacobitism, but it was seldom of the sort that was any real threat.

Politically, then, High Churchmen in Sussex were not marked so much by Jacobitism or the hereditary right of kings, as by a continuing emphasis on divine-right monarchy, passive obedience, and traditionally constituted government. And from all indications, these High-Church tenets reigned supreme among Sussex parsons. There were only a few who ventured contrary opinions, and those few felt themselves to be a persecuted minority.

High Churchmanship and Dissent

High Churchmen, of course, also revealed their true colors by their attitude toward Dissent. Sussex parsons manifested apprehension over Nonconformity and deep-seated unease with the Whiggish/Low-Church tendency to tolerate and/or abet it. Many clergymen felt that Dissenters constituted a fearful threat to the church, and these antagonists had, one way or another, to be checked. William Jenden, for instance, demonstrated his concern about Nonconformity by calling attention to it in the preface of his will:

> I desire all persons to take notice that I live and by God's grace resolve to die in the communion of the Church of England in contradistinction to both Romish and all other Sectarians. And I pray heartily for the prosperity of this most excellent Church as likewise for the Poore distressed estate of the Episcopall (which is the only true) Church of Scotland. Lord give the Sectarians there and their Brethren in England a sight and sense of their grievous and most inexcusable Schism.[31]

Jenden clearly felt that the church was in danger, and he wanted to be put on record for opposing the schism of Dissenters.

The stubbornness of Dissenters frequently kindled the ire of Sussex parsons. William Whitear, Rector of Tangmere and Vicar of Boxgrove, as well as Prebendary of Sidlesham, preached a sermon in the Cathedral Church of Chichester in which he lambasted the Dissenters for their continuing schism. Echoing the earlier work of William Sherlock (see chapter 1), he branded occasional conformity an inexcusable sin, and called for the schismatics to put an immediate end to their "crime" of "separating from us." Dissenters were not honestly mistaken about ecclesiastical government, they were not protecting a weak conscience—they were, rather, deliberately flouting the indisputable authority of the church in its episcopacy, "for there is nothing more plain in every part of History, relating to the Ecclesiastical State, than this unalterable priesthood in the Church, by a constant succession, for more than Sixteen hundred years." There was to be no compromise with Dissenters, since it would only undermine the purity of the church. It is likely that Whitear spoke for many of his clerical brethren, since the sermon was published "at the Desire of the Lord Bishop and the Clergy." Furthermore, Whitear was elected proctor to Convocation by the clergy of the diocese just three years after the preaching of this sermon.[32]

Parochial clergymen had very little patience with Nonconformists. John Needham, future Rector of Storrington and Vicar of Kirdford, poured forth contempt on Dissenters in his two-part sermon, *Considerations Concerning the Origine and Cure of our Church Divisions*. As to the origin of the "division," Needham had no doubt: it arose from the sheer perversity of those who separated from the church. Dissenters frequently could not even give reasons why they had left the Anglican communion. Most of them were simply "of fickle and desultory tempers; ignorant, and pleas'd with any thing, or nothing, just as it happens." Some left because they felt that the established church's services were too "regular and orderly, cool and sober." They wanted more "transport and Heat." Others shifted allegiance because they were stubborn, obstinate, and insufferably arrogant—they felt that they were "cast in a different Mold from other Mortals," and knew better than "all the World," since the verdict of the world was with the Anglicans. Still others thought they could obtain more "profit and Secular Interest" outside of the Church of England.[33] And then there were those who simply wanted an easier religion than Anglicanism—they did not want to struggle toward holiness, but sought a "sensual and worldly Life," which they thought was more readily attainable through antinomianism or predestinarianism.[34]

Despite the fact that Needham promised to propose a "cure" for the schism in this sermon, he was really at a loss for any reasonable solution. Because of the Toleration, he felt that there was very little that could actually be done to win them, other than "to be exemplary in our own Lives and Conversations: this, above all things will set off the cause of our Church to the best Advantage, and will put all our reasonings for it into the best and clearest Light."[35]

Other clergymen, however, had more definite suggestions. William Bridgen, just then M.A. of University College, Oxford, urged that pressure be applied to force Dissenters back into the fold. If that could not be done under the Toleration, he suggested revising or revoking that statute. Furthermore, he advocated that the doctrine of the established church be protected by legislation against trinitarian heresy. In response to the argument that coercion would not make better Christians, he asserted that conformity was still better than unlimited freedom: "Religious Hypocrites are more peaceable Subjects, than heady Rebels and ungovernable Subjects." Control and conformity were more important than liberty of conscience to Bridgen, and in this he was articulating a fundamental of the High-Church ethos.[36]

Many churchmen were anxious, too, about the rise of deism as well as the heterodoxy and republicanism that seemed to be inherent in Latitudinarianism. William Whitear felt that the church was in danger from the infidelity that was spreading rapidly and threatening to overrun the church. "Our soul is among Lions," he lamented, "and the sons of men are set on Fire against us; their teeth are Spears and Arrows, and they shoot out bitter Words; and their Tongue is a sharp sword, they have sharpen'd it like a Serpent, and . . . Adder's Poison is under their lips." Deists had launched a full-scale attack against the church, and churchmen were forced to stand upon the ramparts and defend it against siege of the enemy.[37]

The assaults on the faith, sad to say, often seemed to come from within the ranks of the church's own troops. This is the charge that John Willett, Fellow of Wadham College and soon to be Vicar of Wadhurst, made in a sermon in 1708. He began by excoriating the Dissenters—and the Presbyterians in particular—for remaining outside of the church on account of "a few Innocent Ceremonies, which they can never prove to be Unlawful." Nonconformists were simply peevish, obstinate, and insincere when they persisted in their schism. But worse yet were "those our Comprehensive Friends," the "False Brethren" who questioned divine-right episcopacy in order to appease and woo our "Enemies," the Dissenters. With

Sacheverellian drama, he pounced upon those, "Our Pretended Friends," who were "perpetually Galling and Worrying Us in our Own Camp, and within our Own Walls." They were selling out the true religion for a false one, and trading their birthright for a mess of pottage. In Willett's mind, divine-right episcopacy was not merely an accessory to Anglicanism; it was not an indifferent matter—it was, rather, at the very heart of Christianity and had been "unquestionably made out, and universally Asserted by all Sound and Orthodox Writers." Therefore, those who sought to attenuate it in order to coddle the Dissenters were "False Brethren" and "Treacherous Hypocrites."[38]

Daniel Lafite, the Rector of Woolavington, inveighed against the schemes of Low Churchmen to promote lay religion in his sermon at a visitation of the clergy in Chichester in 1712.[39] To Lafite their efforts represented a plot to rob priests of their rightful authority and denigrate the ministry of ordination. He saw this as all of a piece with the Whig (and Nonconformist) doctrine of "republicanism," which siphoned authority away from the monarch just as lay religion drained it from clerics. He argued from Scripture and history that the priesthood was a divinely instituted office and that laymen had no authority in the realm of religion. Dissenters were flouting God's order, the divinely mandated hierarchy, by reducing the ministry to the same level as shoemaking or farming. And the galling thing was that so many of the Anglican clergymen were not only allowing them to do it, but were assisting them. It was just one more area in which the Latitudinarians were seeking to weaken the church. And, he warned, "Let all our Republicans, and all *Latitudinarians,* therefore consider what they do, and what Hazard they run, in rejecting the *Ministry by whom they were baptized;* they do not only reject and renounce the *Means* of Salvation, and the *Instruments* God hath made use of to convey his *Doctrine,* . . . they renounce a *Fundamental Principle* of the Christian Religion, and *if the Foundation falls, how can the Building stand?*"[40] For Lafite, acceptance and toleration of the Dissenters necessarily entailed the degradation of episcopacy and the Anglican priesthood. When Anglicans started championing Whig tenets, the entire ministry was in jeopardy. Thus, once again, the church was in danger because of the presence of Dissenters and, worse yet, Latitudinarians who capitulated to their republican and egalitarian principles.

There was, however, at least one defender of Latitudinarianism in the county: Humphrey Hammond. Hammond identified himself with the Low Churchmen and Whigs who had, in recent years, been so hounded by

High-Church zealots, and he defended their actions.[41] He started by lamenting the deplorable factions that had developed in recent years amongst churchmen: "Should one of the Primitive Christians arise from the Dead, and behold the Debates, Envyings, Strifes, Backbitings, Whisperings, Swellings, Tumults, that are now among Christians, he would think the very nature of Christianity was changed, and that Holy Religion, which was wont to transform Men from barbarous Cannibals, into harmless inoffensive Beings, had suffer'd a Metamorphosis, and lost all its amiable and native Charms." In his mind there was no real cause for the division. Though he acknowledged "that many of our Brotherhood keep company and converse with those that are bitter Enemies to our Church, and no lovers of the Clergy; hence, some call us Presbyterians," this did not mean that they were selling out the church. On the contrary, there was no cause to think this would be the result of their dealings, for two reasons. First, it was inconceivable that Anglican clergymen would "destroy their own house" for the sake of moderation and charity. They were not selling out the Church of England; they were not allowing heterodoxy and deism to creep in—they were simply trying to call the erring ones back into the church with love and charity. Second, Hammond pointed to the state of the church under these supposed traitors. Their plan was working. "Let us consider," he said, "what great Augmentation our Church has receiv'd under their Administration." Rather than destroying the church as High Churchmen feared, the Latitudinarians' policy of conciliation had actually strengthened it: its enemies were neutralized and it was garnering greater respect.[42]

Contrary to the charges High Churchmen made, Hammond and his Low-Church colleagues were not really happy about Dissenters, nor were they trying to destroy the established church by giving in to them. But their attitude differed from High Churchmen in two significant ways. First of all, Low Churchmen believed that they could live in harmony with Dissenting brethren, without either forcing them into the church or out of society. They could be incorporated into the structure of the culture without threatening the viability or authority of the established church. The prejudices of Nonconformists against Anglican rites were unimportant compared to the "weightier matters of the Law, Righteousness, Judgment, and Faith, or the Love of God," around which Anglicans and Dissenters alike could unite. And they need not be in the same communion to have harmony. Second, the Latitudinarians became convinced that the only possible way of winning over Nonconformists was by example and Christian love: "Charity is the onely way now left to propagate the Gospel of Christ." Force was neither advisable nor effective. Coercion was not only ineffective, it was counterproductive. But that did not mean that the true church was impotent. On the contrary, the way of love was "so excellent a way, that Miracles and Prophecy give place to it."[43]

But Hammond's Latitudinarian opinions were unusual and precocious among the Sussex clergy. Most parsons were still preaching a gospel of control or coercion. One can imagine the murmurs and jeers of the disgusted crowd of clergy and laity as they stood listening to Hammond's words. Certainly he felt hard-pressed on account of his Latitudinarian stand. When he was trying to establish a charity school in Tenterden, Kent, just a few miles away from his parish in Sussex, he complained to the archbishop that the people unreasonably opposed him because he would not "Embarque in their warm way of Politics." They chastised and persecuted him by giving him an "inconvenient Hole" in which to convene his pupils when there were a great many more comfortable and convenient places to hold classes.[44]

Most Sussex clergymen could not be as sanguine as Hammond about Dissent—they were still contending desperately against it. Richard Russel, the Non-juror, though unique in his decision to decline the oaths, was very much in the mainstream in his concern for the church. He evinced a deep apprehension over Dissent in his farewell sermon to his congregation. He had worked diligently, he said, to vindicate the Church of England's "Doctrine and Worship, against Papists on one Hand, and Fanatics on the other." It was the latter in particular that distressed Russel, since it was by Dissenters that "she [the church] has been so much insulted and abused of late." As with other High Churchmen, Russel saw the agitation of Dissenters as challenges to the authority and well-being of the "true Church," and he expressed his hopes that his successor would continue to contend for the faith.[45]

Thus the concern for the church and the fear that it was under attack and "in danger," was a pressing concern for High Churchmen in Sussex and elsewhere in the early part of the century. The issue of the succession had largely fallen away, but the problem of Dissent remained. Thus it was that Bishop Thomas Manningham could report to Archbishop Wake in 1718 that "many of those they call ye Highest in my diocese do declare that they are perfectly at ease concerning the Monarchy of George & the present Succession, but that they have some plans for the Ch[urch] and are much troubled to be soe continuously insulted by the dissenters who pretend to be encouraged to it by the Court. They are doubtless under a mistake."[46]

Manningham appears to have been speaking for himself as much as for his clergy—his communiqués reveal a deep concern about the well-being of the church and a nervousness about the Dissenters that verges on paranoia. He reported to Wake in June of the same year that the town of Lewes was "so miserably overrun with Dissenters, that the Ch[urch] of Eng. has little reputation in those parts, and accordingly the Rectors and Sacred officers are under a great Contempt."[47] He was profoundly relieved when he discovered that Wake intended to vote against repealing the Test Act and considered his decision an act of loyalty to the Church of England.[48] Manningham and the parochial clergy were one on this: "Your last letter, wherein you were pleased to express your resolution of standing firm wth the Ch[urch] of Eng. against all the encroachments of the Dissenters has mightily pleasd all the clergy, whom I have had opportunity to converse wth." This resolution of Wake's, he said, would serve "to be a good introduction to a closer union amongst us." As long as the court dropped its efforts to aid Nonconformists, churchmen could rest easier and would have little compunction against joining wholeheartedly with the administration.[49]

These are the concerns of High Churchmen as revealed by their extant writings. But how representative are they? Did High Churchmen really outnumber Low Churchmen? These are difficult questions to answer, but fortunately there is some evidence that can help us measure the concentration of High Churchmanship in the diocese during this period. The following section will outline this evidence.

High Churchmanship and Sussex Politics

In the years before 1715, the strength of the High Church can be gauged by clerical participation in countywide parliamentary elections. The bond between the High Church and Tory party in this period was so strong that to know the strength of one is virtually to know the strength of the other. After all, the major principles of the Tory party—divine right theories of government, protectionism in church and state, conservatism, and so on—were built squarely upon the concepts that had evolved in the High Church.[50] An analysis of the political activity of Sussex parsons during these years will, therefore, yield significant information about their churchmanship.

There are poll books for 1705, 1708, 1710, and 1713 that record the clerical voting patterns.[51] There is no question that, except for the election of 1708, the Tory clergy outvoted the Whig clergy. Table 1 summarizes the voting record of Sussex clergy for all four elections.

There are a number of observations that need to be made on the basis of these data. First of all, the number of clergymen who did not vote is striking and needs some explanation. If, indeed, the clergy were as zealous for the High-Church/Tory cause in these years as they have been depicted, one would expect there to have been a greater turnout at the polls. But there are some mitigating factors. For one thing, not every parson could meet the eligibility requirements. Not every incumbent owned real estate.[52] They certainly did not have to buy property, since their livings usually included a parsonage with glebe lands attached. Clergymen bought land for investment, not sustenance. There were cases in fact, where opponents of the victors in certain elections charged that there were false votes cast because clergymen who did not own property were polled nonetheless.[53] But this cannot explain the absence of above half of the parsons. In all likelihood, it represented only a minority of them, because, though many of them were thought to be poor, few had no property at all.[54]

There are other possibilities. Sickness or infirmity undoubtedly kept some from making their voice heard. The polls for the county were taken

Table 1.

	1705	1708	1710	1713
Tory	64	30	67	80
Whig	13	26	10	27
Mixed	24	10	6	15
Nonvoters[a]	122	150	120	93
Total	223	216	203	215

a. These figures denote the number of clergymen who were beneficed, but did not vote, in the diocese of Chichester at the time of these elections. They do not indicate eligibility (that is, that they met the 40-shilling freehold requirement). Further, the figures are inexact. Though they are based on the number of clergymen known to hold livings at the time, there are some discrepancies and inaccuracies in that data, such that these numbers must remain approximations (though very good ones).

in alternate election years at Chichester and Lewes, and the journey to the one or the other could be quite difficult and unpleasant. Many clergy suffered from gout or other disabilities that made such a trip torturous, and many of these begged off because of it.

Further, there were some who held their livings in plurality and resided far away (dispensations were sometimes issued to exempt clergymen from the thirty-mile rule). For this reason men such as John Strype, the famous historian, who was the Rector of West Tarring (in addition to that of Low Leyton in Essex) never voted in the county of Sussex. Nonresident Sussex clergymen may or may not have owned property in the county, but they seldom traveled to their distant benefice in order to vote in an election.

Some of the absentees must simply have been apathetic or frustrated with politics. A few High Churchmen came to the realization that their zeal in earlier years may have exceeded acceptable bounds, and resolved not to meddle in politics or disputes any more. Robert Wake, the nephew of the Archbishop and Rector of Buxted, had demonstrated a fiery High-Church temperament in several of his early sermons. He ranted about the dangers facing the church from Dissenters and Low Churchmen, and lambasted his Latitudinarian colleagues for their villainy. Furthermore, he complained that there were so many "meal-mouth'd Cowards now-a-days, who are so much for mincing and moderating everything they should not," that he would have to be so much the bolder.[55] He may have become too bold for his own good—there are hints that his brashness stirred up Whig resentment and opposition just as Sacheverell's had. Moreover, he was probably sympathetic with the Jacobite cause, which did not endear him to the Whigs. In any case, he wrote to his uncle, to whom he owed his preferment, in 1722, and promised that it was his "resolution by the Grace of God to be quiet & peacable under this present government." He acknowledged that his previous High-Church agitation had caused him trouble and that he was tempering his behavior because of it: "The great misfortunes of my wicked, scandalous resolutions and my Family formerly have occasioned my recluse way of Living, & I suppose I shall now never be able to Live otherwise."[56] Wake found that there was indeed a price to pay for overweening zeal, and he had been cowed by it. There is no hint, though, that he was converted to a Whiggish frame of mind, just that he realized that his actions had been immoderate and unacceptable.

The example does not prove that this was the reason that Sussex clergymen failed to show up at the polls—it simply demonstrates a possible scenario. We do know from anecdotes regarding subsequent elections that some parsons decided not to trouble themselves because of the problems it caused them with benefactors and/or parishioners. It is likely, therefore, that some incumbents decided that it was in their best interest not to stir up opposition to their ministries and livelihoods by voting one way or the other.

The puzzling thing about the absenteeism in elections, though, is that so many of the prominent clergy were guilty of it. Neither William Barcroft, Treasurer of the cathedral and proctor to Convocation in 1710, nor William Whitear, prebendary and proctor to Convocation in 1713, nor Josias Pleydell, Archdeacon of Chichester and Canon,[57] nor John Newey, dean of the chapter, appeared to vote at Sussex elections. It may be that some of them voted elsewhere, since many of them had properties and obligations in other counties, but it still seems odd that there should be such a lack of electoral representation among the cathedral clergy.

But not voting could be a statement too. It could demonstrate unresolved conflicts in the electorate. The election of 1708 is a case in point. In this year the Tories were at a serious disadvantage because of a new threat of invasion from the Pretender.[58] Clergymen and others who wished to proclaim their loyalty to the Protestant succession were loathe to vote Tory, since, rightly or wrongly, Toryism was frequently associated with Jacobitism. But because they were not for the Whigs either, many refrained from voting. Thus only 66 clergy in the entire diocese voted, while 150 abstained. Furthermore, the number of votes for the Whigs almost equaled the number for the Tories, which was an unprecedented balance. It is clear, too, that the parsons who voted Tory in this election were die-hard High Churchmen, and many of them were probably sympathetic with the Jacobite cause, if not Jacobites themselves. These voters, almost to a man, voted Tory in every single election they could, and never varied from their party affiliation. Those who cast votes for the Whigs in the 1708 election, however, were much more flexible. Only nine of the twenty-six were consistent Whigs, suggesting that they felt that voting Whig was advisable on this occasion, but not on others. For seven of the Whig voters, it was the only time they ever voted. Several others appear to have voted consistently Tory in other elections. And the clergymen who cast mixed votes were almost invariably Tory. They may simply have been hedging their bets on this occasion.[59]

Several observations can be made on the basis of the data from these early elections. First of all, it is clear that the majority of Sussex clergymen were High Church and Tory. When the individual parsons are followed through all four elections, it can be seen that no fewer than sixty-six of them voted consistently Tory on two or more occasions. Another forty-nine voted Tory (and only Tory) at least once—and many of them only had one opportunity, since they died before 1708. Given these statistics, it is evident that well over half of the clergy in the diocese were High Church and Tory. This is a very conservative estimate: the ratio of High Churchmen was probably much higher.

The number of active Whigs was significantly smaller, though not inconsiderable. There were some twenty-two clergymen who voted Whig (and only Whig) at least two times, and another seven who voted that way at least once (if the 1708 election is included, that number doubles). It may well have been that there was more Whig/Low-Church sentiment than is revealed by these figures, but the Tories clearly had the momentum and they very likely dominated the rhetoric; thus the more reticent incumbents may not have wanted to go against the tide. But, in any case, there can be no question that High Churchmen were in the majority in Sussex in the early eighteenth century, even if their hegemony has been overstated in the past.

The issue of patronage is a difficult one for this period. If there were concerted efforts of patrons to influence their clients one way or the other, those efforts are now shrouded by the mists of time. It is likely that there was a fair amount of campaigning and a concomitant amount of persuasion applied, but there probably was not the large-scale coordinated pressure that was applied by the Whigs under Newcastle.[60] Those who owed their livings to the Crown, for instance, were just as likely to vote one way as the other. It did not seem to matter, either, which monarch presented them. Appointees of the Bishop of Chichester were unpredictable too, and could easily vote against him. And the patronage of the dean and chapter created no clear-cut party alliance.[61] Unfortunately, there are just not enough particulars available to shed much light on this issue for the elections of 1705 to 1713, but it certainly appears that clerical clients maintained a significant degree of electoral autonomy.[62]

After 1713, information about successive elections is scant. There was certainly a hard-fought battle at the polls in 1715, but, other than a final tally of votes cast, little or no data were preserved. The Whigs won, but there is no information about the disposition of the clergy in the affair. Further, from 1715 to 1734 no contest was even recorded, suggesting to many that the Duke of Newcastle, who was building a patronage network in Sussex, had reduced the opposition to quiescence.[63] Undoubtedly it was not that simple. First of all, the fact that there were no polls in the period does not in itself mean there was no dissatisfaction with the Whig party. Second, there are clear instances where Tories rebelled, and at least threatened opposition. In 1722, for instance, John Reynell reported to the SPCK that he had had trouble trying to establish a charity school, largely because of the furor created by the election.[64] Certainly there were contests in some of the boroughs, and it is just possible that the Tories pinned their hopes on those during these years, rather than the county election.[65] But whatever the case, the Tories may have been down, but they were not out—or at least they did not think they were out. Tory sentiment lay dormant in political affairs during these years, but that did not mean that clergymen lost their High-Church identity. High Churchmanship, just like its political concomitant, was inert but not lifeless.

The Convocation elections provide some information about politics and churchmanship in these years. Three individuals were chosen to represent the diocese in the lower house of Convocation for each session, which was called at the same time as Parliament. One of the representatives was chosen by the dean and chapter of the cathedral and one was chosen for each of the two archdeaconries of the diocese by the clergy of each archdeaconry. During the years before the Hanoverian accession, the only proctors elected for Convocation from Chichester, both by the dignitaries and the beneficed incumbents, were High Churchmen. In 1701 Henry Edes, canon residentiary, was chosen by the dean and chapter. In the same year, Conyers Richardson, Rector of Ford, and a staunch High Churchman, was elected for the archdeaconry of Chichester, while Anthony Saunders, another Tory, was sent by the archdeaconry of Lewes. The clergy of the Lewes division chose Saunders time and time again, whereas the incumbents of Chichester chose a different man each session.

The candidate chosen for West Sussex in 1708 was a man who undoubtedly represented the archdeaconry well. He seems to reflect sentiments that mirrored the temper of clergymen in that as well as other years. John Wright was chancellor of Chichester from 1701 until his death in 1719. Wright was a clear supporter of the Protestant Succession, and therefore could not be accused of Jacobitism, but he was no Low Churchman. He published a sermon in his later years (1716), similar to those cited above, in which he argued for the accession of William, Anne, and George to the throne on account of the providence of God, and was probably well known for his stand on the succession in 1708.[66] He was therefore above suspicion in the year in which the Pretender was threatening invasion. Further, he voted Whig in the parliamentary poll in 1708. But Wright was no Latitudinarian and he was not at all happy with the Low-Church tendencies to limit the authority of the ministry and/or give concessions to Dissenters. In 1717 he would react in horror to Benjamin Hoadly's attack on the natural and God-given rights and privileges of the ministry. He argued vigorously for the apostolic succession and, consequently, the independent authority of the clergy, and accused Hoadly of being one of the "False Brethren" in the church. Hoadly and his ilk were enemies "of our own Household," and were selling out the church in favor of the Dissenters, who, in Wright's view, were to be given no quarter in society. The Nonconformists in general, and Presbyterians in particular, were a direct challenge to episcopacy because they did not acknowledge the divine institution of the Church of England.[67] Because of his acceptance of the succession, coupled with his uncompromising High Churchmanship, Wright was the perfect choice for proctor for Convocation in 1708. He continued to be favored by the dean and chapter, and was their representative in 1713 and 1715.

In 1710 the Chichester archdeaconry put up two candidates, both of whom were High Churchmen. John Reynell was the Vicar of Horsham, and though little is known about him, he voted Tory consistently in parliamentary elections. It is telling, also, that he named one of his daughters Henrietta Maria, for this was the name of Charles I's wife. This, in itself, is a good indication of his allegiances; clearly, he was a High Churchman. Dr. Edward Pelling, the venerable old defender of High Churchmanship, was the other candidate. Pelling had been beneficed since 1674, and he was part of the generation that defined High Churchmanship—he authored numerous books in which he stressed sacramentalism, opposed Dissenters, defended divine-right monarchy and passive obedience, contended for an authoritarian ecclesiastical establishment, and execrated the murder of King Charles I. His *Good Old Way* was a classical text of High Churchmanship.[68] In the election, Pelling won handily, beating Reynell by a margin of almost two to one. What is particularly significant here is that not only were there two High-Church candidates rather than one High-Church and one Low-Church, but even some of those who voted Whig in the parliamentary election of the same year voted for Pelling. John Marshall, Saville Bradley, Henry Wright, and Charles Randol Covert all voiced their preference for Pelling. That they voted for either candidate might be surprising, since they both promised to carry on the High-Church fight, but their choice of Pelling is remarkable indeed. Several other known Whigs voted for Reynell, and several abstained.[69]

In 1713 there was a similar contest in the Lewes archdeaconry. There Henry Snooke, Vicar of Ringmer, opposed John Grandorge, Rector of Hartfield and Ashurst. Once again both candidates were on record as Tories. John Grandorge was returned with a 35–26 advantage, and continued as the representative for Lewes into the next session (1716). Only three of the eastern-division Whigs were represented at this election, and those that did appear supported their Tory brethren.[70] No Whig was even considered for the post.

Convocation had been unruly ever since the High-Church/Low-Church split developed, but after George I ascended the throne it became uncontrollable. For this reason, the king prorogued its meetings indefinitely. From 1717 on Convocation did not meet, except once briefly in 1741–42. This continual prorogation amounted to an easy victory for the Whig establishment. It whisked away the main forum of High Churchmen and muted their collective voice. But since Convocation was prorogued rather than abolished, proctors for each session were duly chosen and registered, in case the gathering should proceed. In many places elections continued to be heated, and High Churchmen campaigned for their candidates in a continuing bid for recognition, weak as it may have been in this arena.[71]

In Sussex concern over proctors to Convocation continued only fitfully, with one year being a battle royale and the next being marked by apparent indifference. In 1722 the number of clergymen who appeared at the election for the proctor to represent the Archdeaconry of Chichester was less than a fourth of what it was in 1710: though all clergymen were cited to appear, only eleven showed up. But nine of those eleven were staunch High Churchmen, and so a Tory was returned.[72] In 1727 some twenty-three men assembled, and this time the Whigs had enough strength to elect one of their own, but if there was a contest between the Whig and Tory factions, the Whigs must have just barely overcome the Tories, since the sides were very nearly matched in strength.[73] There was a concerted attempt by High Churchmen in the eastern part of the diocese to return a Tory to Convocation in 1734. Though no record of the election was preserved, there were observations by the Whig parliamentary agents that John Bear, Rector of Shermanbury, was either running against the Whigs or was leading a campaign to vote a High Churchman into the post. Bear and his followers were not successful—the Whigs outvoted them in both elections that year.[74]

The political activity of the clergy during this period indicates that most Sussex parsons were High Churchmen and Tories. This may have gradually changed after the Hanoverian accession, but as we will see, there was still plenty of High-Church/Tory sentiment in 1734.

High Churchmanship and the Cathedral Chapter

It has frequently been assumed that the Whigs "packed" the cathedral chapter with Low Churchmen in order to gain political control over the whole diocese. In this view, the church in Sussex was little more than a "pocket borough" for the Duke of Newcastle, the leading Whig in the county, if not the nation.[75] In actuality, Newcastle may not have had to "pack" the cathedral chapter with Whigs.[76] It appears to be the case that, for some reason, at least half of the dignitaries were Whig already as early as 1710, and that proportion only rose as the century wore on.[77] Why this took place is not at all clear, when the sympathies of the diocese, and perhaps even the bishop, seem to have been the contrary. Bishop Manningham was constantly quarreling with his dignitaries, and some of that antagonism may have come about because he did not like the complexion of the cathedral chapter.

Unfortunately, the years before 1734 are shadowy, since Newcastle's papers are fragmentary in this period, and little documentation of substance was kept in the episcopal archives. Nevertheless, some of the conflict due to the growth of Whiggery can be detected, and the cathedral became one of the stages upon which this drama was acted out. Bishop Manningham seems to have feared that his dignitaries were slipping into a compromising Latitudinarianism. At least that is how he characterized his conflict with the Archdeacon of Lewes, Richard Bowchier. Bowchier, on the other hand, chalked it up to the bishop's peevish nature. In any case, the quarrel between the two men was long-running and bitter. As early as 1716, Bowchier was censured for "speaking words against Bp. Manningham," for which infraction he duly apologized, since his comments had been made "in passion."[78] But the animosity between the two men flared up again in 1721 when Bowchier read prayers in the cathedral. Apparently Bowchier took it upon himself to conclude the service by giving the blessing, which the bishop took as a personal affront and as an affront to the entire episcopal order. Manningham undoubtedly felt that in this episode his archdeacon was departing from tradition and flouting the authority of his diocesan. This only confirmed his suspicions that Bowchier was a Low

Churchman. "This bold and schismatical affront," Manningham was supposed to have written in his register, "deserves a punishment answerable to the exceeding insolency of the crime, of which the Bp will take time to consider."[79] He remained civil to the archdeacon, but as Bowchier told it, he "ran about the Town abusing me, Declaring that I was a Schismatick and antiepiscopate." Bowchier was hurt by this attack and vociferously defended his churchmanship to the archbishop. His protestations of loyalty notwithstanding, Bowchier was well-connected to the Whig establishment, especially the Pelham family, and Manningham may well have been offended at his Low-Church attachments.[80] The dispute between the two men simmered for years, and Bowchier constantly complained about the way Bishop Manningham treated him.[81]

There were other disputes among the cathedral clergy, too, which reflected tensions between High and Low Churchmen. There was a battle, for instance, between the residentiaries and some of the nonresidentiary prebendaries over the chapter choice for Convocation in 1727. The dean at the time was Thomas Sherlock, who was just days away from being created Bishop of Bangor. In November a cabal of Whig prebendaries forced their way into the election and managed to choose one of their own to be the chapter's proctor at Convocation. Traditionally, only the dean and the residentiaries (the four canons who resided in the cathedral close and were charged with most of the cathedral business[82]) were eligible to vote, but in this year Thomas Manningham (another individual of the same name as the late bishop), Daniel Walter, John Peachey, John Pinnell, Isaac Maddox, Bartholomew Cox, and Thomas Ball, mostly nonresidentiaries, orchestrated the election, and even called the meeting in the name of the dean. With the added numbers of nonresidentiaries, they managed to elect Daniel Walter as proctor, and though there was much acrimony over the decision, the dean and the bishop confirmed the decision and sent Walter's name in as the Chichester representative. Undoubtedly the moving spirit behind the petition sent to Archbishop Wake to protest this untraditional procedure was John Parke, the High Churchman and Tory's Tory who was appointed residentiary in 1720. He continued to resent the Whigs' hegemony and stirred up trouble for them for decades.[83]

Thus a bitter rivalry developed in the cathedral chapter as Whig strength and influence grew. Though they had had a majority for some years, they only managed to wrest control away from the Tories in the 1720s. High Churchmen were now proscribed and kept from the upper echelons of preferment and, though their numbers did not really decrease, their sensitivity to Whig pressure grew until they saw themselves as a persecuted minority. The dire predictions of High Churchmen during Anne's reign really seemed to be coming to pass.

To sum up, in the years 1688 to 1734, the clergy of the Diocese of Chichester were predominantly, though not necessarily overwhelmingly, High Churchmen. They accepted gracefully (sometimes jubilantly) the changes in the succession of the monarchy, but did not attenuate their teaching on divine-right monarchy, passive obedience, or the sacraments and liturgy. Indeed, they could not jettison those, since they were inextricably linked to their concept of divine-right episcopacy. These doctrines were all of a piece in their world view, which was based on order by divine mandate. Dissenters threatened that world view, since they challenged divine-right doctrines. For this reason, Sussex parsons contended with Dissenters—Quakers, Presbyterians, and Baptists alike—and if they could not prevail, urged their suppression.

Clergymen, in general, identified with the Tory party, because it was the "church party," and promised protection for the established church. There was a small group of consistent Whigs among the clergy, but they were always outnumbered by the rank and file. This is true everywhere but the cathedral chapter, where Whigs gained early influence. Because of this, there were some bitter feuds among the cathedral clergy. With the consecration of Thomas Bowers (one of the early Sussex Whigs and chaplain and friend to the Duke of Newcastle) as Bishop of Chichester in 1724, the prelacy of the diocese became irrevocably Whig. From this time, too, there was a concerted effort by Newcastle and his allies to gain the allegiance of the clergy by disposing preferment only to those who were loyal to his person and his cause.

All of this notwithstanding, Tory and High-Church sentiment did not just disappear. On the contrary, it was surprisingly vigorous in the 1730s, as the election of 1734 was to attest. But by this time some High Churchmen were beginning to discover what they could not even have imagined during the Sacheverell years: that they could ally themselves with Whig forces without destroying the church.

Notes

1. There is, however, a recent study that argues that High-Church/Tory thought was not so dominant. See William C. Watson, "The Late Stuart Reformation: Church and State in the First Age of Party," Ph.D. diss., University of California, Riverside, 1994.

2. *VCH* 2:47.

3. The fact that the church continued to operate through this tangled, and thus perplexing, structure is one of the main reasons Peter Virgin has called the age one of "negligence" (*Church in an Age of Negligence*). But the impression created by such a label is false—the organization may have needed reform, but that does not mean that those who operated within it were inattentive and lax in their duties. In fact, as Dorothy Owen observed, it was a dynamic organization despite its confusing structure: "There is indeed good reason for perplexity: the society whose records we are to study is as longlasting and complex as any that may be found. Its enduring vitality has constantly given rise, in new circumstances, to new altered organizations; for it has changed much since the remote centuries when it first took root in England" (*Records of the Established Church*, 7).

4. Though the diocese was once divided into rural deaneries, or subdivisions of the archdeaconries, only the peculiar deaneries survived after the Reformation (*VCH* 2:42–44). The deaneries of South Malling, Tarring, and Pagham originated from Saxon land grants given to the See of Canterbury, and were therefore under the jurisdiction of the archbishop. The deanery of Battle was created by the Conqueror as a votive for his victory over the Saxons, and it remained an independent entity until it was abolished in 1846. See *VCH* 2:3–4; Steer, *Diocese of Chichester*, xxii–xxiii. See also Hudson, "Ancient Deaneries."

5. Owen, *Records of the Established Church*, 8. There was a significant political difference, however, between the bishop and the archdeacon: bishops, by right of their office, sat in the House of Lords; archdeacons received no political power on account of their office.

6. These offices probably date from the twelfth century, when they were founded and endowed in order to take care of the increasing administrative and liturgical work for the bishop (*VCH* 3:146).

7. Davies, "Enforcement of Religious Uniformity," 354.

8. Only one canon was required to be in residence at a time. Since there were four canons, therefore, each was obligated to residence three months a year. For the residency patterns of canons, see Brooke et al, "Canon's Residence."

9. *VCH* 3:146.

10. For information on the origin and duties of these parochial offices, see Virgin, *Church in an Age of Negligence;* Spurr, *Restoration Church*, 173–74; and Tindal-Hart, *Curate's Lot*.

11. Lake had been one of the seven bishops who defied James II by declining to read out the Proclamation of Indulgence for Dissenters, which James had or-

dered in 1687. But this did not mean he was ready to endorse William of Orange as King. True to his principles of passive obedience and hereditary right, Lake defied James but remained loyal to him. Though Lake was suspended for his refusal to take the oaths to William, he died before he could be officially deprived. Stephens, *Diocesan Histories,* 236–40.

12. Peckham, "Non-jurors"; Overton, *Nonjurors,* 474–95.

13. Peckham, "Non-jurors," 6.

14. Luttrell, *Brief Historical Relation* 2:352. There is no indication that he was punished for his actions; he seems to have remained PC for Midhurst until 1709, presumably the time of his death. Hennessy, *Chichester Diocese Clergy Lists,* 107.

15. PRO SP 35, vol. 11, ff. 193–94.

16. Peckham, "Chichester Institutions," 71. There is a small possibility that the Meredith Jones prosecuted in Haslemere is a different individual from the one that became vicar of West Dean, but the odds are strongly against such a coincidence: the livings were not very far away from each other and Meredith was not a very common name.

17. See Chamberlain, "Portrait of a High-Church Clerical Dynasty."

18. Shore, *Threnody of the Bow,* 18–20.

19. Heald, *Sermon,* 11–12.

20. The thirtieth of January was a sacred day to High Churchmen because it was the day upon which Charles I had been "martyred" in 1649. On this day clergymen frequently took the opportunity to lambaste the regicides and to press home the idea of passive obedience.

21. Wilson, *Sermon,* 10–11, 17–18.

22. Bridgen, *Duty and Power,* 4–10. There seems to be only one copy of this sermon, and it is deposited in the Public Library, Brighton, East Sussex.

23. Bristed, *Religion and Loyalty,* 9–13.

24. Hammond, *God Save the King,* 8.

25. Spurr, "'Virtue, Religion and Government,'" 61–82, and Straka, *Anglican Reactions.*

26. See Kenyon, *Revolution Principles,* 35–60.

27. Blennerhaysett, *Legal Obedience,* 5–9.

28. For this reason, many parsons were relieved when the new king issued his proclamation regarding the church. Joseph Graves acknowledged his satisfaction to the SPCK in 1714 by writing to them that he was "glad to hear that the King will preserve the Chhs of England & Scotland by his Declaration" (SPCK Abstract Letter Book, CRI 5:4137). Humphrey Hammond expanded on that sentiment in his sermon of thanksgiving for the king's accession. He said that it was "an unspeakable Blessing" that the new king would "maintain the Doctrine and Discipline of the Church of England, as by Law establish'd" (Hammond, *God Save the King,* 7).

29. Richard Russel, *Obligation,* 1–23.

30. Thomas Blennerhaysett complained that he, as a Whig, was hardpressed by "disaffected persons" in and around his parish. Though he seemed to include some clergymen in his indictment, his main complaint was against his patron, Sir John Shelley, who was "a Bigotted Papist," and the Jacobite JPs who would not give Blennerhaysett satisfaction in his dispute with Shelley (SPCK Abstract Letter Book, CRI 4:3817 and CRI 8:5409). Though it is probably true that there were some JPs who harbored Jacobite sympathies (see the Newcastle correspondence, BL Add. MS 32,686 ff. 147, 228), there are no hints of such like attitudes among Blennerhaysett's clerical neighbors. Several of them, in fact, were Whigs.

31. Will 1704, WSRO STCI/30/727.

32. Whitear, *Apology for the Church*, 14, 19–20.

33. He did not explain how or why they thought this.

34. Needham, *Considerations*, 15–28.

35. Ibid., 59–60. Needham had a curious ability to vilify the dissenters on the one hand, and then be gentle to them on the other (he proposed, for instance, treating them "with Humanity and Respect"). Though he did not allow for any compromise (e.g., on the matters of kneeling at the sacrament, using the surplice, etc.), he also did not advocate suppression. He may have been trying to walk a thin line between the High- and Low-Church positions. He accepted patronage from Whigs, and voted with them in later years.

36. Bridgen, *Duty and Power of the Magistrate*, 16–27.

37. Whitear, *Apology for the Church*, 6.

38. Willett, *Nature and Mischiefs*, 8–14.

39. It is not entirely clear to which schemes he is referring. The only thing that is clear is that Lafite objected to the fact that some clergymen were lobbying for laymen to take more of an active part in worship. This was probably part of the Latitudinarian effort to reform Anglican worship so that it would be more conducive to Dissenters.

40. Lafite, *No Lawful Ministry*, 3–19. The only copy of this sermon I have found is at the Brighton Public Library, Brighton, East Sussex.

41. Not only did he fend off the charges of High Churchmen as if they were directed against him, but he also voted consistently Whig.

42. Hammond, *Duty of God's Ministers*, 26–31. Note: there appears to have been no popular request for this sermon to be published—Hammond undertook that on his own.

43. Ibid., 6, 24.

44. Hammond to Wake, 5 March 1716, ArchW Epist. 7, f. 326.

45. Russel, *Obligation*, 23.

46. Thomas Manningham to Wake, 10 July 1718, ArchW Epist. 20, f. 578. I am grateful to Peter Le Fevre for calling this reference to my attention.

47. Manningham to Wake, 26 June 1718, ArchW Epist. 20, f. 557.

48. Wake's own deliberations, with arguments pro and con, are preserved in

his papers. He too sensed the disaster that this bill could wreak on the church: "Consider how they [dissenters] destroyd the Ch of Scotland. . . . Should they ever unite wth their brethren in England, what would become of us? We knew how they used us when they once had power." ArchW Epist. 8, f. 87.

49. Manningham to Wake, 9 August 1718, ArchW Epist. 7, f. 225.

50. Speck, *Tory & Whig,* 1–8, 110–14. Speck notes that there were occasions during this period when both the Tory and Whig interests became divided, but that they were very rare. In general, before 1715 the Whig and Tory parties were cohesive units centered around consistent ideologies.

51. These poll books are to be found in the following collections. The 1705 returns are preserved in a nineteenth-century manuscript in the library of the Sussex Archeological Society, Lewes, and have also been published in *SAC.* The 1708 poll book is housed in the collection of the Brighton Reference Library. The records for 1710 are in ESRO Dan 2188. And the 1713 results are in the Newcastle papers, BL Add. MS. 39,290. I am indebted to Peter Le Fevre for providing me with these references.

52. The wills of some clergymen are barren of legacies of freehold properties. Henry Allen records only leasehold (BL Add. MS. 39,326 vol. 1, ff. 280–81), while Joseph Hoyle (ESRO A.48 f. 65, XA26/29), Peter Pickering (PRO Prob. 11/641, 338 Auber), and Stephen Roborough (ESRO A.51 f.278, XA26/31) leave no land at all.

53. In 1734, for instance, the Tories claimed that John Bristed was not entitled to vote in Lewes because he did not own sufficient lands. Their case, however, was not proven (*Exact State of the Poll Taken,* 9).

54. There are certainly many, in any case, whose wills reveal that they had property—sometimes substantial holdings—and refrained from voting nonetheless. The wills of the following nonvoting clergymen all contain bequests of freehold property in Sussex: Thomas Briggs (BL Add. MS. 38,485 ff. 192–200, copy of his will), Oliver North (PRO Prob. 11/607 77 Plymouth), Thomas Only (WSRO STC I/31/460), Thomas Oram (WSRO STC I/30/828), Samuel Paddy (WSRO STC I/32/152), Nicholas Pennington (PRO Prob. 11/589, 15 Richmond), George Smith (WSRO STC I/31/411), and John Webb (ESRO A.50 f.3, XA26/30).

55. Wake, *Rationale,* preface, 30–31; *Courage and Sincerity.*

56. ArchW Epist. 9, f. 209.

57. Pleydell was a Tory, assuming he did not veer from his pre-Revolution sentiments. In 1681 he preached a couple of sermons in which he denounced exclusionism and Presbyterianism in the same breath. The church was so far from teaching resistance to a lawful monarch, he averred, that "'Tis impossible there should be a Rebellion, while the Principles of the Church of England are Rever'd and Owned." The only reason "republican" principles were even countenanced was because of the meddling of "Rebellious and Traiterous practices, or by Mon-

strous and Damnable Positions" of Papists and Presbyterians (*Loyalty and Conformity,* 8–11).

58. Cooper, "Parliamentary History," 23–24.

59. Thomas Tench, Rector of Harting, for example, voted Whig in this election, even though his patron, John Caryll of Ladyholt, was a Jacobite. Tench never voted in any other election.

60. Speck documents widespread usage of pressure-by-patronage in other counties in these years, and undoubtedly there was much of this in Sussex too. But there was nothing like the concerted organization of the Whig "machine" that developed under the Duke of Newcastle (which will be described in subsequent chapters). Speck, *Tory & Whig,* 33–46.

61. There is no clear pattern of voting amongst parsons who owed their livings to the bishop. Out of thirty-one, nine voted consistently Tory in the elections between 1705 and 1715, ten voted consistently Whig, and twelve mixed their votes between parties. Robert Middleton, Vicar of Cuckfield, demonstrated that incumbents could oppose the politics of their episcopal patron when he derided the Jacobitic connections of Robert Grove, his patron, in 1695. See Beddard, "Sussex General Election." The dean and chapter of Chichester and the Crown had similar records amongst the clergymen they appointed. The dean and chapter preferred five men who voted consistently Tory, one who voted consistently Whig, and six who were mixed in their votes; the Crown appointed sixteen Tories, eight Whigs, and four mixed voters. On the basis of these figures, either politics had little to do with choices for preferment in these years or patrons had little control over their appointees.

62. It is clear, however, from the letter of Robert Middleton that there was considerable involvement by the Earl of Sussex, Lord Abergavenny, and the Earl of Tankerville in the 1695 election. See the copy of his letter to Symon Patrick, the Bishop of Ely, in Beddard, "Sussex General Election," 152–53. But how much influence they had is another question. They did not, in these years, have a substantial number of advowsons to use as leverage with incumbents.

63. Sedgwick, ed., *History of Parliament* 1:332.

64. He could have meant the election for the members from Horsham, Reynell's parish. But the *History of Parliament* (1:335) reports that there was no contest there that year either.

65. See Sedgwick, ed., *History of Parliament* 1:332–38; BL Add. MS. 32,686, ff. 251–58.

66. Wright, *Righteousness.*

67. Wright, *Rights of the Christian Priesthood.*

68. Pelling, *Good Old Way.* See also his *The Apostate Protestant* (London, 1682), in which he defends Robert Filmer and Dr. Hicks; *A Sermon Preached at St. Mary LeBow, November 27, 1682* (London, 1683); *A Sermon Preached on the Thirtieth of January 1678/9. Being the Anniversary of the Martyrdom of King Charles the First, of*

Blessed Memory (London, 1679); *A Sermon Preached Sept. 28, 1692 at a Primary Visitation Held at Chichester by the Right Reverend Father in God Robert Lord Bishop of Chichester* (London, 1693); and *A Discourse of the Sacrament of the Lord's Supper. Wherein the Benefits thereof are set forth, and the Distinction between Christ's Natural and Spiritual Body discussed, with Practical Conclusions drawn from the Whole Discourse* (London, 1692).

69. WSRO EpI/45/14. This could suggest, of course, that some of those who voted Whig in the parliamentary election were actually High Churchmen who cast their votes on the basis of personal loyalties rather than party principles.

70. Peter Pickering and Arthur Coster voted for John Grandorge, and Alan Carr voted for Henry Snooke (WSRO EpII/10/19).

71. Langford, "Convocation and the Tory Clergy"; Lathbury, *History of the Convocation,* 464–79.

72. WSRO EpI/45/16.

73. WSRO EpI/45/17.

74. BL Add. MS. 32,689, ff. 245–46.

75. Browning, *Duke of Newcastle,* 8–9, 28–35; Peckham, "Two Dukes"; Curtis, *Chichester Towers.*

76. As he did the episcopal bench. The distribution of bishoprics was carefully planned by Newcastle and his Whig allies to ensure maximum cooperation in affairs of church and state. See the letter of Sunderland to Newcastle in 1721, congratulating him that nineteen out of twenty bishoprics were now under Whig control (BL Add. MS. 32,686, f. 204). Also see Sykes, "Duke of Newcastle," and Taylor, "Church and State in England."

77. Of those that can be determined, fourteen either were outright Whigs or had Whig leanings, and only seven were solid Tories. There are some fourteen whose sympathies are nowhere recorded.

78. WSRO EpI/17/36 f. 115v.

79. ArchW Epist. 22, f. 63.

80. ArchW Epist. 7, f. 210.

81. He frequently grumbled about this situation to William Nicolson, Bishop of Carlisle. See Nicholson, *London Diaries,* 334, 360, 585, 592, 624, 625.

82. Le Neve and Horn, *Fasti Ecclesiae Anglicanae,* 71.

83. Petition of Dean and Chapter of Chichester to Archbishop Wake, Lambeth Palace Library MS. 1837, f. 27.

3

Patronage, Politics, and Churchmanship: Wooing the Clergy, 1715–34

Patronage destroyed High Churchmanship. At least, that is what the historians have said. When George I came to the throne he constituted a Whig government that systematically purged Tory and High-Church opposition. As the Whigs gained control of national and provincial patronage, High Churchmen were left without any kind of support mechanism and their movement just withered away and died. Thus, as Geoffrey Holmes has written, the Whigs subjected clergymen to "that remorseless patronage system which they found so effective in controlling the politicians," and quickly succeeded "in stifling those clergy who tried to perpetuate" High-Church ideals. "They thus reduced the Church, first to quiescence and Erastian dependence, then to a prolonged inertia."[1]

Unfortunately this view is dependent upon a number of questionable assumptions. First, it presupposes that the political Toryism of High Churchmen was more important than their piety. Once High Churchmanship had been shorn of political content, in other words, there was nothing distinctive left, and these once-ardent opponents of Whiggery would readily submit to new political lords. In this view, religion was not really important to the constitution of the High Church—it was only the language in which politics was couched. It was frequently not meaningful in and of itself, but was "invariably an ideal stick with which to beat" their opponents.[2]

Second, it suggests, with Namierite conviction, that political, ideological, and religious opposition simply masked the real forces of self-interest and aggrandizement. When the opportunity for preferment, status, and monetary gain diminished for Tories and High Churchmen, they quickly changed their colors and proclaimed their steadfast allegiance to the reigning powers. In this view, the clergy were so sycophantic that they dropped their opposition and protested undying loyalty to persons whom they had loathed and to principles that had been anathema to them just a few short years before. The patronage system thus reduced parsons to "inveterate beggars" and unprincipled lackeys.[3]

And third, it implies that patronage was employed primarily, if not exclusively, as a system of control. Patrons used their power to appoint clergymen so that they could maneuver and manipulate for their own gain. The system, in this sense, is frequently portrayed as a modern political machine that either swallowed opposition or rendered it impotent. There was no compassion or mercy in the system, nor was there much purpose to it other than control.[4]

All of these points have some truth to them, but they are all caricatures too, and must be carefully qualified. They ignore some of the underlying foundations of the patronage system—a system that has been much maligned and poorly understood. The nature and meaning of patronage must be discerned before any conclusion can be drawn as to its role in the changing perspectives of clergymen.

Some scholars have begun to chip away at these entrenched assumptions. Political historians such as Frank O'Gorman and Norma Landau have argued that voters were neither entirely deferential to, nor independent of, their patrons in elections. Rather than being "mindless fodder for venal agents" or unprotesting lackeys of their superiors, voters were careful, thoughtful, and responsible in their electoral duties.[5] Stephen Taylor has convincingly demonstrated that patrons such as the Duke of Newcastle had objectives other than just parliamentary management and political control when they made their patronage choices: though "party-political considerations could not be ignored," they did not dominate "ecclesiastical policy."[6] Nevertheless, many historians still seem dependent upon the traditional models that suppose that patronage ultimately determined the politics of parochial clergymen.[7] A close analysis of the workings of ecclesiastical patronage on the local level is, therefore, still necessary.

The Role and Function of Ecclesiastical Patronage

We have already seen, in chapter 2, how the mechanics of patronage worked in the eighteenth-century church. But what were the underlying assumptions? What did the patron expect from his client? What did the client expect from his patron? And how did they view their relationship with one another?

Sharon Kettering has provided a useful definition of patronage. Basing her work on studies by anthropologists, sociologists, political scientists, and historians, she has articulated a composite characterization of patronage that includes four separate elements. First, she maintains, patronage involved a relationship between two individuals that was both personal and emotional. It evoked a bond that was much deeper than a perfunctory contractual arrangement. Second, the participants in patronage were unequal—there was a superior and an inferior. Third, it was a "reciprocal exchange relationship." Each participant had something to contribute to the other, though the values of their contributions may have varied, especially since the patron usually had much more to offer. Fourth, patronage involved a sustained relationship, rather than a "single, isolated exchange." It was an ongoing affair with continuous expectations and interchanges on both sides.[8]

The most common way contemporaries referred to patronage was in terms of friendship. Patrons were "friends" to their clients, and clients were "friends" to their patrons. Thus, when the living of Compton opened up because of the death of the incumbent, the Duke of Newcastle was asked if he had a "friend" to recommend to the benefice.[9] And clergymen frequently thanked their patron for being "a friend to me."[10] The language of patronage was replete with references to friendship on both sides of the relationship.

This tendency to describe patronage in terms of endearment has led some sociologists and historians to assume that the meaning contemporaries attached to it was mythological, hyperbolic, or deliberately overstated because of the grandiosity of patrons on the one hand and the obsequiousness of clients on the other.[11] But it is hard to get away from the fact that contemporaries genuinely thought of patronage in emotional terms, and that they considered it as a bond that went far beyond purely practical arrangements. Stephen Taylor has characterized patronage as a "trust" between two individuals, rather than just an agreement or mutual benefit pact, thereby incorporating a personal and emotional stake on both sides.[12]

The language of friendship in this period, too, ought to be examined carefully rather than dismissed as euphemism or myth. Was usage of the term just a way of glorifying a perfunctory convention? Was it simply a means of dignifying a corrupt and unpleasant practice? If so, then Kettering is correct that we need to "pierce the cloak of language veiling clientage in order to understand it."[13] It will be argued here, on the contrary, that the terminology used by contemporaries was not an attempt at pretense or camouflage. Rather, it went to the heart of what contemporaries understood patronage to be and described very well the relationships in which they participated.

The Georgians appear to have used the term "friendship" in a classical sense. As conceived by Aristotle and amplified by Cicero and then Thomas Aquinas, friendship included three elements: (1) the mutual satisfaction and pleasure of association or companionship, (2) a usefulness one to the other, and (3) a common commitment for the general good.[14] In the ancient world, this frequently meant the interweaving of politics and friendship.[15]

In the eighteenth century, the classical concept of friendship was very much alive. Jeremy Taylor, who had a potent and enduring influence on churchmen, wrote a treatise on friendship in the late seventeenth century in which he emphasized the utility of friendship. "There must be," he observed, "in friendship something to distinguish it from a Companion, and a Countryman, from a School-fellow, or a Gossip, from a Sweetheart, or a Fellow traveler." There must be some mutual benefit out of a relationship if it is to be a true friendship, and "those friendships must needs be most perfect, where the friends can be most useful."[16]

This utility could be demonstrated in many different ways, and so there could be many different kinds of friends. But there had to be some mutual usefulness in friendship, or the effort of the relationship was squandered: "He only is fit to be chosen for a friend who can give me counsel, or defend my cause, or guide me right, or relieve me, or can and will, when I need it, do me good: onley this I adde: into the heaps of doing good, I will reckon [loving me] for it is a pleasure to be beloved; but when his love signifies nothing but kissing my Cheek or talking kindly, and can goe no further, it is a prostitution of the Bravery of friendship to spend it upon impertinent people."[17] "If it were not for pleasure or profit," he concluded, "we might as well be without a friend as have him."[18]

Friendship was noble to Taylor, not because it comprised mutual utility alone, but because it had ramifications for all of society. Two or more friends could do a world of good for themselves, their circle of acquaintances, their society, and their entire civilization. Friends helped each other for a greater purpose: that of nurturing one another to become better, wiser, and more useful to all of society. But friendship without purpose was wasted.

This concept seems to be the pattern that governed the practice of patronage. Patronage was one type of friendship, in which the patron and the client assisted one another. Despite the inequality of the persons in the relationship, each participant counted on the friendship of the other and each had a role to play or a function to perform.

Early moderns were also dependent upon the ancients in their understanding of patronage as the exchange of benefits. Humanists seized upon the sentiments of Seneca and other Stoic writers and incorporated their concepts of mutual benefit into the language of patronage.[19] The Romans had also articulated a view of obligation, whereby the recipient of favors was obliged to return the favor, thereby binding him to the original bestower. This, too, became part and parcel of the English conception of patronage.[20]

In theory, then, patronage was a voluntary friendship between a superior and an inferior who were emotionally bound to each other for the purpose of mutual benefit and assistance. What, then, were the expectations on each side of clerical patronage? How was the patron useful to the clergyman and how was the clergyman useful to the patron?

The first expectation of the patron, of course, was that he provide some post of employment for the client. And it was this expectation that so annoys historians, because it appeared to engender endless, undignified groveling on the part of the clients and either caprice or nepotism on the part of the patrons.[21] But this was not due so much to a failing of the system as it was the insufficient number of positions available, as well as the growth of centralized (or bureaucratized) patronage.

But providing a living was not the only indication of a patron's friendship. There were many other ways in which they expressed their affinity for their clients. Perhaps most important was their support for the church. Patrons frequently donated church plate[22] or service books,[23] assisted in renovation of the sanctuary, and sponsored charity schools. Local patrons were also sometimes involved in the day-to-day operations of the church, acting as churchwardens,[24] advising the rector,[25] and assisting in various and sundry other ways.[26]

Patrons demonstrated their esteem for and favor to their appointees in many ways. Not infrequently they provided them with gifts of venison or fish,[27] offered to be godparents to their children,[28] and assisted in providing educational opportunities for their sons or apprenticing them.[29] Patrons were "protectors," and they were expected to look out for the interests of their clients. When clergymen fell into economic hardship, it was deemed their right and privilege to request help from their patron—and patrons frequently responded, particularly if they had the resources to help.[30] Protection could also mean redress for grievances, advice or arbitration in disputes,[31] or protection from unjust prosecution.[32]

These were not just bribes.[33] They were—or, at least, were taken to be—genuine expressions of friendship. And clergymen respected their patrons and delighted in their attentions. True bonds developed between patrons and clients, and patrons would frequently look after and watch out for the client's family long after the client himself had died. There is no question that these favors were intended to build up loyalty among clients, but that was entirely understood and accepted.

But what about the clients—the clergy? What was their contribution to the friendship? What were they expected to provide the patron in return for his protection? Patrons wanted returns from their investment in the relationship too. This is explicitly stated by John Jewkes, the patron of Pulborough, when his client, Francis Mose, met an untimely death: "I had no other pretence to any interest in Pulborough but by my unhappy friend Mr. Mose, whom I bred up & lov'd most tenderly, & thot it in my power to make a return for any services he could do my friends in which he was as sincere, as I could wish."[34] Jewkes lavished his care on Mose, but felt cheated, in a sense, because Mose had died before he could be of the benefit anticipated by Jewkes.[35] Patronage was usually not entered into as a *quid pro quo* arrangement—as if the parson was hired only to do the bidding of the patron[36]—but some kind of reciprocation was expected from the client, and when it was not forthcoming for one reason or another, the patron was disappointed.

What could clergymen, then, offer their benefactors? The first and foremost thing was gratitude. In theory, no inferior was guaranteed anything, thus when one was favored by a superior, gratitude was expected. And most often, clergymen responded appropriately, if not elaborately—sometimes with effusive displays of gratitude. As William Jenkin wrote to Newcastle, "I begg you would accept of my hearty Thanks, & give Me leave to assure you that I shall embrace all occasions of acknowledging & declaring to the world the gratefull sense I have."[37]

This gratitude of clients was demonstrated by deference, which amounted to allegiance to the patron. Each favor bestowed by the benefactor was taken as an obligation on the part of the parson. This was not an onerous obligation, however, or one that was considered an unwelcome duty; on the contrary, most clergymen were eager to be in their patron's debt because it sealed their friendship and gave evidence of further benefit to come—such as preferment. So clergymen were diligent in acknowledging their appreciation and stating their resolve to honor the favor with obedience and service. In one such acknowledgment of debt, Bishop Waddington thanked the Duke of Newcastle for the "great Honour & service that has been bestowed" both on him and the new dean of the cathedral, John Newey. The regard and preferment they received from their benefactor made them eager to "manifest upon all occasions the sense we have of our Duty & affection (if I may be allowed so familiar a word) to your Grace whose ease & Interest in the High Station (which we earnestly pray to God you may long enjoy in Health & honour) shall ever be the aim of all our Actions."[38] William Clarke was also grateful for Newcastle's care and concern, and informed the duke that he would "always endeavour not to be wanting in any Instance of Duty and Gratitude that I am capable of shewing."[39]

The patron, therefore, expected gratitude, deference, and loyalty from the client in return for favors bestowed upon him. It was in this sense that the patron expected to have control over his client. It was not so much control in a political or party sense as it was an expectation that the client would cooperate with the patron out of personal loyalty and esteem. Newcastle, for instance, seldom made it a condition of a clerical client that he vote Whig (unless, perchance, he was presented shortly before a general election), but he was clearly very disappointed if the appointee cast his ballot for anyone other than a candidate sponsored by the duke. The patron, therefore, assumed that he would be able to influence the politics of his clients, but he did not usually use patronage per se as a means of control.

The largest of patrons, however, did not necessarily guarantee the submission of their clients. Clients were not constrained by the actions of their patron. In the church, if not other realms of patronage, once a man was appointed to a living, that living was his for life, unless he was deprived on account of extreme misconduct. A parson could, therefore, accept a living and refuse to defer to or acknowledge his debt to his patron. But if he chose to defy his sponsor regularly, he was sure to gain a reputation for being monstrously ungrateful, and he risked forfeiting any possible favors or preferment in the future. Even if he gained a new patron, he was suspect, because he had proven himself to be impudent and peevish. Thus Thomas Ball, Archdeacon of Chichester, reported that William Crooke was an "ungrateful & irreclaimable apostate," apparently because he had not bowed to the will of his patron.[40]

In many cases, however, parsons had more than one patron. This was no problem if their patrons were allied with each other in common cause (e.g., in the Newcastle network of "friends"), but it was not unusual that their separate patrons had conflicting desires. If that happened, the client would be forced into the unenviable position of disappointing one or the other.[41] It was actually necessary to disobey a patron sometimes. So obedience was by no means guaranteed through patronage, though it appears that most clients worked assiduously to please their patrons.

Clergymen could perform any number of services for their patrons in order to show their gratitude and deference. First and foremost, they could carry out their office responsibly and according to the terms in which they had accepted it. This was not only expected by patrons, but was regarded as a means of fulfilling the debt of gratitude. Some patrons made specific stipulations as to what they required of their prospective client at the time the living was offered. John Ashburnham, for example, frequently made residency a condition of appointment. Only when his candidate assured him that he would comply with the condition did Ashburnham actually present him to the living.[42]

But whatever specifics were laid down, clergymen were expected by their patrons to perform their duties diligently and act with the piety, industry, and dignity that befit their office. As John Ashburnham told John Fuller, he had "noe other aim in the confering my livings then the good of the Church & the encouragement of a well principl'd & vertuous Clergyman."[43] Ashburnham may have been overstating the purity of his motives to justify himself to a neighbor who wanted another candidate, but he was not lying. When clients of his did not fulfill their duties as he had hoped, he was incensed. Anthony Nethercott, rector of the parish of Ashburnham, frequently was the object of his patron's scorn. First of all, he was an absentee rector, and very seldom even visited the parish. Ashburnham wrote in disgust that Nethercott practically exulted when he "said in his sermon in the pulpit that it was now 26 years since he preached in the church at Ashburnham."[44] But when he did finally preach, Ashburnham was even more disturbed and realized that he would have been just as happy if the rector had extended his absenteeism even longer, for he considered Nethercott's sermons "nonsensical." Ashburnham even tried, unsuccessfully, to have the rector removed from the parish.[45]

Historians have frequently supposed that patrons chose clergymen without any respect for the wishes of the parishioners.[46] But that certainly was not always the case. In 1742, for instance, the vicarage of Hellingly came open and there was a scramble by would-be candidates to apply to the Duke of Newcastle, the owner of the advowson, for the position. At least six clergymen were considered, all of whom had recommendations from prominent gentry or other clergymen.[47] Several of the petitioners, further, averred that they were acceptable to, if not preferred by, the parishioners. As it turns out, one of the candidates, Thomas Brown, who claimed the good will of the people of Hellingly, was either ill-informed or guileful, since the parishioners sent several petitions of their own in favor of another candidate, James Davies. In fact, the people were so opposed to the candidacy of Brown that they warned that "if Mr. Brown succeeds as Vicar all those who are not confined to live at Hellingly will leave the Parish."[48] The successful candidate was James Davies, the parishioners' choice. So sometimes, at least, the parishioners had a say in who was chosen to be their pastor. Patrons chose men who they believed would be good and faithful ministers, and usually they chose well.

In addition to the responsible discharge of their duties, clients could, like Edward Bland, be charged with looking after the affairs of their patron's estate while he was out of town.[49] Or they could act as a patron's emissary to transact business, convey messages, or take care of other personal matters. But most of all, clerical clients were expected to support the "interest" of their patron. This meant participating in the causes he endorsed, helping his "friends," backing him in his endeavors, and voting for the candidates he sponsored in Parliamentary elections. It is because of this last expectation that so many historians attribute the demise of High Churchmanship to the patronage system. This we will examine in detail below.

The patronage system has been criticized and censured by historians for generations. But what did those involved in the process think of it? Was it unsatisfactory to them? Some aspects—like the administration of the distribution of Crown livings—may have been irksome,[50] but by and large it was a system that people not only accepted, but appreciated as virtuous. When the system was equitable and provided both patron and client with what they needed, it was splendid. Clergymen clamored for the patron's favor and exulted when they got it. Thus Henry Ott could say to the Duke of Newcastle that "all your friends are the better for having the happiness to live under your protection."[51] Many others echoed the same sentiment—that through patronage they attained friendship, livelihood, and protection.

The problem with the system came when there were too many clients and too few positions or favors to be granted. Many clergymen tried for years to obtain some favor from their patron, only to fail time and time again. In this situation, many became disappointed and disillusioned. The patronage system could be incommodious, and there was no way of preferment outside of the system. Clergymen frequently, therefore, reminded their patrons of their longtime allegiance, of their faithfulness in duties, of interest they were making, and anything else that they thought might get the attention of their benefactor (or one they hoped would be their benefactor). And if there was no response, the parson was left only with the frustration of his plight. But even when frustration mounted, clergymen frequently remained faithful to their patrons.

Walter Barttelot is a good example of this. Barttelot was from a substantial Sussex family and heir to the manor of Stopham, of which his family had been the lords since the fourteenth century. He undoubtedly felt, therefore, that his rank befitted him for more preferment than what he received as the Vicar of Selmeston and Rottingdean and the Prebendary of Bishopstone.[52] His goal was a residentiaryship in the cathedral. In 1737 Thomas Gooch, one of the canons, was translated to the Bishopric of Bristol. When Barttelot heard the news of Gooch's promotion, he applied to the Duke of Newcastle for a recommendation to the vacant post, since the duke had strong influence with the chapter that elected the canons. Newcastle did not pull any punches in his reply: he informed Barttelot that he was not first in line. The next opening, he said, had been promised to William Clarke, and that had been several years ago. Furthermore, Daniel Walter of Cuckfield also wanted such a position, and his request had preceded Barttelot's and would be granted first. Barttelot was not to hope for a residentiaryship anytime soon, though, the duke added, "I cannot wish any Clergyman in Sussex sooner, to be a member of the Church of Chichester, or in any Station, that may give him Credit & Influence, than yourself."[53]

Newcastle did not, therefore, lead Barttelot on or promise him something he had no intention of delivering, but he did encourage the aging vicar by expressing his respect and esteem for him, as well as offering his best wishes. Barttelot continued to assist the duke as a friend and the duke responded with gratitude. In 1739 Barttelot, buoyed by Newcastle's evident regard for him, petitioned again for advancement. "The obliging notice you was pleas'd to take of me the other day at Glynd," Barttelot began, "encourages me to hope that a letter from Sussex" will "meet with a favourable construction at your hands." Barttelot knew that this new petition was a long shot, and acknowledged as much in his letter: "The request that I beg leave to offer, is of so distant a nature, that I am afraid your Grace will smile at the very proposal." He was old and fragile, and not the most likely candidate for a residentiaryship, but he decided to throw caution to the wind and apply, "since it is possible that I may live to see another vacancy among the Residentiaries in that Cathedral, & more than probable that I may also be too late in any future Application."[54]

Once again, he was disappointed. But his allegiance and friendship to the duke did not flag. In 1741 he was as zealous as any clergyman in promoting Newcastle's candidates in the parliamentary election, even though he knew that at this stage in his life there was no reasonable chance for additional preferment. He not only assured his patron that "not one of my little flock at Rottingdean will go astray," but he personally arranged entertainments for them and assisted other Whig agents in any way he could.[55] Barttelot's disappointments did not dampen his enthusiasm for the friendship and protection of his patron.

Others explicitly stated that no frustrations would cause them to renege on their loyalty to their patron. James Hargraves, for instance, wrote to the Duke of Newcastle that "no change of my condition in this World can ever alter the grateful sense I have of your great goodness to me, And that I shall always receive your commands with the same pleasure I have done formerly and obey."[56] Fortunately for Hargraves, he never had to face the test. But there is no reason to suspect that his sentiments were insincere—many clergymen maintained attachments to patrons who were either ill-equipped or unwilling to satisfy their desires.

Just recognition from patrons, especially when they were as great and powerful as the Duke of Newcastle, could give parsons the sense of prestige and esteem they sought, even if they did not achieve everything they desired. It is for this reason that the famous "Sussex Toast" spoke so glowingly of the Duke of Newcastle, because he was able to befriend his clients in a way that made them feel special:

> At Bishopstone Near to the Sea
> Upon the Sussex Coast
> As good a Duke as Duke can be
> Lives there ______ the Countys Toast
>
> His house and he both open are
> To all that come both near and far
> He has no private selfish Ends
> Esteems his honest Steady Friends

For Proof he Saves not for himself
He loves his country not his Pelf
When Hundreds come to see his Grace
All find a friendly chearful face

His arms are open like his Soul
His friendship full as is his Bowl
Is there a Man who sees him There
Can e're for Sergison appear

You ne're can want while he's your Head
He gives you Freedom, Meat and Bread
Your credit nor your Stocks can't fall
While *Pelham* represents you all

Then fill your Glass Full let it be
Newcastle drink while you can See
With Heart and Voice all Voters Sing
Long live Great Holles Sussex King.[57]

It must be remembered, too, that the parish clergy frequently felt isolated from educated and cultured society. Patrons usually came from the class of people with whom parsons yearned to associate.[58] Patrons could, therefore, represent a clergyman's contact with the civilized world—a contact that the ministers relished and preserved at all costs. Many incumbents seized opportunities to socialize with their patrons (as well as other sophisticated gentry), and dinner engagements, cricket matches, and other social occasions, were common.[59] These were important and gratifying affairs for clergymen, because many of them felt like Thomas Frewen, the Rector of Sapcote in Leicestershire, that such contacts were "one of the greatest happinesses (in my Opinion) that Providence bestows or we enjoy in this Life; for we are by nature sociable creatures & therefore without the enjoyment of Society can be very imperfectly happy at best."[60]

In addition to being good company, patrons held keys to cultural enrichment and were frequently willing to share their resources. Thankful Frewen, Rector of Northiam, for instance, was fortunate enough to have access to his patron's library when the latter was away. This was undoubtedly a supreme pleasure to a man who was known for a love of learning,[61] and he was so careful not to abuse the privilege that he refused to kindle a fire in the fireplace when it was cold and damp even though his patron pleaded for him to do so for his health's sake.[62]

The system of patronage, therefore, had some drawbacks, and could be terribly frustrating, but it is unlikely that many clergymen would have been willing to trade away its benefits. It offered protection, friendship, advancement, and certain amenities in exchange for loyalty and allegiance. It was a paternalism that was in some ways a remnant of feudalism, but scarcely recognizable as such because of the freedom of its participants. It was feudalism shorn of bondage, since there were no vassals in this system, only "friends."[63]

What, then, can be said about the charge that patronage reduced High Churchmanship to ruin? There are a couple matters that need to be examined carefully if we are properly to understand the relationship between patronage and High Churchmanship in Sussex: the development of the Whig patronage network in the county and the response of the clergy to that patronage, especially in terms of politics.

Development of the Whig Patronage Network

Before 1715 there appears to have been limited effort (or at least limited successful effort) to coordinate patronage and consolidate it into a network. Patronage consisted of independent patrons who may or may not have tried to influence their clients politically, but there was nothing like the patronage network that developed in the years after George I's accession.

The coordination of patronage—the pooling of "friends"—in Sussex was due largely to the efforts of one man: the Duke of Newcastle. By the fourth decade of the eighteenth century, enemies were lamenting and friends exulting over the power he wielded in the county. He had managed to set up a network of allies among the patrons so that he influenced, if not controlled, the presentation rights to a large proportion of the benefices in Sussex. How did this come to pass?

Thomas Pelham-Holles was a scion of the Pelham family—a gentry clan that had deep roots in the county of Sussex. In 1711 he inherited the fortune and title of his uncle, John Holles, Duke of Newcastle, though it was years before he was able to use either because of disputes regarding the inheritance.[64] But because of his base in Sussex, Newcastle already had influence and contacts among the clergy. His family controlled the presentation rights of some five livings long before Newcastle's ascent. This was about as many as any other substantial gentry family (excluding peers) in Sussex could claim, though it was nothing compared to the influence the Pelhams would have later under Newcastle's leadership. But Newcastle made important contacts through his family's patronage—contacts that were key to his subsequent ecclesiastical influence in the county.

He apparently became friends with Thomas Bowers on account of Pelham patronage. Thomas Bowers had been appointed to the Rectory of Burwash in 1693 by John Pelham. He resigned that living in 1706, and after barely a year as Rector of Sedlescomb, he was once again appointed by a Pelham, this time to the Vicarage of Hellingly. Hellingly was just a stone's throw away from the Pelham county seat of Halland (which was in the parish of East Hoathly). Bowers was undoubtedly a frequent visitor at Halland, since a close friendship developed between him and the future duke. He may even have acted as a tutor to young Thomas, since his later letters reveal that he continued to hold an avuncular authority over his patron.[65] Bowers was one of the few consistent Whig clergyman in the county before the Hanoverian succession, and however he arrived at this political stance, it was clearly one of the elements that created a strong and lasting bond between him and the duke.

Bowers rose meteorically in the ecclesiastical firmament, undoubtedly due to the duke's patronage. Though he had received no significant preferment in the first twenty years of his ministry, he advanced swiftly after the Hanoverian accession. In 1715 he was created canon of the cathedral of Canterbury, in 1721 Archdeacon of Canterbury, and the following year was raised to the bishopric of Chichester. His diocesan reign was brief, since he died in 1724, but it was by no means insignificant. Bowers was the first avowed Whig bishop in the diocese—and the first in a succession of Newcastle appointees. His diligence in his ecclesiastical duties undoubtedly encouraged many to think twice about the Tory stereotype of Latitudinarian treachery. Bowers was pious, conscientious, and fair in administering the diocese.[66] He was careful about the men he promoted and careful about the men he recommended to others for preferment.[67] He conducted the most comprehensive and detailed visitation the diocese had seen in many years.[68] He assisted the archbishop in administering his peculiars within the diocese, and confirmed on a regular basis.[69] Few clergymen—even die-hard High Churchmen—could object to his diligence and devotion as a bishop. Even the fact that he was a local man must have been a point in his favor in the minds of most Sussex parsons.[70] Newcastle could not have chosen a better man to expand his patronage in the county.

And expand it he did. By virtue of the fact that Bowers was, for all intents and purposes, a Newcastle dependent, all of the livings that he had in his right as bishop came under the influence of the duke—twenty-eight benefices in Sussex alone. The bishop was as eager as Newcastle to fill vacancies with men loyal to the Hanoverian government, but made sure to stipulate to the duke that they be good, honest, pious men. In 1723 he wrote to his friend and patron that he hoped that he would nominate worthy men, "for men of unblemish'd characters are best capable of doing service" to church and country.[71] Bowers died before too many men could be advanced, but he started a precedent that would be continued by his successors. Most of the bishops who followed him conferred with Newcastle before making any clerical appointments.[72]

Aside from extending Newcastle's, and therefore the Whigs', patronage in Sussex, Bowers was pivotal in increasing the esteem for Whig clergymen in the diocese. The bishop was respected by both High and Low Churchmen, and had a sterling reputation among all of the clergy. Through one devoted, conscientious, well-placed man, therefore, Newcastle gained immeasurable influence and esteem in the county.

Newcastle groomed other clergymen too. George Jordan was the son of one of Newcastle's early clerks, and as a favor to the father the duke took an interest in the progress of the fledgling priest.[73] Most likely they were friends, and even possibly playmates, since they were about the same age. Furthermore, the young George must have come to know Thomas Bowers and his family well—undoubtedly from contact at the Pelham household—since Jordan married one of Bowers's daughters.

Bowers attempted to advance his son-in-law by giving him the office of Vicar General for both archdeaconries, but there may have been some opposition in the chapter to Jordan at this time, since he was never confirmed. Bowers did succeed, however, in collating him to the prebend of Sidlesham in 1723, but there his help was to end, since he died the next year.[74]

Bishop Waddington, Bowers's successor, elevated Jordan (undoubtedly at Newcastle's behest) to the chancellorship of the diocese in 1725, a post he held until his death in 1754. Though Jordan's colleagues may have been resentful of him at first, they came to respect him highly, since he was an observant pastor and hard-working office holder.

Chancellor Jordan was important to Newcastle's interest. He was the foremost clerical agent for the duke when it came to canvassing for the Whigs at election time. In 1734, in particular, he crisscrossed the county campaigning for the Whig candidates. But Jordan's political involvement did not affect his colleagues' appreciation for him. In 1737, when he was presented by the Duke of Newcastle to the sinecure vicarage of Burwash, three out of four testimonials he obtained were from staunch Tory parsons, who maintained that he had "behav'd himself soberly, carefully and diligently in his station" and that he was entirely orthodox.[75] Jordan was another exemplary clergyman who won the approval of the clerical community despite his solid Whig connections. Nobody dared assert that Jordan was a "false brother" because of his Whiggery.

The fourth person who signed Jordan's testimonial in 1737 was another of Newcastle's favorites—James Hargraves. Hargraves came in contact with Newcastle at Clare College, Cambridge, and there he became the future duke's tutor. He must have impressed Thomas and befriended him, because he and Newcastle appear to have had a special relationship until Hargraves's death in 1741. Hargraves originally came from Wakefield, in Yorkshire, but was brought to Sussex by the duke in order to be his chaplain. He too received preferment due to Newcastle's influence—he became Rector of the parish of East Hoathly in 1718 (the location of the duke's estate of Halland), Prebendary of Thorney in 1723 (once again, during Bowers's tenure as bishop), Rector of St. Margaret's in Westminster and Prebendary of Westminster in 1724, and, finally, Dean of Chichester in 1739. Furthermore, he continued to tutor various Pelhams down through the years.[76]

Hargraves was important to the duke's interest too, and he spent much of his time and effort campaigning for Whig candidates in elections. He was clearly a Whig by principle, since he admitted in 1724 that he was one of the number who were suspect to High Churchmen. The suspicion, he said, "has been but too generally entertain'd of us; and that we, more than any other Order of Men, have lain under the misfortune of being represented as secret Enemies to that Establishment, which we are, by so many Obligations, bound to support."[77] Furthermore, though he was not happy about the Dissenters' separation, he counseled patience and moderation rather than suppression. "A visible Reformation of our Lives and Conversations," he exhorted, was much more effective in the church's "Defense and Preservation" than restrictive measures against conscientious objectors. Hargraves was a firm adherent of Anglicanism, but he did not feel that he had to impose it, or coerce anyone to accept it just because he believed in it. It was enough to live it. This, he claimed, "will be found more successfull in making Converts, than all the Arguments of the most loud and forward Zeal without it."[78] This was a distinctively Latitudinarian position.

But Hargraves, like Bowers and Jordan, could not be faulted as a pastor. His parish was well-provided for, his duties faithfully executed, and his orthodoxy and loyalty to the church unimpeachable. Hargraves's emphasis on converting through example must have had some effect—but not so much on the Dissenters as High Churchmen. He undoubtedly converted Tory clergy from their unreasonable suspicions of the Whigs on account of his piety and concern for the church.

These men were the first fruits of Newcastle's ecclesiastical patronage in Sussex. They all became premier Whig clergymen and campaigned vigorously for the interests of the duke. But they were also important for convincing High Churchmen of the sincerity, loyalty, and piety of Whig clergymen. The reputation they collectively earned convinced many clergymen that the Whig clergy—especially Newcastle's appointees—could be trusted. Their reputation evidently reflected back on Newcastle and the Pelhams too. When the duke and his family chose such outstanding clergymen, it was much harder to accuse them of being "false brethren" in the church.[79]

Newcastle's clerical patronage in Sussex grew in other ways also. Though he was not "ecclesiastical minister" until the 1740s,[80] his influence over Crown and Archiepiscopal appointments was substantial early on, and grew until both the archbishop and crown relied heavily upon his recommendations. By the early 1720s, Newcastle seems to have had a large measure of control over both sources of patronage, since his preferred candidates were being presented both by the archbishop, who controlled thirteen livings in the diocese, and by the Crown, which held presentation rights to twenty-five Sussex benefices.[81] As early as 1718, in fact, Henry Pelham seemed to consider the living of Cliff near Lewes, though it was in the archbishop's right, virtually as his own gift. Accordingly, he had no difficulty getting Archbishop Wake to accept his recommendation of Thomas Peirce for the benefice.[82] In 1720, Peirce, undoubtedly on recommendation of the Pelhams, was preferred to an additional living by the Crown. John Board recognized that Newcastle was responsible for getting his friend Thomas Turner into the Crown-appointed living of West Hoathly in 1721, and acknowledged the duke's goodness in giving the benefice to him.[83] Though Newcastle and his family were undoubtedly not the only ones who had influence with the archbishop and the king when it came to livings in Sussex, their clout was formidable.[84]

By the early 1730s, Newcastle's influence over both Crown and Archiepiscopal patronage was well-established. At that point, applications for positions in the right of either were not likely to be successful unless they were made to the duke himself (or one of his agents). This can be illustrated with the case of Ringmer living. Ringmer was a peculiar of the archbishop, and thus in his right of patronage. In 1733 the incumbent, Thomas Hurdis (who himself had been a Newcastle client),[85] died, and a successor was sought. The Tory interest hoped to gain the post and frustrate the designs of the Whigs in the parish, so upon Hurdis's death, they immediately "posted away to London" with a delegation to the archbishop to lobby for the appointment of one of their own.[86] They even intended to tip the scales in their favor by proposing to the archbishop that if he would present their candidate (Charles Dixon), one of the country gentlemen (Henry Snooke, son of the Vicar of Ringmer who preceded Hurdis) would, in turn, augment the living 50 pounds per annum in perpetuity.[87] This offer, which smacked of bribery, did not persuade the archbishop—he waited for Newcastle's recommendation, and when it came, he quickly nominated the suggested person to the living. The successful candidate was Robert Talbot, a graduate of Newcastle's beloved alma mater. Ringmer may have been in the archbishop's gift, but it was essentially a Pelham living.

Newcastle did not stop with influence over the Crown's, the archbishop's, and the Bishop of Chichester's patronage: he also began to accumulate allies among the gentry and nobility in the county. The Pelhams, of course, had had their share of Sussex alliances before Newcastle's ascent, and the duke merely assumed most of those. It was undoubtedly these connections that enabled Newcastle to triumph in the 1715 election in Sussex. The duke at this time sponsored Spencer Compton (later speaker of the House and Earl of Wilmington) for Knight of the Shire, and from this association a close and undying friendship grew between the two men. Wilmington continued to bolster Newcastle's interest in the county all of his life.[88]

The Pelham interest grew swiftly with additional associations that Newcastle forged. In 1723 he sponsored the Duke of Richmond's interest in Chichester elections, which inaugurated a close alliance between the two dukes.[89] Newcastle's connection with the Duke of Richmond went far beyond political cooperation—their letters to each other reveal the development of an intimacy that was unparalleled in their other associations.[90] The Newcastle/Richmond coalition was a powerful one, since they were the two most influential men in Sussex, Newcastle in the east, and Richmond in the west.

As early as 1718, William Neville, the Earl of Abergavenny, was declaring his complete devotion to Newcastle and was cheerfully filling up positions with persons recommended by the duke.[91] Abergavenny built his estate in East Grinstead, and was able to marshal some influence in and around that parish. Richard Lumley, the Earl of Scarborough, also aligned with Newcastle and Richmond. His interest came from his estates in Arundel, which had been inherited from the Earls of Arundel.[92] Charles Bennett, second Earl of Tankerville, was a Whig and was eager to please Newcastle and Richmond. He was based in the extreme western portion of the county—at Uppark in the parish of Harting—and was able to promote the Whig interest there. And at some point in the 1720s or 1730s, the Ashburnham family established ties with the Pelhams. This was a coup for Newcastle, since the Ashburnhams, as descendants of royalists, had been staunch Tories.[93] But their conversion was sincere and permanent: they consistently supported Newcastle's interest, and Newcastle, in turn, assisted them in their designs.[94]

Newcastle also made common cause with the Duke of Dorset, who, though based in Kent, had much influence in Sussex. Despite the fact that they were often at odds at court,[95] they almost always cooperated in matters of patronage. The Duke of Dorset supported the Pelhams in elections and appointed men who would be loyal to their interest as well as his own.

There were a couple of peers in Sussex, however, whom Newcastle could not co-opt. The Duke of Somerset, whose seat was at Petworth, was a constant thorn in the Pelhams' side. Somerset had been a moderate Whig, and one of the members of the Junto under Queen Anne, but he steadfastly refused to bow to Newcastle's influence. He refused Newcastle's request to help reform the commission of the peace in 1719 in order to oust troublesome Jacobites,[96] he would not cooperate in important elections,[97] and he even called into question Newcastle's strategy for defending the country at the time of the Jacobite invasion of 1745.[98] Somerset stood aloof from Newcastle's charms, and as the "proud duke," probably resented being eclipsed by the influence and power of the younger man. But as the years went by, Somerset's influence in the western part of the county waned while Richmond's burgeoned, so he became less and less of an impediment to the Newcastle/Richmond interest as he grew older.

The Earl of Thanet and the Earl of Derby both had control of some livings in Sussex, and neither one of them were under Newcastle's spell. But even their combined patronage only governed six livings, so their influence was, in and of itself, not terribly troublesome.

There were, of course, many notable gentry families who aligned themselves with the Pelhams too. The Pooles of Chailey and Lewes joined the Pelham coalition when they married into the family.[99] William Hay of Glyndbourn, MP for Seaford, 1734–55; Sir William Gage of Firle, MP for Seaford, 1722–44; John Jewkes of Petworth, a lawyer and MP for Bridport, 1730–34 and Aldborough 1735–43; and William Battine of East Marden, who was Mayor of Chichester in 1742, all professed themselves in Newcastle's debt and put their influence and patronage at his disposal.[100]

It can be seen, therefore, that Newcastle built an extensive and loyal patronage network in the county. Because of the alliances he established, he had significant influence in the patronage of at least 131 benefices in Sussex (there may have been a few more in private hands that were influenced by the duke). That is close to, but not quite, half of all of the livings in the county. The interesting thing is that Newcastle never had to purchase a single advowson to gain such influence—he owned no more in 1750 than he did in 1720.[101] He gathered patronage by association.

The Compatibility of Whig Patronage and High Churchmanship

Did this mean, then, that High Churchmen were systematically being replaced by Low Churchmen in the county, or that beneficed High Churchmen were being bribed and therefore seduced away from their ideals? The big question is, What did Whig patronage mean to churchmen? Did it mean that they had to lower their standards, repudiate their beliefs, or adopt positions that they felt, deep down, were compromising? Did High Churchmen have to roll over and play dead for Whig patrons?

There is abundant evidence to suggest another conclusion: that Whigs succeeded in shaking their negative image among churchmen. In Sussex, Whigs came to represent protectors of the church, not detractors. Of course, that is what Whigs and Low Churchmen had believed all along, but with the favor the Whigs bestowed on the church in the county over the course of years, it became clear that the Whigs really did have the church's best interests in mind, and that to align with them was to preserve, not ravage, Anglicanism. To some degree, then, the Tory party lost its distinctiveness as the "church party," because more and more clergymen became convinced that the Whigs also were guardians of the establishment.

It may be helpful, at this point, to review the distinctive elements of High Churchmanship and then to examine whether Whig patronage affected or undermined them. High Churchmanship was rooted in a world view steeped in divine order and purpose. According to this world view, God had devised an intricate plan for society and government—a blueprint—and humans were obligated to follow that blueprint as closely as possible. *Jure divino* monarchy and episcopacy were part of this plan.[102] So were the sacraments and liturgy. Though the rites and liturgy of the church had been established in the sixteenth century by human agents, they were about as close to the divine pattern as possible. Therefore they, too, were considered virtually sacrosanct. Dissent threatened the order—the divine order—of church and state and could not, for that reason, be tolerated or accommodated. It had to be eliminated. Heterodoxy also was a danger, and anyone who breached the bounds of orthodoxy was to be treated with like severity. The divine order had to be maintained, whatever the cost.

As we have seen, the Protestant succession (and the Hanoverian accession) did not undermine High Churchmanship. Whiggish support for the Protestant succession was, therefore, not a significant problem for High Churchmen (except for the few who were Jacobites). When patrons stipulated that their clients had to be "well affected to the government,"[103] that was no major hurdle—most of the clergy in the diocese were "well affected to the government" in one sense or another. As Edward Waddington, shortly after his consecration as Bishop of Chichester, confided to Archbishop Wake, "I thank God I hear of few or no complaints to make me uneasie. The Clergy are, I believe, as regular & as well affected to our present happy constitution both in Church & State as they are in any other Diocese whatsoever."[104] Even the Tory opposition candidates during the election campaign of 1734 advertised themselves as "zealously affected to his Majesty King George" and "the Protestant Succession."[105] The requirement of the Whigs that their clerical clients be loyal to the government, therefore, was not a major hurdle for clergymen who were offered their patronage.

High-Church zeal for ecclesiastical order and authority was not a hindrance to Whig patronage, either. The desire of High Churchmen to preserve the doctrine of *jure divino* episcopacy and to safeguard the Articles and liturgy from destructive recension or diminution was not affected by Whig patronage. The Whigs made no attempt at all to force these issues. Perhaps they had learned a lesson through the Bangorian controversy earlier in the century, but for whatever reason, Whigs did not demand that their clients drop the rigid High-Church understanding of the ecclesiastical constitution in favor of a more flexible (or "Latitudinarian") one.[106] Many churchmen who received preferment from Whigs remained staunch advocates of *jure divino* episcopacy[107] and many held strictly to the liturgy as it was handed down to them by tradition.[108]

Whig patronage did not entail Erastianism in the minds of parsons, either. It did not follow that when clergymen allied themselves with the interests of their patrons that they thereby subverted the church's rights and privileges. The two were not necessarily related. Just because clergymen were not opposing the government or administration does not mean that they had become servile—just that they were not unhappy enough with the status quo to revolt.[109] Patronage was not a method of reducing the church to subservience. Newcastle and the Whigs were as responsive to the demands of the church as the church was to the Whigs.[110] And clergymen were never so subdued by the Whigs that they could not or would not rise against their policies, if they felt that those policies were detrimental to the church. Patronage was a mutually beneficial arrangement, not a dictatorial one on the part of the Whigs.

And that is what made the arrangement work and what allowed many High Churchmen to ally themselves with the duke. Newcastle was himself a devoted Anglican,[111] and he assisted the church in Sussex in various ways. In 1729, for example, he and his Whig allies in Sussex were instrumental in the efforts to rebuild the Church of All Saints in the town of Hastings. The church was in poor repair and needed such extensive renovation that the poor parish was incapable of raising the necessary funds (the cost was estimated at above 1,249 pounds). Though the church's patron and rector were Tories, it was the Whigs who promoted its rebuilding. The Pelhams rallied their forces: Newcastle, his brother (Henry Pelham), three other Pelhams, Lord Wilmington, the Ashburnhams, and the Bishop of Chichester all acted as trustees for the project. And Newcastle himself pleaded with the Lord Chancellor to grant the necessary funds for the renovation of the church.[112] This episode was one of many in which the Whigs proved their devotion to the Anglican Church in the county of Sussex. In this instance, Newcastle was unsuccessful in gaining the goodwill of the rector, Thomas Broadway. Broadway continued to oppose him. Hurt by the rector's ill will and ingratitude, Newcastle asked the Lord Chancellor to block his preferment.[113] But other clergymen responded eagerly to the duke's benevolence and manifest concern for the church. If Newcastle had not been watchful of the church, the clergy would not have been so ready to bow to his authority. They were deferential because, in their estimation, he merited the deference.

But were there other stipulations that might make High Churchmen reluctant, if not loathe, to accept the sponsorship of Whigs? The only issue that remained that could be an impediment to High-Church/Whig alliance was that of the management of Dissent. It was, after all, primarily the fear of Dissent that had driven High Churchmen into opposition in the early years of the century. Much of the clerical motivation for voting Tory in those years was the fear of Whiggish concession to Dissent and the hope of passing Occasional Conformity or Schism bills to thwart their designs. What, then, happened between High Churchmen and Whigs on this issue?

First of all, it must be noted that, in real terms, the threat of Dissent was diminishing rapidly nationwide in the early eighteenth century. The Low Church's leave-them-alone-and-they-will-go-away strategy seems, in large measure, to have worked.[114] Not only was the Dissenting zeal gone, but the number of congregations declined or were destroyed from within by doctrinal and trinitarian disputes.[115]

In Sussex, the decline was palpable. Between 1676 and 1724 the strength of Sussex Nonconformity was reduced by at least one quarter. The number of Dissenters dropped from some 4,300 to roughly 3,300 or less.[116] But even more significant than the numerical reduction was the modification that occurred in the local parishes. In the 1724 visitation, Bishop Bowers asked the clergy to report the number and type of Dissenters in each parish. The results manifest a marked decline when compared to the figures from the Compton Census of 1676. In 1676 only about forty-nine parishes reported being entirely free of Dissenters. By 1724 that number had doubled: almost a hundred parishes—over a third of the total—had no Dissenters at all.

Furthermore, some parishes revealed a dramatic reduction in the strength of Nonconformity within their boundaries. Horsham, for instance, had a community of one hundred Nonconformists in 1676. By 1724 there were only thirty-four: fifteen Presbyterians and nineteen Anabaptists. The Rector of Hurstpierpoint reported twenty-two Dissenters in his parish in 1676, but his successor could only find three. Similarly, Lurgashall may have seemed overrun with twenty-seven Nonconformists in 1676, but in 1724 there was only one Quaker in the entire parish. And Maresfield's population of Dissenters dropped from twenty to only two.

Traditional centers of Nonconformity suffered attrition too. The Compton Census reported some three hundred Nonconformists in Rye. This concentration was largely due to Protestant refugees from France. By 1717, when John Evans collected information in order to lobby parliament for

Dissenting interests, there were only 140 "hearers" at meetings.[117] The congregation had been so depleted by the time of Bishop Bowers's visitation that the rector reported only two families of Quakers and ten others in his parish.

Lewes had also been a stronghold of Dissent. In 1676 the pastors of four Lewes parishes reported that there were 149 Nonconformists in the region. When John Evans collected his data, he noted that there were two principal Dissenting congregations left in Lewes. The larger of the two—Thomas Barnard's meeting—could still attract 425 hearers, though its membership was hardly a quarter of that. But Barnard's membership register, which is extant, reveals that his congregation was dwindling even as the ink was drying on Evans's list. The register is bustling with admissions until about 1710 or 1711, when only two or three individuals a year were added to their number. Furthermore, deaths were exceeding admissions. The entries stop entirely in 1717. Barnard may have still been able to draw a crowd in that year, but his influence was waning.[118] By the 1724 visitation, the Anglicans noted only fifty-seven Dissenters in the entire town. Nonconformity had not disappeared in Lewes, but it had certainly been drained of much of its vitality.[119]

It would seem, given the evidence from the John Evans manuscript, that most of this decline occurred after the Hanoverian accession. This would make sense given the shrillness of High-Church rhetoric during the first decade and a half of the century—during that time Dissent was still a real threat to the church. As late as 1718, Bishop Manningham bemoaned that Lewes was "miserably overrun with Dissenters."[120] But if the decline occurred primarily after 1715, then Nonconformity decayed with remarkable rapidity. The erosion of Dissent would seem to have continued at least to mid-century, if not even later. The change was so marked in these years, as Caplan observed, that "Nonconformity ceased to be a source of real concern to the Established Church."[121]

Clergymen were very much aware of the diminution in the strength of Nonconformity. Certainly Dissenters did not seem nearly as troublesome or as threatening to churchmen in Sussex in the third and fourth decades of the century as they had seemed earlier. William Simmonds, Dean of Battle, reported to Wake in 1725 that "In my time have been in Otham [his living in nearby Kent] Quakers, Independents & Anabaptists, & now there is not one Dissenter."[122] James Cranston observed this decline in his own parish of St. Clements, Hastings. Cranston had been instituted to the rectory in 1690, and must have known a good many Nonconformists at that time (the Compton Census reported the number at twenty). But by 1713 he had already noticed a marked change: in that year he informed the SPCK that the number had dropped to "not above 10 Dissenters."[123] Within five years the Dissenting presence in his parish was all but gone. In 1718 he exulted that in Hastings "among 5000 souls there are not above 2 Dissenters."[124] Cranston watched as Nonconformity dwindled in his parish, and he was clearly delighted at the development.

This atrophy in the camp of their opponents allowed many High Churchmen to drop their guard and to stop lobbying for repressive measures. After all, if Nonconformity was in the process of self-destruction, there was no need to persecute it. For this reason, High-Church passion did not need to be expressed. High Churchmen became less strident in their rhetoric because there was no reason for them to manifest anti-Dissent zeal.

Just the same, some parsons were haunted by the specter of Dissent even after its corporeal presence vanished. Many who had lived through the Sacheverell era simply could not believe that the church was secure. These parsons still distrusted the Whigs and continued to doubt their loyalty to the church whether or not they sensed a diminution in the vitality of Nonconformity. For this reason, Thomas Curteis, a Low Churchman, lamented in 1733, that some men would never "think *the Church out of Danger* so long as their great grievance, *the Toleration Act* is subsisting."[125] The danger was past, but those of "coercive sentiments and misguided zeal" would simply not believe it. These skeptical, fearful clergymen constituted much of the remainder of Tory opposition.

The important thing for our purposes here is that Dissent—the most significant impediment to High- and Low-Church solidarity—had markedly diminished in the years after the Hanoverian accession. As Nonconformity faltered, the number of clergymen who decried Whig governance and patronage plunged, because the alliance of Whigs and Dissenters was not nearly the threat to the Anglican Church that it had once been.[126]

But just because parsons were not as intimidated by Dissent as they had been in the past, that did not mean that they were willing to allow the Whigs a free hand in promoting the interests of Nonconformists. Incumbents frequently aligned with the Whigs only on condition that they continue the policy of exclusion of Nonconformists from society. Anthony Springett is a good example of this. Though he was appointed to his living of Westmeston in 1716 by a committed Tory, Springett accepted the sponsorship (and, therefore, patronage) of the Pelhams and other Whigs in various endeavors. He was, for instance, their candidate for proctor to Convocation from the Archdeaconry of Lewes in 1734, and he undoubtedly supported the Whig candidates in the parliamentary election of that year.[127] The year before this, Springett attempted to start a charity school near Lewes. Once again he obtained the sponsorship of the Pelhams: Newcastle, William Hay, and three other Pelhams agreed to be trustees. But Springett demanded, much to their dismay, that the school be restricted only to children who were members of the established church. "The Boys," William Hay reported to Newcastle, "are to conform to the Church; which is a Point Mr. Springet[t] absolutely insists on." Hay and the Pelhams wanted to admit any and all, in hopes that the Whigs might thereby persuade the Dissenters to vote for them, but Springett would not have it.[128] In order to stress this point and make it an irrevocable restriction, Springett made it an item in his will. "I will and appoint," he recorded, "that all children which shall be admitted to partake of the Charity or Schooling by this my will appointed shall during the time they shall be taught resort to the service of the Church of England only and not to any Dissenting Meeting."[129] Springett was happy to join with the Whigs, and held the Pelhams in great esteem, since they were obviously benefactors of the church and its charities, but he would not capitulate to Low-Church pressure and indulge the Dissenters. Springett may have aligned with the Whigs, but he was a High Churchmen in sentiment.

Newcastle himself was quite sensitive about this issue. He knew that many of the churchmen he had incorporated into his patronage network were still zealous in their High-Church sympathies, and he was, in general, very careful not to alienate them by making agreements with the Dissenters. Though he himself was tolerant and accommodating,[130] he knew that his clerical clients (as well as many others with High-Church sentiments) would not stand for further concessions to Nonconformists. It was for this reason that he counseled patience for Dissenters who petitioned him for relief of one sort or another. When solicited by Nonconforming interests in 1734 for repeal of the Test Act, Newcastle observed that at the present time it would be impossible because there was too much resistance to the notion: "Those, in the Administration to whom the Dissenters have applied upon this Subject, have endeavored in the most friendly manner possible, to dissuade them from the attempt, as what could not fail of greatly affecting the peace and quiet of the kingdom, and raising a Flame, which it was greatly to be feared, might prove, in the End, prejudicial to the Interest of the Dissenters themselves and could not possibly be attended with success."[131] Newcastle's constant fear was that his carefully built, but nonetheless fragile, patronage network could be undone with one stroke. "I am very apprehensive that such a handle will be taken from an attempt of this kind . . . to foment, & raise a Spirit in the Nation" that would create just such a backlash as had occurred with Sacheverell in 1710. Therefore, he counseled forbearance. The clergy were still protective of the church, and they were happy with the Whig administration, but only as long as the administration protected the church from incursion by Dissenters. Newcastle and the other Whigs found that they had to cater to the demands of High Churchmen in order to win their loyalty, and they had to continue accommodating themselves in order to retain that loyalty.[132]

Though it is true, therefore, that the Whig patronage network co-opted High Churchmen, it would be just as true to say that High Churchmen succeeded in modifying Whiggery. Patronage did not destroy High-Church sentiment, it merely provided the medium whereby High Churchmen and Whigs could join in common cause. High Churchmen did not capitulate and relinquish their ideals; on the contrary, they discovered that the Whigs could, in fact, be faithful benefactors of the church, and they accepted their support as long as it could be had without undermining High-Church principles. The Whig patronage network did not, therefore, subjugate High Churchmen—if anything, it assisted them. The Whig/High-Church alliance was a marriage of interests, not a divorce of principle. High Churchmen found that they could be "friends" with the Whigs, since their interests were not imperiled by that association as they had once imagined they would be.

Of course, not all High Churchmen came around; not all were convinced that Whig patronage and benevolence toward the church were genuine. But a few examples will demonstrate the effectiveness of the Whig effort in winning over clergymen in these years. James Cranston, the Rector of Hastings who was so pleased by the retreat of Dissent, is a case in point. He had been an ardent Tory and High Churchman and had campaigned for the "country party" in the early part of the century.[133] But by the end of the first decade of the eighteenth century, he was apparently cultivating a friendship with Sir Nicholas Pelham, as a fellow corresponding member of the SPCK.[134] Though he died before the election of 1734 (and, hence, was not included in the detailed and revealing correspondence of the Duke of Newcastle), it is evident that he began to form alliances with the Pelham family as his opposition to the Whig party eased. This evidence comes primarily from the actions of his children. His daughter, Mary, married John Collier, an ardent Whig client of the Duke of Newcastle, and future mayor of Hastings. And his son, James, voted Whig in 1734 and was actively involved with the Newcastle network.[135] Cranston was a consistent Tory during Queen Anne's reign, but as Dissent diminished and as his respect grew for the Pelhams, he and his family had no reservations against aligning with the forces of Whiggery.

Charles Bettesworth, Rector of Terwick and Kingston-Kewsey, was also won over by Newcastle and his associates. Bettesworth had been a steady High Churchman and Tory. Though he had voted Tory in every election in the early part of the century, in 1733 he informed John Jewkes that he would support the Whig candidates because they were "for the Church."[136] The old caricature of the Whigs as "false brethren" had worn thin by this time, and Bettesworth and others had come to respect the Pelhams for their churchmanship and believed they had good intentions regarding the church.

Many other High Churchmen also came to trust the Newcastle Whigs— William Brownsword, John Bullis, John Hawes, John Wright, Daniel Gittins, and Julius Bate, to name just a few, had been persuaded to ally with the Pelhams precisely because it was their best hope of defending and protecting the church. They were still High Churchmen at heart, and had not altered their perspective on the constitution of church or state, but they no longer saw the Whigs as a threat to that constitution.

A significant shift had, therefore, occurred between 1715 and 1733, but that shift was not from High Church to Low Church, but from High-Church distrust of the Whigs to High-Church confidence in the Whigs' intentions and actions in respect to the Church of England. "Enemies" had been turned into "friends," not by subversion or bribery, but by goodwill and benevolence. Patronage had indeed been an effective means of wooing the clergy into the Whig camp, but it was not at the expense of High Churchmanship. The shrill opposition of High Churchmen was quickly becoming a thing of the past, and their distinctiveness was waning. But that is not because they had been coerced or bought by the patronage system. High Churchmen had been co-opted, not muzzled or bribed.

Notes

1. Holmes, *Politics, Religion and Society,* 211–12.

2. Ibid., 202. See also, Bennett, *White Kennett,* xi, 26, 57–58, and passim. Stereotyping and politically motivated name-calling did, of course, occur. Jan Albers has documented this quite well in eighteenth-century Lancashire. See her "'Papist Traitors' and 'Presbyterian Rogues': Religious Identities in Eighteenth-century Lancashire," in Walsh et al., eds., *Church of England,* 317–333; and Albers, "Seeds of Contention." But this does not mean that religion and piety were only pretexts.

3. Bateson, "Clerical Preferment"; Sykes, "Duke of Newcastle"; Porter, *English Society,* 188–90. A rather extreme caricature of this is Curtis, *Chichester Towers,* which portrays the posturing for preferment during a vacancy in the deanery of Chichester in the same sardonic tone as Anthony Trollope employed in his criticism of the church in his own day, hence the play on *Barchester Towers.*

4. Holmes, *Politics, Religion and Society,* 211–12; Plumb, *Origins of Political Stability,* 188–89; and Sykes, *Church and State,* 175. Even D. R. Hirschberg, who has debunked the idea that through patronage "the Church of England was Erastian in the worst sense of the word," seems to take for granted that the main purpose of patronage was management and control ("Government and Church Patronage"). J. B. Owen was, for a long time, a lonely voice in opposition to this prevalent view. His view of patronage is remarkably well-rounded even today. See, for example, his rebuttal of J. H. Plumb in "Political Patronage in 18th Century England," as well as his earlier work, *The Rise of the Pelhams,* 62.

5. O'Gorman, *Voters, Patrons and Parties,* 384–89; Landau, "Independence, Deference, and Voter Participation."

6. Taylor, "Government and the Episcopate," and "Church and State," 87–122, esp. 120. Note also John Brewer's care to separate the patronage system from the venality and graft that occasionally infiltrated it. Patronage did not in and of itself create a corrupt or machine-like organization. In fact, despite the degree to which England was dependent upon patronage, "by the standards of other European administrations of the period . . . the British executive was remarkably uncorrupt." See Brewer, *Sinews of Power,* 69–79.

7. See, for example, Baskerville, "Political Behaviour of the Cheshire Clergy," 81, and Albers, "Seeds of Contention," 286–88, both of which attribute political partisanship almost entirely to patronage.

8. Kettering, *Patrons, Brokers and Clients,* 13. For another more involved, but nevertheless similar, description, see Eisenstadt and Roniger, *Patrons, Clients and Friends,* 48–49; and Eisenstadt and Roniger, "Patron-Client Relations."

9. John Dear to Newcastle, BL Add. MS. 32,696, f. 74.

10. See, for example, Thomas Powell to Newcastle, 14 March 1740, BL Add. MS. 32,696, f. 228.

11. Sydel Silverman, for instance, feels that the participants in patronage should

not be taken at their word: she asserts that there was a profound discrepancy between their values and behaviors ("Patronage as Myth").

12. Taylor, "Church and State," 89. On the issue of trust and patronage, see also, Eisenstadt and Roniger, *Patrons, Clients and Friends,* 29–42.

13. Kettering, *Patrons, Brokers and Clients,* 12–14.

14. Aristotle, *Nicomachean Ethics,* books 7 and 9; Cicero, *De Amicitia,* and Aquinas, *Disputations: De Caritate.*

15. See Hutter, *Politics as Friendship.*

16. Taylor, *Measures and Offices,* 31–32.

17. Ibid., 31.

18. Ibid., 36.

19. Peck, *Court Patronage,* 12–14, 18, 225.

20. Salmon, "Stoicism and Roman Example."

21. Bateson, "Clerical Preferment," 685–96; Sykes, "Duke of Newcastle," 59–84; Curtis, *Chichester Towers,* 7; Hirschberg, "Government and Church Patronage," 125–27. Note: patrons have been vindicated from the charge of choosing clients on account of interest rather than ability by several recent historians. Stephen Taylor has cleared Newcastle and his circle from the charge of preferring incompetent lackeys in ecclesiastical patronage, and John Brewer has observed that the quality of the administration in England was second to none, despite the patronage system (Taylor, "Church and State," 110–22; Brewer, *Sinews of Power,* 69–79).

22. Couchman's "Sussex Church Plate" details the extant church plates that are inscribed with marks (and sometimes coats of arms) of the presenters. It is clear from this that the majority of gifts were given by the patron of the parish. Newcastle and the Pelhams were not remiss in this duty either.

23. John Bear, Rector of Shermanbury, recorded in the parish register that "on December 22d 1734 I received a large five Common Prayer folio . . . bind for the service of Shermanbury Church from Thomas Frewen of Brickwall in Sussex, Esq. which was presented to me by his son in our said Church, & accordingly used on December 25th Being Christmas Day. . . . the said Thomas Frewen was further pleased to bestow on our Church a large folio Bible printed at Oxford, which I received also from the hands of his son on March 10th 1734 being Sunday & was then used in public service for which pious generosity may God reward him, & his in this world and the next." WSRO PAR 167/1/1/1.

24. ESRO FRE 1290.

25. Thomas Frewen advised his client Thankful Frewen not to choose a Mr. Batchellor as a churchwarden even though he was the rector's son-in-law, because Batchellor, as a physician or chirurger, was so forward as "to try experiments upon me when I was ill." ESRO FRE 1295.

26. Thomas Frewen, patron of Northiam, for instance, was churchwarden repeatedly. The rector was pleased to accept his recommendation for increasing the

frequency of communion from three to four, and he was influential in the decisions regarding to whom alms should be distributed (ESRO FRE 1302, 1291–92). Surprisingly, even Roman Catholic patrons sometimes took an active interest in the affairs of their church. John Caryll, patron of Harting, was evidently in attendance when some affairs in that parish were being decided. WSRO Par 98/12/1.

27. Thomas Powell thanks Newcastle for fish, 14 March 1740, BL Add. MS. 32,696, f. 228.

28. The Duke of Newcastle was godfather to Thomas Browne's son (BL 32,688, f. 582). Thomas Frewen was godfather to William Lord's son (ESRO FRE 1359).

29. See John Woodham's request to Newcastle for help to apprentice his son (27 October 1739, BL Add. MS. 32,692, ff. 433–34). William Jenkin acknowledges Newcastle's influence in getting his son into the Charterhouse school in BL Add. MS. 32,693, f. 287, 17 May 1740.

30. Note in particular the financial straits in which John Bristed of Lewes constantly found himself. His patron and his patron's friends helped satisfy Bristed's creditors, even if they did not extricate him from debt. William Hay, acting on behalf of the Duke of Newcastle, noted in 1733 that "when I called on Mr. Bristed, he was confined to his house for fear of his creditors; & on conversing with him I found him so honest a man, that I was resolved to do something to set him at liberty: he told me Ashby was the only Creditor that would not come to terms with him: I ordered a Letter of Licence to be drawn up for his other Creditors to sign; & have collected some money amongst my Friends & have paid Ashby" (10 November 1733, BL Add. MS. 32,689, ff. 15–16). It is noteworthy that despite all of the apprehension of the clergy regarding financial affairs, and all of their plaintive petitions for help, I have not discovered a single one in Sussex that was actually thrown into debtor's prison.

31. John Ashburnham advised his client, Alexander Cunningham, the Rector of Ampthill, to accept the arbitration of the bishop in a dispute between Cunningham and another of Ashburnham's clients, Anthony Nethercott. Cunningham was not happy with the solution that he expected the bishop to propose, and resisted. Ashburnham warned him that it was his best option, and that it was not wise to spurn the goodwill of the diocesan (ESRO Ash. 841, ff. 23–24).

32. John Bristed's "friends," for example, promised to "support him" in a threatened lawsuit. Hay to Newcastle, 6 June 1734, BL Add. MS. 32,689, f. 263.

33. As G. H. Nadel took them to be. Nadel wrote that these were simply "corrupt practices, euphemistically called favours." In his view all such "favours" were immoral and unconscionable. Unfortunately, Nadel's analysis was based on an incomplete understanding of the events, since he relied entirely on secondary sources. He did not go through the correspondence or other primary sources himself, and so missed a lot of evidence that indicates that there was much more to patronage in the eighteenth century ("The Sussex Election of 1741").

34. John Jewkes to Newcastle, 16 September 1740, BL Add. MS. 32,695, ff. 77–78. Note that he described the relationship with terms of endearment, even to a third (though not disinterested) party. This reveals the emotional bond involved.

35. Nevertheless, the Mose family was cared for by Jewkes and other Whigs. Mose's boys were educated and apprenticed, and his wife was adequately housed and fed. Jemima Mose to Newcastle, 14 June 1741, BL Add. MS. 32,697, f. 192.

36. Clients still remained free agents, and could disagree with their patrons or go against their wishes on particular matters without jeopardizing their overall allegiance (or "friendship"). The point here is that parsons were much more than lackeys of their patrons.

37. Jenkin to Newcastle, 17 May 1740, BL Add. MS. 32,693, f. 287. These exclamations of gratitude may have been exaggerated at times, but this is no reason to believe that they were merely self-interested obsequies. Kettering, *Patrons, Brokers and Clients,* 15.

38. Waddington to Newcastle, 23 June 1728, PRO SP 36, vol. 7, ff. 57–58.

39. 17 July 1738, BL Add. MS. 32,691, ff. 248–49.

40. Ball to Newcastle, 28 July 1740, BL Add. MS. 32,694, ff. 337–38.

41. Kettering, *Patrons, Brokers and Clients,* 22.

42. Thus he wrote to his client, Richard Thorneton, "My son having assur'd me of your willingnesse to reside att Dallington when you are possess'd of that living, makes me cheerfully declare to you my deseign to oblige you with the Presentation most heartily wishing it were tenn times better for your sake" (ESRO Ash 846). Many patrons required their clients to be resident. Archbishop Wake frequently made residence a condition. ArchW Epist. 7, f. 214. So too did Lord Chancellor Hardwicke. Taylor, "Church and State," 116–17.

43. ESRO Ash 846.

44. ESRO Ash 975.

45. ESRO Ash 931, p. 6.

46. "The clergymen of England were imposed upon their congregations overwhelmingly from the top or from the outside" (Hirschberg, "Government and Church Patronage," 114).

47. The Newcastle papers contain a document entitled "Abridgment of Letters & Petitions to my Lord Duke of Newcastle about Hellingly Living," from which most of this information is derived. BL Add. MS. 33,085, ff. 449–50.

48. Ibid. Brown, it should be noted, was not a popular clergyman, even in his own parish of Litlington. In response to a report that his parishioners were dissatisfied with him, he replied that their disaffection was due to the "spitefulness & misrepresentation of many whom I could not humour in their romantic Bigotrie and Jacobitism." Brown to Newcastle, 20 January 1741, BL Add. MS. 32,696, ff. 40–41. But Brown was simply not a likable man, for other clergymen described him as "troublesome." James Hargraves to Newcastle, 7 March 1740, BL Add. MS.

32,696, ff. 200–201. Though Brown promised time and again to support the Whig cause, he never received any other preferment.

49. Letters from Edward Bland to Thomas Pelham informing him of the state of affairs on his estate. BL Add. MS. 33,085, ff. 480, 494.

50. Hirschberg, "Government and Church Patronage," 125.

51. Ott of Newcastle, 18 February 1741, BL Add. MS. 32,696, f. 103.

52. It is a bit unfair, I think, and certainly uncharitable to call him a "clerical beggar," as Curtis did in *Chichester Towers*, 7.

53. Bartellot to Newcastle, 4 April 1737, BL Add. MS. 32,690, ff. 268–69; Newcastle to Bartellot, 7 April 1737, BL Add. MS. 32,690, f. 270.

54. Bartellot to Newcastle, 3 September 1739, BL Add. MS. 32,692, ff. 266–67.

55. Hurdis to Newcastle, 13 September 1741, BL Add. MS. 32,698, f. 41; Bartellot to Newcastle, 1 October 1741, BL Add. MS. 32,692, ff. 92–93; Curtis, *Chichester Towers*, 8.

56. Hargraves to Newcastle, 26 August 1724, BL Add. MS. 32,687, f. 147.

57. N.d., BL Add. MS. 32,698, f. 82.

58. Regarding social classes and the clergy, see chapter 1 of my Ph.D. dissertation, "The Changes and Chances of This Mortal Life: The Vicissitudes of Politics and Churchmanship among the Clergy of Sussex, 1700–1745" (University of Chicago, 1992), esp. 61–100.

59. The journal of John Ashburnham reveals that clergymen were often in his company and at his table. ESRO Ash 931–33.

60. ESRO FRE 1326.

61. ESRO FRE 1290.

62. ESRO FRE 1300.

63. Kettering, *Patrons, Brokers and Clients*, 20; Peck, *Court Patronage and Corruption*, 3.

64. Browning, *Duke of Newcastle*, 5.

65. The tutorial post would have put him in a superior position in the relationship, at least for a while. Bowers's authority as mentor may have lasted long into the relationship, despite the fact that Newcastle, as patron, would have become Bowers's superior. In a letter dated 30 October 1717, for instance, Bowers proceeded to lecture Newcastle on his poor financial management. It is doubtful, if Bowers had been a mere client, that he would have had the impudence to counsel his patron in this manner. BL Add. MS. 33,064, ff. 131–33. See also Browning, *Duke of Newcastle*, 41–43.

66. Apparently Bowers was known for years as a fair and impartial judge, since he was sought as an arbitrator in disputes between clergymen. See ESRO Ash 841, ff. 23–24.

67. He asked for references and testimonials, and refused to sign testimonials for men he hardly knew. See ArchW Epist. 10, f. 57, and ArchW Epist. 22, f. 261.

68. The records left from the 1724 visitation are the most complete source of information about the diocese for the entire eighteenth century. WSRO Ep I/26/3. See also Caplan, "Visitation."

69. ArchW Epist. 9, f. 276.

70. There appears to have been significant anti-outsider sentiment in the county. An anonymous letter to the Duke of Newcastle complained (ca. 1740) that it seemed that two-thirds of the available livings were going to "foreignors." In the author's opinion, outsiders "crowd down here in such numbers," that they created resentment and bitterness among the residents, and especially among the local candidates for preferment, when they usurped places that should have been reserved for Sussex men. This petitioner thought that it was "high time to convince" such interlopers that it was "not worth their while" to apply for positions in Sussex. BL Add. MS. 32,992, ff. 119–20.

71. BL Add. MS. 33,064, f. 240.

72. And Newcastle, for his part, conferred likewise with the Bishop, particularly if he did not know a candidate. It was more a cooperative effort than a dictatorial one on the part of Newcastle. Nevertheless, Newcastle's wishes could not be ignored.

73. Jordan to Newcastle, 5 December 1724, BL Add. MS. 32,698, ff. 63–64.

74. Ibid.

75. WSRO Ep I/66/1/58.

76. On 5 November 1737, Hargraves reported to Thomas Pelham on the progress of his son's studies. BL Add. MS. 33,085, f. 529.

77. Hargraves, *Sermon Preached in LAMBETH-CHAPEL*, 17–18.

78. Ibid., 16.

79. Taylor emphasizes that patrons wanted to choose well because the behavior of the client reflected on them ("Church and State," 90). Newcastle chose extraordinarily well, and his reputation among clergymen rose significantly because of it.

80. Ibid., 70–76; Sykes, "Duke of Newcastle," 59–84.

81. Stephen Taylor rightly observes that both the king and archbishop could reject a recommendation by Newcastle and act independently. But a veto of the Pelhams in their own county was rare ("Church and State," 76–86).

82. Pelham to Wake, 26 June 1718, ArchW Epist. 7, f. 214.

83. Board to Newcastle, 8 September 1733, BL Add. MS. 32,688, f. 289.

84. In the 1720s alone, the hand of the Pelhams can be detected in all of the following Archiepiscopal and Crown presentations: Robert Lamb (Stanmer, 1724, presented by archbishop), Edward Bland (Stanmer, 1727, presented by archbishop), John Carpenter (Pagham, 1729, presented by archbishop), William Clarke (Buxted, 1724, presented by archbishop), John Hancock (Bersted, 1723, presented by archbishop), Thomas Hurdis (Ringmer, 1727, presented by archbishop), Edward Lund (Cliff, 1725, presented by archbishop), Thomas Turner (West Hoathly,

1721, presented by Crown), and James Barker (Newhaven, 1727, presented by Crown).

85. Bishop Waddington wrote to Newcastle in 1727 that "I hear his Grace of Canterbury say that the person to whom he gives Ringmere shall take care in a particular manner to support your Graces Interest in the Countrey" (PRO SP 36, vol. 4, ff. 14–17). When William Hay reported Hurdis's death to the duke, he observed that "your Grace has lost a Voter and a wellwisher" (9 October 1733, BL Add. MS. 32,688, f. 480).

86. Thomas Hurdis Jr. to William Hay, 11 October 1733, BL Add. MS. 32,688, f. 490.

87. William Hay to Newcastle, 15 October 1733, BL Add. MS. 32,688, ff. 504–5.

88. Browning, *Duke of Newcastle,* 8–10.

89. Newcastle to Bishop Bowers, 6 June 1723, BL Add. MS. 32,686, f. 253; McCann, ed., *Correspondence,* xxiii.

90. McCann, ed., *Correspondence,* xxiii–xxviii.

91. BL Add. MS. 32,686, f. 125, and 32,687, f. 79.

92. McCann, ed., *Correspondence,* xxx.

93. John Lord Ashburnham's Tory sympathies were clearly demonstrated by his campaign directions to his associates. He used at least one of his clerical clients—Richard Thorneton—as a Tory agent. See ESRO Ash 843, ff. 411, 416–17, 425–26, 434, and 454. Furthermore, the poll books reveal that the Ashburnhams were voting consistently Tory before 1715.

94. Newcastle preferred William Ashburnham, son of Sir Charles, the baronet, rapidly. In 1739 Ashburnham was granted his first living in Sussex (Bexhill). By 1741 he was Dean of Chichester, and in 1754 was consecrated Bishop of the diocese.

95. Von den Steinen, "Fabric of an Interest," 28–34.

96. Henry Pelham to Newcastle, 17 September 1719, BL Add. MS. 32,686, f. 147.

97. Somerset refused to back Newcastle's Whig candidate (Lord Middlesex) in the bi-election of 1741 for two reasons: he was, first of all, "under Engagements to Sir Cecil Bishop [a Tory!]," and, secondly, he wanted a man from the western division of the county (Middlesex was from Kent). 28 May 1741, BL Add. MS. 32,697, f. 92.

98. PRO SP 36 vol. 70, ff. 130–31.

99. J. Brent, "Pooles of Chailey and Lewes."

100. One illustration of the operation of the Pelham patronage network is the involvement of both Francis Hare, the Bishop of Chichester, and the Duke of Newcastle in the presentation of a clergyman to the living of Maresfield, which was in the right of William Gage. There was, as usual, a scramble among parsons who wanted to succeed to the living when it fell vacant early in 1739. No decision

was reached for months and Hare was eager to get the living filled. In August he wrote to Newcastle and asked him if he "and Sr Wm Gage are come to any resolution upon Meresfield." Hare favored giving the first refusal of the benefice to Henry Michell and advised Newcastle of this. The duke reassured him that he would take care of it, and Michell was in due course presented to the living. This demonstrates that appointing incumbents was often a cooperative effort with Newcastle as the coordinator. Hare to Newcastle, 8 August 1739, BL Add. MS. 32,692, f. 212, and 14 August 1739, BL Add. MS. 32,692, f. 238.

101. The ownership pattern of the advowsons changed very little over the period of this study. Though many advowsons changed hands, they were usually transferred to new owners who resembled the old in class and politics. The Archbishop of Canterbury neither lost nor added any livings, and the Crown's and the Bishop of Chichester's patronage rights also remained constant. The vast majority of transfers and purchases were between gentry families of roughly the same social status. An advowson owned by a clergyman also tended to stay in ecclesiastical ranks even after it was sold. Though there was a fair amount of changeover in patrons over the years, therefore, the proportion and complexion of patronage in the diocese of Chichester remained very much the same. The faces may have changed, but the patrons, in effect, did not.

102. There is some question whether or not High Churchmen still maintained the doctrine of *jure divino* episcopacy in the mid-eighteenth century. Edmund Gibson, who is frequently thought of as a man with High-Church proclivities, adopted the older idea of episcopacy as *bene esse* (i.e., important for the well-being of the church), rather than *jure divino,* apparently so that he could consider continental Protestant churches legitimate (see Spurr, *Restoration Church,* 136). How common this tendency was is unclear. But the common conception of high churchmanship still entailed the idea of *jure divino* episcopacy.

103. Bishop Bowers to Newcastle, 9 November 1723, BL Add. MS. 33,064, f. 240.

104. ArchW Epist. 10, f. 66.

105. "A Copy of the Paper fix'd upon the Market House and other Publick Places, on Sunday in the Night the 22d July [1733]," BL Add. MS. 33,058, f. 331.

106. Newcastle, for instance, laid down almost no doctrinal or ecclesiastical conditions at all, as long as clergymen could prove to be orthodox and regular churchmen. He did, however, tend to exclude the most controversial theologians and polemicists from high office. S. Taylor, "Church and State," 101–5.

107. If anything, the tendency even in Low-Church circles was to increase rather than diminish the importance of episcopacy. No less a dignitary than Archbishop William Wake had written against Edward Stillingfleet's *Irenicum.* He argued that episcopacy was an apostolic, if not a divine pattern, and not merely a convention as Stillingfleet maintained. And other Low Churchmen applauded his efforts to bolster episcopacy. As Thomas Curteis, a Low Churchman in most

matters, observed, "I am glad to find the three distinct orders of Bps Presbyters & Deacons so clearly trac'd to the Apostolic Age." Curteis to Wake, 23 November 1717, ArchW Epist. 7, f. 53. See also Mather, *High Church Prophet,* 4–5.

108. There is little reason to believe that the liturgy was treated any differently in the eighteenth century than it was in the Restoration period. The liturgy was never revised, nor were the Thirty-Nine Articles. Visitation returns seem to indicate that clergy were relatively diligent in following the liturgy as it stood. The only parson I have found who objected to the liturgy, or substantially modified his use of it, was William Hopkins, Vicar of Bolney (whose unorthodox sentiments were not clear until after the period this study covers). Hopkins gravitated toward unitarianism and began to publish writings in the 1750s that defended William Whiston and Lord Bolingbroke. Eventually he published *The Liturgy of the Church of England . . . reduced nearer to the Standard of Scripture* (London, 1763). For a short history of his life and his difficulties with traditional orthodoxy, see Disney, *Short Memoir.* He did apparently have influence with a rector, John Tench, in a neighboring parish, who acknowledged "regard and friendship for" Hopkins in his will. Tench seems to have harbored heterodox ideas too, but he feared that overt profession of them might harm his livelihood. He refused to acknowledge his doubts even in his will because, he said, "I must by no means do anything that might seem to injure my dearest wife the above little legacies." PRO Prob. 11/975 74 Taverner. This would seem to indicate that even late in the century open profession of heterodoxy was rare, and when it was discovered, it was hounded.

109. As we have already seen, clergymen in many areas protested against the perpetual prorogation of Convocation by continuing to elect proctors, long after that act had significant meaning. This reveals that they had not accepted Erastianism, despite the fact that many (if not most) of them accepted the administration's good intentions regarding the church. See Langford, "Convocation and the Tory Clergy."

110. See below, in response to clergy fears over dissent.

111. Browning, *Duke of Newcastle,* 82–83.

112. PRO SP 36 vol. 15, ff. 193–96.

113. Newcastle to Lord Chancellor, 23 June 1730, PRO, SP 36, vol. 19, f. 62. Newcastle undoubtedly felt at this point, like Jeremy Taylor, that it was "prostitution of the Bravery of friendship to spend it upon impertinent people" (Taylor, *Measures and Offices,* 31).

114. Watts, *Dissenters,* 382–93.

115. Ibid., 371–82.

116. Caplan, "Outline of the Origins," part 3, 70–71. The figures come from two separate sources. The first was from a nationwide survey commissioned by Archbishop Sheldon to ascertain the number of Dissenters throughout the land. It was conducted by Henry Compton, the Bishop of London, in 1676, and is generally referred to as the "Compton Census." See Anne Whiteman, *The Compton*

Census of 1676. A Critical Edition (London: The British Academy, 1986), and J. H. Cooper, "A Religious Census of Sussex in 1676," *SAC* 45 (1902): 142–48. If anything, the Compton figures are low. Colin Brent has demonstrated convincingly that there were many more people—at least in Lewes—who could be counted Nonconformists than were reported in the Compton Census ("Lewes Dissenters," 198–99). The 1724 figures are derived from Bishop Bowers's Visitation Book, WSRO Ep I/26/3.

117. "Hearers," it should be stressed, were by no means committed nonconformists. They were simply those that had come to hear a sermon. Many were regular Anglicans who wanted a change of pace from their regular fare. The Anglican church did not emphasize preaching, and many hungered for more exposition than they received from their parish church, so they sought alternatives. "The John Evans List of Dissenting Congregations and Ministers 1715–1729" (manuscript in Dr. William's Library, London), 116.

118. ESRO NU 1/1/1. I am grateful to Peter Le Fevre for this reference.

119. It is uncertain how the other main Dissenter congregation (Westgate Chapel) in Lewes fared in the eighteenth century, since its register has been lost. Nevertheless, as Colin Brent has recently demonstrated, theological differences, personality disputes, and other problems took their toll in Lewes: Nonconformity in the town was not thriving. Brent, *Georgian Lewes,* 152–57.

120. ArchW Epist. 20, f. 557. I am grateful to Peter Le Fevre for this reference.

121. Caplan, "Outline of the Origins," 2.

122. ArchW Epist. 20, f. 209.

123. SPCK Abstract Letter Book, CRI 4:3509.

124. SPCK Abstract Letter Book, CRI 8:5535.

125. Thomas Curteis, *An Appeal to the Reason and Consciences of all True Englishmen, concerning their unhappy Prejudices and the Fomenters of them* (handwritten manuscript submitted to the Duke of Newcastle for his approval, but apparently never published). BL Add. MS. 33,344, ff. 86–87.

126. The obverse is also true—where dissent remained strong and vital, High Churchmanship continued to be vigorous and unyielding. See Albers, "Seeds of Contention," 389–474.

127. James Hargraves to Newcastle, 27 May 1734, BL Add. MS. 32,689, ff. 245–46.

128. 3 January 1733, BL Add. MS. 32,689, ff. 128–29; Springett to Hay, 18 March 1734, PRO SP 36, vol. 36, f. 2.

129. PRO Prob. 11/675 44 Derby.

130. He was a solid Anglican churchman, but he was friendly with Dissenters and attempted to assist them in whatever ways he could. Early in his tenure, for instance, he voted for repeal of the Occasional Conformity and Schism Acts, as well as the Test and Corporation Act. See ArchW Epist. 8, f. 89. See also Browning, *Duke of Newcastle,* 78–80.

131. Newcastle to Mr. Attersol, BL Add. MS. 32,690, ff. 115–17.

132. Occasionally the Whigs miscalculated. In 1736 Walpole and his adherents attempted to pass a bill that excused the Quakers from paying tithes to Church of England ministers. This undertaking created a High-Church backlash of unexpected proportions, and reminded the administration once again that they had to accommodate churchmen on the issue of Dissenters. See S.Taylor, "Sir Robert Walpole."

133. He had, for example, acted as an agent in Hastings for the Tory John Ashburnham. ESRO Ash 843, f. 419; 845, f. 130.

134. SPCK Abstract Letter Book, CRI 1:1634.

135. BL Add. MS. 32,692, f. 1.

136. Jewkes to Newcastle, 4 October 1733, BL Add. MS. 32,688, ff. 462–63.

4

Toryism, High Churchmanship, and the Election of 1734

In 1734, the Whigs in Sussex faced their toughest electoral battle in two decades. The Tories—or Country Party—had chosen to put up a fight, and they gave the Whigs a good run for their money. A large percentage of the clergy participated in the contest, some quite vigorously. This election and the events surrounding it are telling indicators of clergy sympathy in the period, since they generated so much correspondence regarding clerical allegiances and attachments. We can discern not only the numbers of clergymen who voted Whig and the numbers who voted Tory, but also why they chose these paths and what the choices meant as far as churchmanship was concerned. The election of 1734 was something of a watershed because it virtually sealed the hegemony of the Whigs. It is important for our purposes, too, because it revealed some of the key differences between Whig and Tory clergymen.

The Campaign

Before evaluating the clergy's disposition and role in the election, it is necessary to understand the general outline of this event and get acquainted with the chief participants. There were, of course, two categories of parliamentary elections. First, there was the election of Knights of the Shire—the countywide campaign for the representatives for Sussex. Some four thousand voters—all of them qualified by ownership of at least 40 shillings worth of property—cast their votes for two members to represent their county. Then there were thirteen separate borough elections (Arundel, Bramber, Chichester, East Grinstead, Hastings, Horsham, Lewes, Midhurst, New Shoreham, Rye, Seaford, Steyning, and Winchelsea), all of which returned two members to Parliament. But because the number of voters for most boroughs was small (ranging from a high of 440 in Chichester to a low of 36 in Bramber and East Grinstead) and the debates much more parochial,[1] not nearly as much is known about the contests in them. The records for these contests are simply not as copious, nor as helpful, as those for the election for the Knight of the Shire. Nor are they as significant for our purpose, since each borough election could involve only one or two clergymen (except for the large towns of Lewes and Chichester). Accordingly, we will concentrate primarily on the countywide election.

As noted in chapter 2, the county elections were not contested between the years 1715 and 1734. In 1715 the Whig candidates—James Butler and Spencer Compton—were elected with a comfortable margin in a contest. Spencer Compton continued to be returned for the county in succeeding elections until he was raised to the peerage in 1728. But in 1722 Henry Pelham was elected in the place of James Butler. Hence began his long and illustrious career as MP and, ultimately, Prime Minister. He was returned continually as a member from Sussex from this time until his death in 1754. After Compton was called to the Upper House upon the receipt of his peerage, Butler was chosen to replace him, and he sat as MP once more. In 1734 the Whigs again put forward the team of Pelham and Butler, the sitting members.[2]

Frustration with Robert Walpole's government had been growing for some time, and opposition seems to have galvanized in the county after proposals for new taxes were made known.[3] By early July 1733, the Tories were making noises that the Duke of Newcastle and his Whig allies could not ignore. John Fuller, one of the Tory JPs for the county, had already declared himself an opposing candidate for the election, and as Robert Burnett, one of the Duke of Newcastle's election agents, reported, he had vowed to campaign vigorously: he "sayd he would shake every freeholder by the Hand in the County & kiss theire wives before Christmas Day."[4] His Tory partner, Sir Cecil Bishopp, declared his candidacy the following month at the Steyning horse races.[5] It was a fitting place to announce his plans to run, since the whole event symbolized for the Tories the start of the electoral race. Fuller and Bishopp bolted onto the track at this time and galloped for the finishing line with more power than the Whigs could have imagined.

The Pelhams were nonplussed by this opposition, and they could never quite explain why after all these years of relative quiescence such a vigorous challenge arose, or why it attracted such numbers. Newcastle himself observed that the opposition was "unexpected," and appeared to be quite hurt by it. As he wrote to Thomas Sherlock, the Bishop of Bangor, "we shall have a good deal of trouble, which I think we don't deserve either from the County or even from these Gentlemen [the Tories]." He took it as a personal affront and was disturbed that many, like John Parke, one of the canons of the Church of Chichester, would oppose him so vigorously, because "I am persuaded Mr. Parks cannot say, we ever did any thing personally to offend him; and I was in hopes our Publick behaviour would have recommended us to his Favour."[6] Newcastle was also disconcerted by the opposition that emerged in the borough election at Lewes, in which two of his cousins were candidates. He sent out a circular letter to his supporters in and around the town in which he observed that "the chief design" of the opposition was "not only to destroy my Interest at Lewes, but if possible to drive me out of the Country." He felt betrayed by this. "I am very positive," he lamented, "I have not deserved this usage from the town of Lewes of all places."[7] In Newcastle's mind, deference and consensus were still central to society and politics, and when they did not function, he was surprised, bewildered, and hurt.

Nevertheless, there was opposition, and there was a lot of it. It took the Whigs by surprise, and only gradually did they comprehend the scope of the challenge. At first they were confident, but as the months went by, the Tories appeared to gain more and more ground until it appeared that, as an anxious Henry Pelham reported to his brother, "the whole Country almost is poison'd" by them.[8]

Both parties had numerous agents who "ridd up and down the country like Devils," campaigning for their respective candidates.[9] In the case of the Tories, the "burgessers" included the candidates themselves, the principal Tory gentlemen of the county (many of whom were JPs), and certain clergymen. The Duke of Newcastle had the advantage here, however, since he had more agents than did the Tories, as well as a wider spectrum of them. Newcastle relied, first of all, on paid agents like Robert Burnett, whom he employed to be his eyes and ears in the county and organize campaign events.[10] Burnett's detailed and colorful reports provide us with a great deal of information about life in Sussex as well as the election.[11] Newcastle utilized, secondly, the Whig JPs, borough representatives, and other gentry as agents. William Gage and William Hay, both MPs from Sussex boroughs, were very important in the countywide Whig electoral effort.[12] The mayors of Chichester (John Dear) and Hastings (John Collier) were involved too, pressing for votes and providing intelligence. Other prominent gentlemen, like John Jewkes and John Board, also played a large role in the campaign. Newcastle depended, thirdly, upon clergymen. James Hargraves and George Jordan, two of his early favorites in the county, played a large role—they canvassed not only their own parishes, but parishes across the county. Other trusted members of the clergy received commissions from Newcastle too: Thomas Hurdis, John Penfold, Thomas Ball, and James Barker all were assigned roles in the campaign. The duke even authorized Barker to treat the men in his parish (and perhaps elsewhere) at the great man's expense, in order to woo them into the Whig camp.[13] The biggest problem for Newcastle was that his candidates did not do their own canvassing very often. Henry Pelham was engaged much of the time in London; James Butler made the rounds, but his face was not as familiar as his opponents'; and Thomas Pelham, one of the candidates for Lewes, was, according to some of the other agents, simply indolent. If victory eluded them in that borough race, William Hay alleged, "the loss . . . must be imputed entirely to Mr. Pelham's inactivity."[14] Agents may have been beneficial to the cause, but the people wanted to see the candidates themselves, and since the Tories were more diligent about this than the Whigs, they gained points with the voters. As William Hay wrote Newcastle, the "People would not Promise your Grace's Servants; but expected to be waited on by Persons of a Superior Rank." The Tories, on the other hand, had their best men doing the burgessing: their "Gentlemen of Fashion had ask'd votes in all Places throughout the County, & in many two Months before the Candidates had declar'd."[15] The Whigs constantly had to play catch-up to the Tories here.

The chief ammunition in the Tories' armory of arguments was the Excise Bill, which Walpole and the Whigs sponsored in 1733. The irony of this was that the Excise Bill was a measure adopted by Walpole largely to appease Tory landowners, who had been suffering under the burdens of the land tax, by reducing the land tax and levying an excise on certain commodities like beer and tobacco to make up the shortfall.[16] Unfortunately for Walpole and the Whigs, this conciliatory move backfired badly and was bitterly attacked by Bolingbroke and Pulteney in the *Craftsman*.[17] Since this was an issue that affected everyone, the Tories could (and did) exploit it in order to damage the reputation of the Whigs and lift their own standing in the election. The hue and cry raised everywhere by the Tories was "No Excise." They united around that platform, and even the Whigs had to acknowledge that it was an effective one. The Bishop of Chichester found it such a powerful argument against the Whigs that he lamented that the bill had been proposed "so near the expiration of a Parliament." In his view, it was not well conceived, and was easily blown out of proportion amongst the common people "who are so little inclined to think favorably of a ministry which they have for so many years been taught to look on as enemies to this Country."[18] The Tories were able to get many freeholders angry over the bill, and it was not unusual to find a group staying up late "huzzaing No Excise."[19]

The voters frequently got the impression—and the Tories did precious little to disabuse them of it—that the excise applied to basic foodstuffs as well as luxuries. The Whigs found themselves running around putting out fires created by the propaganda (or even misinformation) campaign of the Tories. In the parishes of Hellingly and Hailsham they found that the voters "had heard that Bread & Meat" had almost been included in the bill.[20] And others elsewhere had gotten the same idea. As William Hay bitterly complained to the Duke of Newcastle, "those who told them these stories [i.e., the Tory candidates and their agents] knew them to be false; & did it to make them & other honest people uneasy in their votes, & I believed with a very ill design . . . that they ought to resent such Usage & vote against them."[21]

The "Common Cry against the Excise" served the opposition well through much of the campaign. The Whigs were so hard pressed by this issue, that they were eventually forced to drop the scheme. And as word spread that this was no longer an impediment to the Whig cause, the candidates and their agents were able to breathe a collective sigh of relief. As John Crawford observed, "the Bugg-bear Word Excise seems to decrease pretty much, so that I am hopefull they will be obliged to think of some other art to gain people."[22]

Thus the campaign proceeded. But what did this election mean for the clergy? And what can we gather about High Churchmanship from it? Those are the next questions to be addressed.

The Shift among the Clergy

Several Tory canvassers noted with surprise and dismay that the clergy seemed largely to have defected from the Tory to the Whig camp. On one occasion when the Tory candidate, John Fuller, encountered Robert Burnett he marveled "that there should be such an alteration amongst the Clergey. That when he stood last he had all of them & now but very few." He was puzzled at this and "none of the Gentlemen" he asked about it had "the least answer."[23]

Similarly, Thomas Spence, an agent for the Duke of Newcastle, was riding along the Downs one day on his way to James Butler's parish "to Enquire into the present State of the Protestant interest" in those parts, when he was met by a Mr. Middleton, who was obviously on a Tory errand. They had a cordial conversation, as Spence put it, in a "Jocular Stile," and spoke of many things. But at one point Middleton "took notice that he understood we had made a great impression amongst the Clergy in our favour, and wonderd from whence that arose." Spence's response revealed that he thought the answer was obvious: "Now I told him, he must certainly Joke, for You that are a thinking man cannot but be sensible, that as they have now had time to weigh and consider the merritts of *Our Cause,* we may with reason hope to have their friendship and assistance."[24]

These episodes demonstrate a couple of things. First of all, the Tories still expected the clergy to be with them. The clergy had been Tory for so long that it was almost as if Tory sympathy was part of the clerical duty, despite the fact that the opposition was now forced to create a coalition out of groups with disparate political and ideological stances. Second, as Spence observed, many, if not most, clergymen no longer looked upon Whiggery as a threat to the church. In fact, he believed that they ought to join the Whigs because the cause was just and, undoubtedly, good for the church as well.

Though Fuller and Middleton both seemed to feel that some sea-change had taken place and that they had been abandoned by the clergy, the reality is much more subtle. It is true that more clergy voted Whig than Tory on this occasion, but there are mitigating factors to be taken into account. This section will examine the voting pattern of the clergy in this election and attempt to form some conclusions on the basis of it.

Scrutiny of the polling results suggests that clerical sentiment had indeed shifted in favor of the Whigs. The 1734 poll book[25] reveals the following: eighty-three clergymen voted Whig, sixty-two voted Tory, fifteen split votes between Whig and Tory, and forty-two did not vote at all.[26] Of those who voted (160 total), then, some 52 percent were Whigs, 39 percent Tories, and 9 percent mixed. This is not the two-to-one margin reported by some historians.[27] The balance had, therefore, certainly been tipped from the previous elections from Tory to Whig, but the shift is not as substantial as it has frequently been seen to be.

Furthermore, if the unregistered Tory (as well as Whig) sentiment is taken into account (as much as it can be determined), the gap narrows even further. On the basis of indicators other than votes, it appears that there were at least another ten Whig supporters among the clergy and an additional sixteen for the Tories.[28] If nonvoters had expressed themselves, therefore, the margin of the Whigs' victory among the clergy might have been shaved considerably—this would drop Whig support some six percentage points (to 46 percent), while Tory and mixed results stayed virtually the same. Some 8 percent of the clergy would still remain unaccounted for in this construction.

Thus the Whigs pulled off a victory among the clergy, but not by more than thirteen percentage points, and their real ascendance may have been considerably less (9 percent or less). This cannot be considered political dominance. In fact, the biggest gain for the Whigs seems to have come from the ranks of the nonvoters in previous elections—the majority of those who voted Whig were voting for the very first time. The Whigs may simply have been more effective in getting clergy to express their sentiments by mobilizing them to go to the polls. Nevertheless, given the actual results, the balance of power had shifted noticeably to the Whigs. What do these results indicate?

The Role of Patronage

First of all, it is important to dispel the notion that patronage alone had won this election amongst the clergy for the Whigs. Though John Jewkes believed that most of the clergy "will go as enjoyn'd by their patron,"[29] the Bishop of Chichester was less sure. He observed that there were a lot of considerations for the clergy, and that patronage was no control. As he put it, the clergy "have their relations, friendships, Interests and opinions as others have, and therefore it can't be expected they should act all alike, or as one could wish, in affairs of this nature." This he said in order to explain the lack of effect from his own efforts as a "poor patron."[30] And, indeed, the clergy did not act solely as their patrons wished—out of the sixty-two parsons who voted Tory, nearly half (twenty-eight) had Whig patrons, and over 10 percent of those who voted Whig had Tory patrons (nine out of eighty-three).[31] In addition, most of the forty-two who refrained from voting had either an active Whig or Tory patron, but the efforts of those patrons were not sufficient to goad their clients into action (unless, of course, those parsons abstained from voting in order to satisfy their patrons).

Patronage was, of course, important, and patrons pulled all of the strings they could in order to get their clients to vote according to their wishes. The clergy too could be threatened if they did not comply with the instructions of their patrons. But most of the attempts to intimidate incumbents had less effect than the ones directed at vulnerable tradesmen, for clergymen were appointed for life, and it was very difficult to dismiss them. They were not impervious to pressure, as we shall see, but they were resistant to it—at least much more resistant than other freeholders. One illustration of this is William Lamb, the Rector of Ditchling. The Whigs lobbied Lamb to support them on the basis that he owed them gratitude for his living, which was in the right of the Chancellor of Chichester, George Jordan, Newcastle's right-hand man. Lamb did not give in, and refused to acknowledge their claims to his allegiance. This frustrated and irritated the campaigners. As one agent wrote to Newcastle, "the parson who of all others in the neighbourhood ought to have embrased this opportunity of shewing himself gratefull refuses to promise."[32] Lamb kept up his resolve to the end: he voted Tory, and probably managed to convince a few of his parishioners to do the same (eight out of the twelve freeholders from Ditchling voted Tory).

The pressure was undoubtedly intense at times. Edward Wilson, for example, knew what it meant to withstand pressure. Wilson had been appointed Vicar of Rye in 1700. Rye was a difficult place for a minister of the established church, because Dissenters practically outnumbered Anglicans in that location. Sometime before 1724, Wilson's patron (Thomas Bromfield) either died or sold the advowson, for in Bishop Bowers's Visitation the patron is listed as Spencer Compton, the indefatigable Whig. Though in 1734 virtually the whole town voted Whig, Wilson steadfastly held to his Tory principles and registered his choice for Fuller and Bishopp. His patron had become Whig and he was outvoted eleven to one by his parishioners (out of eighty-eight voters in Rye, only eight voted Tory), yet he resolutely stood against the tide.

There was a unique pressure put on those who had both Whig and Tory patrons. William Bridgen, Bell Carleton, and Richard Nairn were all clergymen who were indebted to Whigs for one of their livings, yet they voted Tory. And William Jenkin, Edward Martin, Thomas Newcombe, and John Smith all had a Tory patron in addition to their Whig one, and they voted Whig. But many in this predicament were not so lucky, especially if their patrons had some influence over them other than a benefice. Thomas Turner had been presented to the living of West Hoathly by the Crown (on the recommendation of the Duke of Newcastle), but he was also the curate of the nearby parish of Lindfield, by which he supplemented his income. The problem was, the lessee of the tithes of Lindfield (for all intents and purposes the controller of the curacy)—Peter Short—was an implacable Tory. Turner was inclined to vote Whig, but was intimidated by Short. As John Board reported to Newcastle, "poor Mr. Turner to whom your Grace was so good as to give the living of West Hoathly is on acct of his gratitude and fidelity to your Grace on this occasion [the election] like to loose the Cure of Lindfield, from which my neighbour Mr Peter Short . . . has declared he will remove him, for promising his vote and Interest to Mr. Pelham and Butler."[33] Turner was safe in his benefice, but not in his curacy. When the poll was taken, Turner appeared and cast his vote for the Whig candidates. It is not known whether he managed to retain his curacy or not.

Thus patronage was a significant force in politics, but it was unusual that it forced conscientious men to vote against their wills. Pressure from patronage might, however, keep clergymen from voting at all. Some steadfastly refused to get involved with politics despite the pressure of their patrons. When Thomas Denham's patron turned Whig after being Tory, the rector withheld his vote, as if he was protesting against his patron's volte face. The same was true of William Harvey and Henry Hodsden.

Some of the nonvoting clergymen refrained voluntarily and some were prevailed upon to stay away for one reason or another. Some, like Henry Baker, just seemed to shy away from politics in general. Baker never once voted in Sussex, though he had a living there from 1699 until his death in 1739. William Hawkins and John Scott also lived in Sussex throughout these political contests and never ventured a single vote. Henry Pellat, on the other hand, was a professed Tory, yet his brother, who was in favor of the Whigs, thought he could keep him at home.[34] Others undoubtedly were pressured into abstaining too.

There was, of course, another reason for not voting: infirmity. The election of 1734 took place at Chichester, and if an individual was not fit enough to make the journey, his choice would not figure in the tally. This appears to be the reason that the names Gabriel Thorne, Edward West, and John Scott, did not appear in the poll book. Gabriel Thorne professed himself "always ready & willing to joyn in the Interest of the Duke of

Newcastle."[35] Unfortunately, his interest was quite limited, since he was a paralytic and lived as a shut-in. He may have backed the duke's candidates, but his support was intangible and was not registered in the poll. Similarly, John Scott told the Whig agents that he would vote for Pelham and Butler "if he was well enough to go to the Election."[36] Scott must not have been feeling well in May, since his name did not appear. Edward West seems to have battled some kind of debilitating disease, for his will indicates that he had to be taken care of during a "long illness."[37] It is always possible, too, that parsons who did not want to involve themselves or make a commitment could use ill health as an excuse.

Some clergymen were apparently uncertain or afraid of the consequences when they refused to commit themselves. Charles Lyddell was evidently one such waverer. He probably did not face the pressure that some other incumbents did because his patron was his father (who may very well have been dead by the election of 1734). When Whig agents pressed him, he resisted their attempts and kept his sympathies to himself—at least at first. This, according to the Whig campaigners, allowed the opposition to get a leg up in his parish, even though Lyddell had not declared for them either. But he finally decided to align himself with the Whigs in late September, and even helped them campaign. John Board was delighted with Lyddell's decision to join them, and he hoped that his "declaration to his Parishioners" would "have the desir'd success" of winning them over to the Whig cause as well.[38] Despite this commitment, Lyddell must have had doubts or pressure from another quarter, because when the poll was actually taken the next May, he cast his votes for Fuller and Bishopp rather than the Whigs. It may be that Lyddell had remained Tory in sympathy all along, but capitulated under the Whig barrage (or even feigned surrender) for a time, only to decide later that his submission to the Whigs was ill-advised or unnecessary.[39]

Some clergymen compromised when they were caught in a dilemma between conscience and obligation. John Citizen, the Rector of Aldrington, seems to have been a Tory in sympathy,[40] and was close to John Fuller, the Tory candidate.[41] But Lord Wilmington pressured him to vote Whig. Wilmington thought at first that he was hopeless,[42] but when the election rolled around Citizen split his vote—casting one for Fuller and one for Pelham. This was good enough to oblige Wilmington, who presented him with the vicarage of Westham in 1741.

Thomas Ball was also one who compromised. Ball was a firm believer in Whiggery and a devoted "friend" of the Duke of Newcastle. But he had been appointed to his living of Boxgrove by the Tory Earl of Derby, to whom he was deeply obliged. A letter he wrote to the Duke of Newcastle in October reveals the struggle he faced in having two patrons with different political orientations and expectations. He began by informing Newcastle of Derby's decision to sponsor both Fuller and Bishopp in the Sussex elections. He continued:

> Whatever effect this may have upon others I am sure it operates in this manner upon me; I cannot give up those Principles for which I formerly suffer'd & in which his Lordship [Derby] so generously supported me; I cannot give up or oppose the Whigg interest in Sussex (of which I take your Grace and your Family to be the main supporters) tho' I am sure of forever forfeiting his Lordship's favour by acting otherwise at this crisis, tho' I am under greater personal obligations to his Lordship than to any man liveing and tho' no private views of my own cou'd ever divert me from embracing every honourable occasion of shewing my gratitude. This I shall take the liberty to signifie to his Lordship in the most respectfull Terms as soon as occasion offerrs.[43]

Ball may have been genuinely resolved upon this course, but he apparently did not follow through. Though he campaigned vigorously for Newcastle's candidates (both of them),[44] when the poll came he voted for one Tory and one Whig. His obligations to the Duke of Derby were simply too weighty, and he could not bring himself to defy one to whom he owed so great a debt.

Thomas Leyland was another parson who wavered. Leyland was a Tory in sympathy, but was pressed by Newcastle and his allies to vote Whig. Leyland had been presented in 1727 to the vicarage of West Dean by Thomas Sherlock, then Dean of Chichester. But Sherlock had been translated to the Bishopric of Bangor shortly thereafter. Sherlock had himself had a reputation as a Tory. In fact, he was the only Tory to be appointed to a See after the Whig ascendancy at Court. Despite this, he had succumbed to the influence of the Duke of Newcastle such that when Newcastle wrote to him to ask if he might request Leyland's interest for the Whigs, he readily complied.[45] This apparently had its effect on Leyland, but it was not enough to put him wholeheartedly in the Whig camp. At the election, Leyland cast one Whig vote (for Henry Pelham), to oblige his patron, and one Tory vote (for John Fuller), to oblige his conscience.

But such compromises were comparatively rare (after all, there were only fifteen mixed votes, and some of those were due to conscience, not coercion). Most often clergymen were able to maintain their principles despite the patronage system. This could mean either wholehearted agreement with their patron or abstention from voting entirely, but sometimes it meant outright defiance. When Newcastle wrote to Sherlock to use his influence with Leyland, he also asked him to entreat John Parke, the most implacable opponent of Whiggery in the cathedral chapter, to vote for the Whig candidates.[46] This time the plea fell on deaf ears. Parke not only refused to vote Whig, but he proceeded to campaign actively and noisily for the Tories, an action that constantly irritated the duke and his allies in the chapter. Patronage held little or no power over Parke.

Patronage failed in a number of other cases too. Bell Carleton, for example, was indebted to Whigs for his preferment. He had, first of all, been chaplain to the Duke of Richmond. Then he was presented to the vicarage of Amberley by the Bishop of Chichester, at which time he had professed wholehearted devotion to the Whig cause. Nevertheless, when the election of 1734 came along, neither the duke nor the bishop could persuade him to join forces with them. Carleton became a die-hard Tory, bent on opposing the Whigs at every turn. In 1740 his neighbor, Edward Prattenton, Rector of Bury, recalled the measures Carleton had taken in 1734 to spur on Whig defeat:

> The Vicar of the next parish to me [Carleton], pretending to be very uneasie about the present Ministry and especially about the Excise Bill, sent a great number of Reflecting Balads to be printed and dispersed about this Country. After that he got into his intimate acquaintance one Thos Day an Excise-man in my Parish: This Excise-man (in order to oblige some certain People) did all that lay in his power to persuade the Country, that all necessaries of life were to be Excis'd, and to convince the Ignorant but well-meaning people of the truth of what he said, he at last took a paper in his hand, went into the poor people's Gardens, and told them, that Paper was an Act of Parliament, for this very Excise, and that he must and would have the Excise of their Gardens.[47]

Whether Carleton stooped to unconscionable tactics or not is really unclear (he may not have known any better than his people what the excise was to cover), but it is clear that he neither trusted nor heeded his patrons. They not only failed to receive his vote, they failed to receive his respect.

There are many other examples of parsons defying their patrons in politics. William Willes was indebted to Charles Eversfield for two separate livings. Eversfield had been a Tory MP for the borough of Horsham, but after 1715 his endorsement declined until he came to some agreement with the Duke of Newcastle. From about 1722 on, Eversfield voted with Newcastle and sponsored his candidates.[48] Willes, however, did not follow Eversfield into the Whig camp. In 1734 he voted Tory against his patron's will. Nevertheless, he was not penalized for his principles, since Eversfield gave him the opportunity for further preferment if he wanted it: directly after the election Willes was offered the right of refusal for the vicarage of Hollington, apparently with the consent of the Duke of Newcastle.[49] This kind of response to the pressure of patrons occurred time and time again: Thomas James, Thomas Kelway, Richard Nairn, John Stuart, John Story, John Tattersall, and William Jenkin all rebuffed the influence of their patrons by voting the opposite way.

Patronage, therefore, had influence, but not control, in the election of 1734. Most often there was no conflict at all. Most of the parsons who voted with their patrons did so because they believed in them and their cause. But when there was a conflict, resolution was possible either through compromise or abstention, and it was very possible simply to defy one's patron. The very presence of such intensive campaigning is itself evidence that patronage did not lock in results in elections.

Ideology of Clerical Toryism

What prevented clergymen from all becoming Whigs? If, as we saw in chapter 3, there were fewer and fewer impediments to making common cause with the Whigs (at least with the Pelhamite Whigs in Sussex), why did so many continue to resist their charms? Who were the Tories among the clergy, what forces held them in the Tory camp, and why did they resist Whig hegemony?

There appear to be two main reasons that many remained Tory: ideology and reinforcing mechanisms. Ideology amounted to the things Tory clergymen told themselves—they were the premises that they put forward as justifications for opposition. The reinforcing mechanisms were those social structures—education, friends, family, tradition, and so on—that kept men from changing their ideological stances. These acted as effective blocks to new ideas and new alliances.

It is no simple matter to discern the ideologies involved in clerical Toryism in Sussex at this time, since few clergymen left self-conscious statements detailing their opposition principles (most of the extant documents were written by Whigs). But a number of things can be said. First of all, there were undoubtedly a few—though only a few—who leaned toward

Jacobitism. The Whigs, at least, thought that this was the reason that many incumbents were so intractable. Lord Tankerville, for instance, hoped in 1740 that he could get some Whig votes in Trotton "in spite of that Jacobite Parson, [John] Alcock."[50] The Duke of Richmond, too, once characterized the Rector of Slindon, Robert Styles Launce, as a Jacobite, though he was not too worried about him because "he is so eternally drunk with rum and brandy that he does us no harm."[51] These characterizations may merely have been pejoratives hurled at opponents and not real, accurate descriptions at all. But it is likely that some clergymen were steeped in Jacobitism. Certainly there were clergymen who harbored romantic Jacobite sentiments.[52]

The leaders of the Tory party and the opposition among the clergy certainly felt that they were the ideological heirs of the past. Though the years had produced significant changes to which the Tories had to adjust, they still felt continuity with the party of Anne's reign, even though its heyday was long past (they did not, however, know that its heyday was past—in their minds, there was always the possibility of resurgence). They saw themselves as the torch-bearers of their generation, carrying on High-Church and Tory principles, despite the fact that they had to soften or attenuate their rhetoric in order to attract enough followers to create a viable opposition. There was still enough use of High-Church vocabulary for John Mills of Hellingly to observe that "the common langague [*sic*] which was genaraly and most in use in the four last years reigne of Queen Ann is now by many extold to be the newest and best moad of talking." He alleged that "Things are now in an unsettled posture," because men of High-Church temperament were making "noys and clamour" against the Whigs like they had many years ago.[53] Thomas Curteis, too, maintained that in Kent the upheaval of the election was comparable to that which occurred in 1710: "The Middle Sort," he said, "are as mad as in the Time of Sacheverell."[54] Nevertheless, the old High-Church/Tory slogans were deliberately muted so that, for elections purposes, there would be a broader base to the party. This is undoubtedly why Robert Burnett felt that the Tories did not know "what they wass for."[55]

Though they forged a "Union of Parties" so that they could be "able to make a strong opposition,"[56] most participants were cognizant of the fact that these were "unnatural alliances," and that they would not last. This was especially evident in the alliance of High Churchmen and Dissenters in the borough of Lewes. Thomas Sergison was known as a High Churchman, and no matter how much he courted the Dissenters, and despite the fact that he accepted Nathaniel Garland (a Presbyterian) as a running mate, there was real doubt in their minds about the advisability of accepting his support. This became very clear in one particular Presbyterian worship service when a visiting minister came to preach. The guest preacher lambasted his hearers for even considering aligning with the opposition against the Whigs, for the Whigs, he said, had been friends to the Dissenters. "By opposing those who have been their friends," he continued, "they must onely expect to bring in the Torys, who when in wou'd be their ruin." This harangue was aimed specifically against Nathaniel Garland's partnership with Thomas Sergison in the race for the borough of Lewes. Garland, who was a Dissenter, had the misfortune to be present at this occasion. He sat through the service enduring this verbal abuse and, undoubtedly, wishing with all his heart that he was elsewhere. This tongue lashing was too much for Garland: "there were twenty stories that he came sick out of the meeting & stop't at two or three places before he got to his Lodgings."[57] It did not, however, dissuade him from running.

There is evidence, too, that as the campaign went on, there were real strains between Sergison and Garland and their respective followers. In October Burnett informed Newcastle that the opposition in Lewes "bragg that they gett ground, and that Mr. Sergison is before Mr. Garland, by which I could perceive, that the Dissenters are likely to be jealous."[58] And again it was observed by a loyal Whig that "that unnatural alliance between the Dissenters [and the Tories] will be at last two [*sic*] their confusion, for there can be no Love between them at the bottom, but only malice mixed with a spirit of dissatisfaction is at present sowen among the people."[59] So even though there was this marriage of convenience, the Tory reputation for persecution of Dissent was still intact, and some clergymen, at least, remained Tory because they felt that in the end a Tory government would regulate and control Nonconformity much better than a Whig administration.[60]

The Tory candidates for Knight of the Shire had unsullied reputations as High Churchmen. Though the campaign seldom focused on specifically High-Church issues, the voters—especially clergymen—knew where they stood on such matters. Their reputations were well established and they did not have to campaign on matters where their sympathies were obvious. It would, therefore, be a mistake to discount the role of conservative ideology in this election.

Certainly many of the incumbents had not yet been convinced of the Whigs' devotion to the church. Thomas Lewis, whom the Duke of

Richmond called "a mad Welsh enthusiast, a sort of Whitfeild," was "violent for Butler because he sayes he knows him to be a churchman, butt he looks upon Mr. Pelham to be a presbyterian," and so would not vote for him. This despite the fact that the Presbyterians themselves objected "to Mr. Pelham's too great attachment to the Church."[61]

The clergy may have been right to be cautious at this point, however, for though the Whigs in general supported the church, they certainly wanted the Dissenting vote and they quietly, surreptitiously, went about campaigning for it. William Hay was frequently out and about telling Nonconformists that the Whigs intended to repeal the Schism Bill, and make other concessions.[62] Furthermore, the Whigs frequently kept the clergymen—even their committed clergymen—from canvassing Dissenters, for fear that the parsons would not be pleased with the Whig flirtations with Nonconformity. Thus Thomas Pelham refused to send Edward Bland, the rector of his parish of Stanmer and a close associate, to certain areas where the inhabitants were chiefly "Anabaptists."[63] The relations between the two were by no means cordial enough for that.

But "country" ideology was much more pronounced than High-Church polemic in the Tory platform of 1733–34. Neo-Harringtonian ideas had been woven into the fabric of the Tory ethos by this time, and they frequently formed the stated basis of opposition. Deprecation of standing armies, political corruption, placemen, oligarchy, and long Parliaments all figured prominently in this propaganda, as did an insistence on observance of the ancient constitution (however understood).[64] Tory campaigners complained that "the debt of the nation," which of course they considered the fault of the Whigs, "wou'd be the ruin of it."[65] They feared that the country was being dominated by a cabal whose stranglehold jeopardized the rights of all free Englishmen. At one gathering, the Tories spent much time "ennumerating up all the Places enjoyed by the Pelham family with all Invidious reflections that are possible against the Ministry."[66] This was the principal rallying point for the opposition in this election. There was a rage against exclusion and proscription that was so powerful that groups as disparate and hostile as High Churchmen and Dissenters banded together, albeit uneasily, to fight the danger of oligarchy.[67]

Propaganda from the neo-Harringtonian perspective inundated freeholders. John Board observed that he had heard that the "other side" was putting out a number of pamphlets along these lines.[68] Likewise Thomas Ball, one of Newcastle's agents among the clergy, reported that "I wish we had some proper news Papers &c to disperse here," because Tory pamphlets were common and forceful and there were no equivalent organs on the Whig side to rebut them.[69] Undoubtedly the *Craftsman* was a persuasive vehicle of propaganda for the Tories. It certainly was distributed assiduously. Ball complained that "the Craftsman is very industriously sent down to the Tory coffeehouse [in Chichester] every weeke,"[70] and Thomas Curteis maintained that "the Weekly Letters in the Craftsman . . . are continually poysoning the nation."[71] Some clergymen, we know, were avid readers of the *Craftsman,* and they were evidently affected by the arguments they found there. John Newlin, Rector of Harting, for example, read the magazine and was quite pleased with it. He was particularly "delighted to see Religion shine" in its pages.[72] Many others must have perused the *Craftsman* and been influenced by it too.

Tory ideology in this period was, therefore, a strange mix. The core leadership of the party, which included the clergy, still retained much of the ethos that was evident during Queen Anne's reign. But the ideology had expanded with the adoption of neo-Harringtonian principles, and it was these ideas that united the disparate groups that made up the opposition against the Whigs in 1734. For most clergymen, the fear of Whiggery and a distrust of its leaders lay at the bottom of their persistence in Tory opposition.

Reinforcing Mechanisms for Clerical Toryism

Why was it that so many High Churchmen continued to hold this fear and antipathy of the Pelhamite Whigs when so many others were coming to trust them? This section will analyze several possible mechanisms that reinforced Toryism and will ascertain which ones were most consequential for the clergy.

Patronage

As we saw earlier, patronage was not the deciding factor in the election in Sussex. Neither was it, by itself, the key to understanding the persistence of Toryism among the clergy. It had its effect, certainly, but only in conjunction with the other ingredients below.

Education

University education could have had something to do with the decision to remain Tory. After all, the universities in the late seventeenth and early eighteenth centuries were notoriously political, with Cambridge emerging as the champion of Whiggery[73] and Oxford clinging to the old values of High Churchmanship and Toryism.[74] What then, was the university affiliation of the Whig clergy compared with the university affiliation of the Tory clergy?

There seems to be a slight correlation: the Whigs did proceed more often from Cambridge and the Tories did proceed more often from Oxford. Of the clergymen voting Tory in 1734, some thirty-one attended Oxford (53 percent), while twenty-three (41 percent) had been educated at Cambridge. Only five of them (8 percent) went to both universities. The Whig clergymen displayed a different pattern. Out of the seventy-nine whose university affiliations are known, well over half (forty-two, or 53 percent) attended Cambridge. Only eighteen of them (23 percent) went to Oxford. However, a significant number of them—many more than the Tories—split their education between Oxford and Cambridge: no fewer than eighteen of them (23 percent) could claim both schools as alma maters. And this last statistic could be significant, because with only one exception, they all matriculated at Oxford and transferred to Cambridge, where they completed a degree. This could indicate a dislike of the Tory politics at Oxford and a desire to immerse themselves in the more conducive Whiggish environment at Cambridge. If this shift is taken into account, it means that three out of four of the clergymen who voted Whig in the 1734 election attended Cambridge.

But the university was probably not as important in influencing the cleric as the individual college that he attended, for political perspectives varied widely among the colleges. And here the links between education and later voting patterns become weak. Eight different Whigs (10 percent) attended Clare College, Cambridge, which might be expected since Clare College was strongly Whig and was the alma mater of the Duke of Newcastle. But, surprisingly, nearly 7 percent of the Tories also attended Clare, one at the very time that Newcastle was there. Likewise, a large number of Tories (six, or 10 percent) came from the staunchly High-Church St. John's College, Cambridge. But so did many Whigs. In fact almost the exact proportion of Whigs attended that college (seven, or 9 percent). Given this record, it is difficult to make any kind of generalizations about the influence of education on the later political behavior of the clergy. There seems to have been no hard and fast rule: those educated in high Tory schools were just about as likely to vote Whig as Tory, and those taught by Whigs were frequently to be found in the ranks of the Tories at election time.[75] What this seems to indicate more than anything else is that the university education of a student, partisan though it may have been, did not necessarily predispose him toward one political party for the rest of his life.

Tradition

It might also be argued that the clergy who remained Tory were basically an old guard, a superannuated generation that was firmly rooted in tradition. It is true that the older generation tended to cling to Toryism. There were very few conversions among them. Those that had been staunch Tories in Queen Anne's reign were almost always staunch Tories in George II's as well. John Alcock I, Jeremiah Dodson, Thomas Hooper, Nicholas Lester, Thomas Milles, Edward Powell, Adam Sixsmith, John Tattersall, and Edward Wilson all continued to vote Tory. Concomitantly, those who were Whigs in the earlier period were invariably Whigs in the later. John Clifton, Arthur Coster, Charles Randol Covert, Bartholomew Cox, John Eresby, Humphrey Hammond, Theobald Michell, John Milner, John Peachey, John Penfold, John Pinnell, and Thomas Wellings illustrate this tendency. And we have already seen that the clerical leaders of Newcastle's Whig network had adopted Whiggery early—they were not converts from Toryism. In fact, of all the clergymen who voted Whig in 1734, only a handful had been consistent Tories in the earlier period. Despite all of the campaigning and pressuring done by the Whigs, only John Bullis, William Burrell II, John Hawes, Charles Bettesworth, and John Smith defected from the Tory side. Less than 10 percent of the older clergy, therefore, decided to change sides at this time. There were some others who did not vote, but that can hardly be seen as successful conversion.

But the Tories were not all elderly. On the contrary, there were plenty of young men who voted Tory. If it were true that the Tory ranks were comprised mostly of superannuated clerics, then the maturation of the party would manifest itself in the age differences between Whigs and Tories: the Tory clergy would be on average significantly older than the Whig clergy. But no such correlation appears in Sussex. The Tory clergy actually averaged slightly younger (at 42.7 years of age) than the Whigs (at 43.2 years apiece).[76] The only significant difference came from those who refrained from voting: their average age was 48.7, which means that they were over five years older than their voting colleagues. This may indicate that the older clergy had more trouble making the trek to the location where the poll was being held. In any case, on the basis of this data, it cannot be said that the Tories were, overall, a particularly mature lot.[77] They may have been more conservative politically, but that does not mean that they were, on average, older chronologically.

Family

The most significant reinforcing mechanism for clergymen appears to have been their family ties. The younger generation usually followed their fathers' example. Most of the young Tories were sons of old Tories. Of those clergymen who were appointed after the Hanoverian accession and voted Tory, well over half came from Tory families. And many of the rest may have, but their backgrounds are too sketchy to be sure. Furthermore, if one came from a household in which the father was both a parson and a Tory, it was almost certain that he would remain Tory. There were a few desertions, but not many.

The majority of the old High-Church families persisted in Tory opposition. The Alcocks, the Bartons, the Burrells, the Chatfields, the Cluttons, the Evanses, the Fortries, the Frewens, the Hamptons, the Hoopers, the Lathams, the Lewises, the Tattersalls, the Wilsons, and the Woodwards are all examples. These families were fixtures in Sussex, and they could all be called clerical dynasties. There was something in the traditions or heritages of these clans that perpetuated resistance in their progeny to the Whigs in general and the Duke of Newcastle in particular. It was more than the fact that they were country gentlemen, since many country gentlemen of equal or greater social-economic status aligned with the Pelhams. There was something about the dynamics of a clerical tradition that kept these men anchored to the old ways. And their resistance did not occur simply because they hung on to some patronage, for, as has been shown, many accepted patronage from Whigs but then refused to vote their way. The family legacy was more important than patronage in determining the vitality of clerical Toryism.[78]

A few illustrations will suffice to demonstrate this trend.[79] Let us begin with the Alcocks. The Alcock clan had settled in Midhurst centuries before the Hanoverians came and were an important gentry family for local and central government: many Alcocks were MPs during the Tudor/Stuart era.[80] Laurence Alcock was the holder of the family estate in the late seventeenth century, and he sired John, who was to take orders in the church and become a rector in the county. John was appointed to his first living—the rectory of Trotton—by his father in 1705, and he, not surprisingly, sided with the Tories during the political turbulence of Queen Anne's reign. John continued to align himself with the Tories and he supported them in the 1734 election, much to the frustration and disgust of Newcastle's agents, since he managed to convince most of his parishioners to vote Tory. John's son, also a John, followed in his father's footsteps and entered the ministry. He was appointed Rector of Treyford in 1729 by Robert Allwyn, a Tory gentleman. He too voted Tory, and must have encouraged his parishioners to do the same, since Treyford produced many more Tories than Whigs. The Alcock sons followed in their fathers' footsteps.

Perhaps an even better example is the Hoopers. The Hoopers do not appear to have had the roots in the county that the Alcocks did, but they did manage to establish themselves quite well in the parishes of Beckley and Mayfield by the late seventeenth century, and they began to buy up advowsons in the region.[81] During the period of this study alone, some four Hoopers became clergymen in Sussex: Thomas Sr., Thomas Jr., Odiarne, and Robert. Thomas Sr. was the first to gain a living. He was presented to the rectory of Beckley in 1699, and from that time until 1804 a Hooper occupied the post. Thomas voted Tory in every election from 1705 to 1734. In fact, the whole family did. Nevertheless, their Toryism did not stop them from requesting favors from good Whigs. In 1730, George Hooper, a gentleman of Mayfield (and a brother of Thomas Hooper of Mayfield) wanted to present his son to the vicarage of his parish, but he had a problem: his son was too young. Fortunately his brother's son, Odiarne, was in orders and of age. So he wrote to Robert Burnett, and had a Whig friend of his—Humphrey Fowle—write directly to Newcastle, to allow him to appoint Odiarne temporarily, until his son was of age. Newcastle apparently obliged him in this request, and recommended to the Archbishop of Canterbury that this procedure be allowed. Odiarne was appointed for three years, at the end of which time Robert, George's son, took over the benefice. Despite this help from the Whigs, and despite the fact that George had promised Burnett that "my Brother and my self shall be ever obliged to his Grace," the Hoopers remained 100 percent Tory.[82] Their family ties were strong enough to maintain a rigid Tory perspective, even though they at times needed help from Whigs.

Hugh Evans Jr. also held to a Tory family tradition, despite the fact that he accepted Whig patronage. In 1727 the Whig Earl of Scarborough appointed him to the rectory of Singleton. Even with the influence that this patronage created, however, Scarborough was unable to get him to promise the Whigs in 1734. Evans remained tied to the Tory party, as his father before him. Family tradition simply had more influence over him than patronage.

This tendency to follow family tradition can also be observed among the sons of clergymen who took up another trade. One of the most rabid Tories in Sussex was Henry Snooke, son of the late Rector of Ringmer. Snooke's father—also Henry—had been a consistent Tory in the decades of Queen Anne's reign.[83] He died in 1727 and was replaced by the Whig Thomas Hurdis, an appointment that disgusted his son Henry. The reader will remember that when Hurdis died at the height of the 1734 Parliamentary campaign, it was Snooke and his Tory friends who made a pitch, unsuccessfully, to the archbishop for a Tory successor. Snooke was an unyielding and bellicose Tory, and his opposition seems to have come from principle instilled by his father. That he had imbibed a staunch loyalty to Laudian religion and monarchical prerogative is evident from a notation he made in the parish register of Ringmer in 1737. He discovered at that time an entry made in 1641 by the then vicar, William Cooper, and the majority of the parishioners, apparently protesting the Laudian canons. Snooke was livid at the impudence of these malcontents, and he scrawled his own comment next to theirs in the register: "May the memory of such Rebellious Rogues Perish and their names be forgotten so wishes Henry Snooke of Ringmer 1737."[84] A legacy of High Churchmanship in Snooke's family continued to influence him years after his father had passed away.

The propensity for sons to continue to hold their father's (or family's) principles held true in Whiggish families too. No less than 82 percent of the younger Whigs (fourteen out of the seventeen whose fathers' sympathies can be determined) were following in their fathers' footsteps when it came to politics. John Bristed was the son of an early Whig whom we have already had occasion to notice.[85] John carried on his father's tradition and professed loyalty to the Whigs in 1734. Thomas Curteis specifically charged his son with the responsibility of carrying on his politics, and even provided him with a freehold in Sussex so that he could support the Whig cause in the county. As the elder Curteis apprised Newcastle, "I have supply'd my own unavoidable Deficiency [i.e., his own inability to continue making an interest in Sussex due to his age and infirmity], by making my Son a Sussex Freeholder with the Sole view of serving your Grace's Interests, which I know he will be zealously active to promote, as far as lies in his Power."[86] And the son did not disappoint the father. Even a father's conversion could bring with it the interest of his son. When John Hawes defected from the Tory camp, he brought his son with him. Thus, though John Hawes Sr. had voted Tory in every election before 1715, both he and his son—John Hawes Jr.—voted Whig in 1734.

Thus family loyalty seems to have had priority even over patronage. It was certainly a much better indicator of whether a clergyman would be Whig or Tory in 1734. There were some changes: Thomas Turner, John Lloyd, and John Frewen all went against the grain of family loyalties, but this was only a small minority of the cases. The Whigs simply did not make much headway among clerical dynasties.

Gentry/Clerical Alliance

Linda Colley has called attention to the importance of gentry alliances in bolstering Tory opposition.[87] These associations were important for the clergy too, although they do not appear to have had quite the force of kinship. Clergymen certainly liked to associate with others of similar principles and encourage them to maintain their ideals.[88] But where this mechanism seems to have been most influential was with clergy who emigrated into the county—those who had no strong local kinship ties. And it is here, too, that patronage was most effective, since it functioned in conjunction with the broader phenomenon of alliance. When newcomers came into the county, they were dependent upon new connections—patronage, friendship, and other associations—and if they established such connections with Tory gentry and clergy, they invariably became earnest Tories, and if they fell in with the Whigs, they usually voted Whig.[89]

Richard Nairn will serve as an example on the Tory side. It is not certain what Nairn's upbringing was, except that he was raised in Kent by his father, who was a maltster. It may be that his father was a Tory, for Richard chose to attend St. John's College, Cambridge, but his reasons are not at all clear (especially since so many Whigs were drawn there too). In any case, in 1725 he was presented to the living of Westfield by the Bishop of Chichester, Edward Waddington (a Whig). By the very next year he had forged strong bonds with Tory clergy and gentlemen. In 1726 Thomas Webster, one of the county's leading Tory gentlemen, presented him to the rectory of St. Clement's Church in Hastings. Nairn also seems to have struck up friendships with the Frewens, and very likely with William Simmons, the Dean of Battle. These associations held him fast to the Tory side of politics. Both in 1733 and 1740 he campaigned vigorously with some of these men for the opposition.[90] Furthermore, his daughter, Martha, married Sir Whistler Webster, another die-hard Tory.

The Whigs were more successful in securing adherents by alliance than the Tories. It was, in fact, where their biggest gain in support came from. Though the Tories managed to attract the allegiance of sixteen outsiders, the Whigs' drew twice that number. After the old Whigs and their offspring are accounted for, the largest category of Whigs came from those who migrated into the county and had little or no family or tradition to guide them. The majority of young Whigs (twenty-nine out of thirty-three, or 88 percent) who were not part of a Whig clerical dynasty originated outside of the county of Sussex, most of them from long distances away. Moreover, two out of three of them were from nonclerical families. This is not to say that the Whigs imported people for the purpose of gaining adherents, only that they found their additional support—the support they needed to overcome the Tory opposition—in the newcomers to the county. It was these who were the most susceptible to the power of patronage, since they needed friends and sponsorship much more than those who were natives in the county. And since so many were from nonclerical backgrounds, they may not have had the legacies of High Churchmanship and Toryism that scions of Tory clerical families had.

Edward Bland is a good example of an outsider who was influenced by the Whigs. Bland was raised in Killington, Westmoreland, far from the Sussex Downs, and he appears to have had no kin in the region.[91] Bland was hired out of Christ's College, Cambridge, to be the curate to Anthony Springett at Westmeston. Springett, as we have already had occasion to notice, was a High-Church Whig. Bland must have gotten along well with Springett, and he quickly gained the favor of the Pelhams, just like his rector. He must, too, have become comfortable with the Whig leadership of the county, for soon he was presented by Thomas Pelham to the rectory of Stanmer. Bland became so close to the Pelhams, in fact, that he acted as a steward for Thomas when the latter was away from the village, and he was more than willing to campaign for the Whigs in Sussex. By the election of 1734, there was no question which way Bland would vote: he had been adopted by Whig churchmen, and he, in turn, had adopted their politics. In subsequent years he was chaplain to Lord Ashburnham and obtained the Whig-appointed rectory of Pyecomb.

In chapter 3 we observed that several of the Duke of Newcastle's favorite clergymen—the ones he was closest to and relied on the most (for example, James Hargraves and George Jordan)—were imported into the county by the duke. Another was William Clarke. One would not have guessed that Clarke would do as well as he did, given his origin. He was born to an obscure farmer and raised in a small village near Shrewsbury. Whether his father or he had any particular political affiliation is not known, but after attending Shrewsbury school he matriculated at St. John's

College, Cambridge, where he took a B.A. in 1715 and an M.A. in 1719. He had become a fellow of his college in 1717. Shortly thereafter he was nominated by the college to succeed Richard Lloyd (who had resigned) as headmaster of Shrewsbury school. But there ensued a lengthy court battle between the corporation of the town and St. John's over the right of presentation, because the corporation had another candidate in mind. Eventually, Clarke withdrew himself from consideration, since the archbishop presented him the living of Buxted in Sussex in 1724, probably as a consolation prize. This is the way he entered into the county. Clarke appears to have had no other ties in Sussex than those that the archbishop recommended to him. And, of course, that meant, first and foremost, the Duke of Newcastle and his friends. Clarke must have made quite an impression upon the duke, and the two readily made common cause. Clarke was preferred regularly—prebendary 1727, canon residentiary 1739, chaplain to Newcastle 1743, proctor for Convocation 1754, and Chancellor of Chichester 1770—and he, for his part, unflinchingly supported the duke's interests.[92] Clarke, as a newcomer to the county, attached himself to the Whig interest either at the time of his arrival or very soon afterward, despite the fact that he had been educated at a traditionally Tory school. The reasons for this are by no means certain, but it would seem that the recommendation of the Archbishop of Canterbury, coupled with the duke's interest, was enough to motivate him to attach his loyalty to the Whigs.

There were, therefore, two factors that swung the advantage in clerical votes to the Whigs. The first was that the Whigs exploited previously untapped support by mobilizing voters. The second was that they were successful in importing clergymen who did not have the reinforcing supports that local Tory clergymen did. If the Tories had been able to draw on as many outsiders as the Whigs, they might have equaled, if not surpassed, the latter's numerical strength.

The Bishop of Chichester, it appears, was correct when he observed that the clergy "have their relations, friendships, Interests and opinions."[93] This seems to represent accurately the situation: relations mattered first, then friendships, and then patronage and individual opinions. If a person did not have the first within the county, then he cast about for the second and the third, and since the Whigs were ascendant, it was frequently no contest which they would choose.

What are the implications of all of this for High Churchmanship as a whole? First of all, though the connection between politics and churchmanship was substantially weaker than it had been in previous times (such that many Whigs held High-Church principles), the Tory party still had the weight of tradition behind it. The churchmanship of Whigs and Tories was frequently identical, but most of those who had been reared in traditional clerical families could not bring themselves to throw in their lot with the Whigs. Family and friends acted as support mechanisms, as networks that reinforced traditional allegiances, even after those allegiances had lost much of their purpose. The contest between Whigs and Tories was no longer, in general, a battle between Low and High Church—those issues had largely fallen away, and all that was left was the specter of past contests that haunted tradition (though that specter could still motivate through the medium of tradition).

The new Whigs were not by any means all Low Churchmen. On the contrary, many if not most of them were High-Church Whigs who held the Whig leaders accountable for preservation of the church and control of Dissent. But they no longer had reservations about Whiggish control, because they, unlike the traditional Tories, could see that no harm had come to the church under their guidance. The traditional Tories were still jaundiced; the new Whigs were placated, largely because they did not have the extensive reinforcement in the old attitudes that the Tory clergy did. In many cases, in fact, the Tory clergy could see as well as their opponents that the Whig leaders were neither detractors nor destroyers of the church. But the momentum of heritage and tradition kept them clinging to the Tory party nonetheless.

High Churchmanship had not disappeared, but it had been muted. Toryism was increasingly outmoded, because, for the clergy anyway, it was a mere shell of what it had been. The old High-Church values that had given it distinctiveness had become non-issues, and clerical Tories found themselves either boxing with shadows or inventing new—and not distinctively Tory—issues. Family and custom might carry them in their opposition for a while, but eventually even that resolve would fade.

Notes

1. Frequently, of course, these were "pocket boroughs," whose candidates were put forth by the owner of the majority of burgages in the parish. Bramber was such a borough. See Sedgwick, ed., *History of Parliament* 1:331–38.

2. Sedgwick, ed., *History of Parliament* 1:331–32.

3. Brent, *Georgian Lewes*, 172.

4. Burnett to Newcastle, 9 July 1733, BL Add. MS. 32,688, ff. 19–21. Burnett observed later that "its plaine this oposition have bin hatching longer then one would have Imagind for my Lord Fuller told me that he Dind att Mr. Fullers [the Tory candidate] Last summer & they wass joking about Mr. John Fullers standing & my Lord Fuller answard when he stood he would Give him a vote." Burnett to Newcastle, 29 August 1733, BL Add. MS. 32,688, ff. 198–99.

5. Burnett to Newcastle, 14 August 1733, BL Add. MS. 32,688, ff. 92–93; James Hargraves to Newcastle, 16 August 1733, BL Add. MS. 32,688, f. 125.

6. Copy of letter from Newcastle to the Bishop of Bangor, 4 September 1733, BL Add. MS. 32,688, ff. 257–58.

7. Newcastle to agents, 16 October 1733, BL Add. MS. 32,688, ff. 510–11.

8. When William Hay initially heard the Tories' boast of their popularity (based on their own polls), he dismissed it. He felt that their evaluation was due to the proclivity of the "Gentlemen" in the opposition to "magnify their own Interest, and to give each other more flattering accounts, than any your Grace is like to receive from your own agents." Hay to Newcastle, 12 September 1733, BL Add. MS. 32,688, ff. 325–26. Later his tune was very different. In November his reports bordered on alarmist: "I tell your Grace that things grow worse and worse; and if some speedy remedy is not found out the election will be in great danger." 3 November 1733, BL Add. MS. 32,689, ff. 7–8. Henry Pelham's letter to Newcastle, 29 September 1733, is BL Add. MS. 32,688, ff. 421–23.

9. Thomas Spence to Newcastle, 5 September 1733, BL Add. MS. 32,688, ff. 261–63.

10. In the early part of the campaign Burnett acknowledged that his commission, as Newcastle had issued it, was "not to make any publick entertainment but to go Quietly about to feind the Disposition of the people." Later he would be very much involved in the entertainments. Burnett to Newcastle, 9 July 1733, BL Add. MS. 32,688, ff. 19–21.

11. Burnett's letters were full of every sort of gossip. His language is rather coarse and his spelling abominable, but these eccentricities contribute a sort of rustic charm to his reports.

12. For characterizations of these men, see Brent, *Georgian Lewes*, 66, 171, 172, 174–75, 178–79.

13. In October he thanked Newcastle for "the commission you have given me." He was pleased to receive it, he said, for "it will be an agreeable office, & I shall take care to put your Grace to as little charge as possible." BL Add. MS. 32,688, f. 524.

14. William Hay to Newcastle, 3 November 1733, BL Add. MS. 32,689, ff. 7–8. Hay repeatedly complained about Pelham's inertia in the campaign. See his letter to the duke, 15 November 1733, BL Add. MS. 32,689, ff. 24–25. See also, Brent, *Georgian Lewes*, 174.

15. William Hay to Newcastle, 12 September 1733, BL Add. MS. 32,688, ff. 325–26. See also Thomas Ball to Newcastle, 3 October 1733, BL Add. MS. 32,688, ff. 445–46.

16. On the history, purpose, and mechanics of the Excise, see Brewer, *Sinews of Power,* 68, 145–53.

17. Williams, *Whig Supremacy,* 180–82, 195–96.

18. Hare to Newcastle, 18 August 1733, BL Add. MS. 32,688, ff. 135–36. It is hard to believe, however, that the people had been as indoctrinated against the Whigs as Hare thought, since they had returned them to Parliament for the last twenty years (three separate elections). But his point that the people were moved by the arguments about the Excise Bill are well founded—almost everyone admitted that.

19. As they did in Hailsham in August. Thomas Johnson to Peter Forbes, 25 August 1733, BL Add. MS. 32,688, f. 179.

20. Hay to Newcastle, 14 August 1733, BL Add. MS. 32,688, f. 98.

21. Hay to Newcastle, 16 August 1733, BL Add. MS. 32,688, ff. 121–22.

22. Crawford to Peter Forbes, 30 August 1733, BL Add. MS. 32,688, f. 224. See also BL Add. MS. 32,688, ff. 319, 522.

23. Burnett to Newcastle, n.d., BL Add. MS. 32,688, ff. 127–28.

24. Thomas Spence to Newcastle, 5 September 1733, BL Add. MS. 32,688, ff. 261–63.

25. *Poll Taken by Henry Mountague.*

26. Ascertaining the clerical vote is not as simple as it might seem. Most clergymen were identified in the poll with the designation "Cl" after their name. Given this, one might easily assume that they were all so identified. But that is not the case. Many of them were not set apart in this manner, so a name-by-name search was necessary. At least forty clergymen appear without the designation "Cl." Furthermore, clergy did not always vote with the parish that they served, since they had property elsewhere. When there are several persons by the same name in the poll, therefore, it becomes extremely difficult to know who was who. Nevertheless, though identifying them has been a time-consuming process, it is fairly certain that the above representation closely approximates the exact totals.

27. Langford, "Convocation and the Tory Clergy," 118–20. Langford undoubtedly did not count those who were not designated with "Cl" in the poll book.

28. This statistic is based on the following indicators. First of all, some parsons declared their allegiances to certain campaigners, and unless there was any dispute between the Whigs and Tories, this declaration has been assumed to fairly represent the individual's attachment. So for example, Charles Bettesworth has been considered a Whig, even though he did not vote, because he promised Pelham and Butler. John Jewkes to Newcastle, 4 October 1733, BL Add. MS. 32,688, ff. 462–63. Second, some clergymen voted consistently one way in previous elections, and there is no reason to suspect that they would change their vote in 1734,

particularly if they still had patrons who concurred with their past behavior (this assumption is bolstered by the fact that very few clergymen ever switched from a Tory to a Whig vote—see below). Henry Hodsden and Lewis Beaumont, for instance, had both voted Tory in no fewer than three previous elections. Both have been counted as probable Tories. Others were children of committed clergymen on one side or the other, and showed signs of following in their fathers' footsteps. Paul Batchellor II was the son of a Whig clergyman and was clearly part of the Newcastle organization. Batchellor, further, campaigned for the Whigs in 1740. Thankful Frewen was part of a loyal Tory family, and he expressed his solidarity with the family sympathies frequently (see my "Portrait of a High Church Clerical Dynasty"). He was considered to be a Tory. It must, of course, be stressed that this tally is suggestive, not conclusive, even though I have been quite conservative in my reckoning.

29. John Jewkes to Newcastle, 4 May 1734, BL Add. MS. 32,689, f. 281.

30. Francis Hare to Newcastle, 18 August 1733, BL Add. MS. 32,688, ff. 135–36.

31. This only includes the patrons whose politics are known. No information is available for nearly a quarter of them.

32. Elfred Staples to Newcastle, 11 September 1733, BL Add. MS. 32,688, ff. 311–12.

33. Board to Newcastle, 8 September 1733, BL Add. MS. 32,688, f. 289.

34. Butler to Newcastle, August 1733, BL Add. MS. 32,688, ff. 111–12. His brother was wrong—Pellat voted Tory.

35. Gabriel Thorne to John Collier, n.d. (ca. summer 1731), BL Add. MS. 32,687, f. 392.

36. William Hay to Newcastle, 16 August 1733, BL Add. MS. 32,688, ff. 121–22.

37. PRO Prob. 11/717, 136 Trenley.

38. John Board to Newcastle, 1 October 1733, BL Add. MS. 32,688, ff. 429–30.

39. John Board to Newcastle, 30 August 1740, BL Add. MS. 32,694, ff. 530–31.

40. He voted Tory in 1705 and was close friends with other Tory clergymen.

41. Fuller used him as a manager of his business on at least one occasion. See ESRO SAS RF 15/25, f. 76.

42. He informed the Duke of Newcastle on 20 September 1733 that "Citizen . . . your Grace knows I must despair of." BL Add. MS. 32,688, ff. 359–60.

43. Ball to Newcastle, 3 October 1733, BL Add. MS. 32,688, ff. 445–46.

44. Francis Allen reported to Robert Burnett that "Here's also a worthy clergyman Mr. Ball who is also very Zealous & active and does abundance of good for the Cause." 7 September 1733, BL Add. MS. 32,688, f. 285.

45. Newcastle to Bishop Bangor, 4 September 1733, BL Add. MS. 32,688, ff. 257–58, and Bishop Bangor's reply to Newcastle, 8 September 1733, BL Add. MS. 32,688, f. 297.

46. Newcastle to Bishop Bangor, 4 September 1733, BL Add. MS. 32,688, ff. 257–58.

47. Prattenton to Newcastle, 12 August 1740, BL Add. MS. 32,694, f. 465.

48. Sedgwick, ed., *History of Parliament* 2:19–20.

49. Eversfield to Newcastle, 19 September 1734, BL Add. MS. 32,689, f. 407.

50. Tankerville to Newcastle, 9 October 1740, BL Add. MS. 32,695, f. 237. It is, in reality, highly unlikely that Alcock was a committed Jacobite, since he voted at least partially Whig in 1708.

51. Richmond to Newcastle, 1 December 1742, McCann, ed., *Correspondence,* 93–94.

52. See, for example, my "Portrait of a High Church Clerical Dynasty."

53. Mills to Newcastle, 30 October 1733, BL Add. MS. 32,688, ff. 622–23.

54. Curteis to Newcastle, 3 September 1733, BL Add. MS. 32,688, f. 246.

55. Burnett to Newcastle, 29 August 1733, BL Add. MS. 32,688, ff. 198–99.

56. Thomas Hurdis to Newcastle, citing Henry Campion, one of the chief Tory gentlemen, 16 August 1733, BL Add. MS. 32,688, f. 110.

57. Thomas Pelham to Newcastle, n.d. (ca. 1 September 1733), BL Add. MS. 32,688, ff. 240–43.

58. Burnett to Newcastle, 23 October 1733, BL Add. MS. 32,688, ff. 573–74.

59. Thomas Fuller to Newcastle, 25 October 1733, BL Add. MS. 32,688, ff. 590–91.

60. Thus the Frewens supported Sergison because they believed that he, as a High Churchman, would restrict the Dissenters more than would the Whigs.

61. Richmond to Newcastle, 30 July 1740 and 5 September 1740, McCann, ed., *Correspondence,* 38, 43.

62. Hay to Newcastle, 9 August 1733 and 16 August 1733, BL Add. MS. 32,688, ff. 56–57, 121–22.

63. Thomas Pelham to Newcastle, 18 August 1733, BL Add. MS. 32,688, f. 137.

64. Colley, *In Defiance of Oligarchy,* 85–117; Dickinson, *Liberty and Property,* 160–93.

65. John Welby to Newcastle, 18 October 1733, BL Add. MS. 32,688, ff. 522–23.

66. John Collier to Newcastle, 22 October 1733, BL Add. MS. 32,688, ff. 556–57.

67. See Colley, *In Defiance of Oligarchy,* 177–235.

68. John Board to A. S., 30 October 1733, BL Add. MS. 32,688, ff. 449–50. The *Address to the Freeholders of the County of Sussex* (n.p., 1741) is illustrative of propaganda from the Sussex Tories. It combined neo-Harrington arguments

against oligarchy and placemen with High-Church concern regarding control of Dissent.

69. Ball to Newcastle, 4 November 1733, BL Add. MS. 32,689, ff. 9–10.

70. Ibid.

71. Curteis to Newcastle, 26 September 1733, BL Add. MS. 32,688, f. 393.

72. Newlin to John Caryll, 4 September 1735, BL Add. MS. 28,229, f. 52.

73. Gascoigne, *Cambridge in the Age of the Enlightenment,* 71–114; and Winstanley, *University of Cambridge,* 37.

74. Ward, *Georgian Oxford.*

75. It must be remembered, too, that colleges were never 100 percent Tory or Whig. As John Gascoigne has shown, political divisions existed in the most homogenous of colleges (*Cambridge in the Age of the Enlightenment,* 96–101).

76. These statistics are quite different from those of Paul Langford, who, surprisingly, maintained that the Whigs in Sussex were four to six years *older* than the Tories ("Convocation and the Tory Clergy," 120).

77. The evidence from Bishop Secker's Diocese Book, compiled for the diocese of Bristol when Secker was bishop there, ca. 1735–37, seems to suggest that age was not a major difference between the parties there either. Bristol Record Office EP/A/2/2. See Elizabeth Ralph, ed., "Bishop Secker's Diocese Book," in *A Bristol Miscellany,* ed. Patrick McGrath, *Bristol Record Society* 37 (1985): 23–69, for published portions and Bristol Record Office for the rest.

78. As J. B. Owen has said, "Tories were born, not made" (*Rise of the Pelhams,* 69). See also Colley, *In Defiance of Oligarchy,* 85, and Brewer, *Party Ideology and Popular Politics,* 42–43.

79. The best illustration from Sussex is the Frewen family. For a full explication of their Tory/High-Church traditions, see my "Portrait of a High Church Clerical Dynasty."

80. *VCH* 4:76.

81. *VCH* 4:148.

82. Fowle to Newcastle, 8 June 1730, and Hooper to Burnett, 18 June 1730, PRO SP 36, vol. 19, ff. 49–50.

83. In an unpublished paper, Ronald Tibble claimed that Henry Snooke, the Vicar of Ringmer, was "a staunch supporter of the Whigs." Tibble apparently came to this conclusion because in 1705 Snooke voted for J. Morley Trevor, one of the Whig candidates. But this represented only one of his two votes, and the other he cast for the Tory candidate. But this seems to be a case of personal connection, because Trevor owned Glynde Place, which bordered on Ringmer, and to a man the Ringmer freeholders voted for him. In every election after this, Snooke voted a straight Tory ticket. Snooke was a High Churchman, and had been educated at Christ Church, Oxford. For all of these reasons, Tibble's assumption that Snooke was a Whig must be disputed. See Tibble, "Rev. Henry Snooke."

84. ESRO PAR 461/1/1/4.

85. See chapter 2.

86. Curteis to Newcastle, 21 June 1740, BL Add. MS. 32,693, f. 406.

87. Colley, *In Defiance of Oligarchy,* 118–45; and Colley, "Loyal Brotherhood of the Cocoa Tree."

88. But they also formed associations and alliances with individuals of the contrary persuasion. Sussex society was not so divided that it could be neatly partitioned into two social groups. At election time each party had its club, but there is little evidence that organizations or associations along party lines were the norm in the interim. Even during a campaign, gentlemen and clergy intermixed freely.

89. It is likely, of course, that many of them moved to Sussex because they already had some ties with the county gentry or clergy.

90. BL Add. MS. 32,688, ff. 17, 556–57; 32,695, ff. 75–76.

91. At least, his will betrays no connections. PRO Prob. 11/952 364 Bogg.

92. BL Add. MS. 39,326, vol. 20, ff. 1362–63.

93. Hare to Newcastle, 18 August 1733, BL Add. MS. 32,688, ff. 135–36.

5

The Clergy and the End of Tory Opposition
in Sussex, 1740–46

The road to clerical acceptance of the Whig leaders had its ups and downs. Some High Churchmen, as has been shown, saw no impediment and joined the coalition early. But many others—particularly those that had solid support networks—lingered long outside of the Whig camp. This final chapter details the process by which virtually the whole of the ecclesiastical establishment in Sussex came to accept the leadership of the Pelham coalition. In the election of 1741, more clergymen were recruited by the Whigs, and it might have appeared that clerical opposition was dead then and there, had it not been for the bi-election of 1741. This last event apparently stirred up the clergy—if not the rest of the freeholders—such that opposition was renewed and rapprochement with the Whigs delayed. But the bi-election was the last formal occasion of opposition for many years. It was, in essence, the twilight of clerical opposition to Whiggery. The threat of the Jacobite invasion of 1745 drove the vast majority of remaining High Churchmen into the arms of the Whigs, for the purpose of presenting a united front against the foe. This event was the catalyst that secured a lasting alliance between the Whigs and the clergy.

None of these events visibly affected the ethos or churchmanship of Sussex parsons. High Churchmen remained High Churchmen, and Low Churchmen remained Low Churchmen. The only difference was that, after the partnership had been struck, the participants on each side were less adversarial than they had been in preceding decades. Thus the chronicle of clerical submission to Whig leadership is not a tale of High-Church dilution or decay, but one of cooperation and mutual support. There were some compromises on both sides, to be sure, but there was no wholesale capitulation.

The Election of 1741

The Tory opposition in 1741 was a mere sputter of a campaign in comparison to that of 1734. And though not a few clergy resolutely opposed the Whigs, many parsons began to waver in their resistance because the support mechanisms of family and tradition were not strong enough to hold them. Much of the reason for this is that the coherence of the Tory party was gone—Toryism fell apart, and most of the remnants of High-Church loyalty for Toryism disappeared. There just was not enough reason to defy the Pelhams. The election of 1741 was significant since it revealed the weakness of Toryism.

In the 1733–34 Parliamentary campaign the opposition had caught the Pelhams off guard. As Newcastle wrote to Thomas Pelham, "All the trouble we had last time, was occasioned by our setting out ill, and letting the enemy early get the start of us."[1] The Duke of Newcastle was determined not to let that happen in 1740–41. So, before any opposition had even crystallized, he planned to get the jump on the Tories by consolidating the Whigs in a huge rally to announce the candidates. "The first thing to be done is, to get a good meeting of considerable Friends at Horsham," which was the site of the next assizes. The duke compiled a list of all of the principal men of the county, "all the Baronets, Esquires, and most of those that are called Gentlemen, and all the Clergy," and had his agents personally invite each one to attend the Horsham meeting as a show of Whig strength. The strategy was not so much to overwhelm with numbers as it was to impress with quality, thus Newcastle chose the "considerable" men of the county and avoided descending "too low." Even before the meeting took place, Newcastle was ebullient: "Except for the Clergy [i.e., the unbeneficed clergy, who were too numerous] . . . I think there are not twenty people that could have been left out [of the invitations]."[2]

Emissaries of the Duke of Newcastle approached the clergy. Thomas Ball, the Archdeacon of Chichester, was asked to canvass the incumbents in his rape (an ancient geographical division of the county). Though he was at his country parish when he received the duke's call (due to an outbreak of smallpox in Chichester), he was quick to respond. Ball reported that the clergy were "improv'd in these parts," meaning that he expected less opposition this time around. Of the twenty-six parsons he solicited, nine made definite commitments to attend the meeting at Horsham. Several were "entirely in the Interest," but were either too old and frail to make the journey to Horsham or simply wanted to "avoid all publick appearances." In fact, of those he spoke to, Ball could only find one who was irreconcilably in the opposition. And the archdeacon was sanguine about his chances to enlist several "of those that us'd to oppose."[3]

With the response that Ball and others got, Newcastle was confident that the clergy would "behave well." Though the number of incumbents who actually showed up was limited,[4] their enthusiasm was encouraging. Since, as the duke exulted, the Whigs gathered "a greater Number of considerable gentlemen, & Persons of Distinction, than was ever known upon the like occasion,"[5] the campaign was off to an auspicious start.

The Tory campaign, on the other hand, never got off the ground. Though the Tory gentlemen announced in July that there would be an opposition (in an advertisement in the *London Evening Post* that inflamed the Whigs),[6] that opposition was slow in taking shape. The Whigs heard only rumors and speculation about who would stand against them. Early on the gossip was that Sir Cecil Bishopp would run, but in the end he declined.[7] The Tory gentlemen simply could not agree. As John Pelham gloated, their meetings were inconclusive—even chaotic—because the participants "all ended in naming different persons." This boded well for the Whigs, Pelham thought, since it meant that the Tories were "unlikely to produce anything terrible."[8] Ultimately, the Tories could only find one acceptable and willing candidate to stand for the county. Edward Medley declared and was offered the support of Sir Cecil Bishopp and most of the other country gentlemen. Despite the endorsement, however, Medley had to shoulder most of the burden of this contest on his own. Though his Tory associates were ready and willing to ask votes for him, the candidate had to "treat himself everywhere for his friends say they will be att no expense."[9]

Medley was industrious and campaigned hard, but he was fighting an uphill battle. He and the other Tories knew that they had little chance for success. Despite this, Medley vowed to fight to the end—he was determined, he said, to "stand a poll if he had but fifty votes."[10] The Pelhams knew that the Tories were desperate. For this reason, they suspected that their opponents were out more to discomfit the Whigs and make things difficult than to win the election. As Thomas Pelham lamented, "It is very plain that none of our Enemys expect success either for the County or Town, but several of them are determin'd to give us as much trouble & uneasiness as they can."[11]

It is quite likely, however, that Thomas Sergison, the candidate for the borough of Lewes, thought he had a good chance for victory in that race. After all, in the previous election he lost by only eight votes. He was, therefore, buoyant at the beginning of the campaign. But as he began canvassing, he discovered that his popularity in the town had slipped, and his spirits began to sink. As William Gage discovered, Sergison found time and time again that his former clients had gone over to Newcastle's side. Because of this, he grew "sick of his Interest there."[12] For a time, in fact, Sergison abandoned the town when he found that he might be able to obtain a seat from the borough of Steyning instead.[13] But he returned to Lewes for a final attempt when he heard that internal squabbling had disrupted the unity of the Whig party there.

In fact, the Whigs caused most of their own problems. In one borough after another the Whig interest ruptured, and wherever possible the Tories leapt into the breach. This indicates that the chief threats to the Whig party in this election came not from the external opposition of the Tories, but from internal tensions and conflicts within their own party.[14] Even with these apparent flaws in the Whig organization, the Tories were unable to gain much ground. They were simply not strong enough or sufficiently organized to muster a serious challenge in this contest, despite the opportunities that the Whig disputes opened up.

The clergy did not pose much of a threat to the Whigs either. The majority of them had been either pacified or reconciled to the Whig party. Those who had voted Whig in 1734, as might be expected, also lined up with the Pelhams on this occasion. Whig agents solicited individual after individual, and one by one they promised to continue to support the Whigs. There was only one exception: John Bristed. Bristed was a disgruntled Whig who abandoned Newcastle and his friends not out of principle, but out of discontent that grew from his frustration with the way he was treated in Newcastle's patronage system. Bristed was the son of one of the early Whig clerics (Ezekiel Bristed, who was noted in chapter 2), which accounts for his initial attachment to the Pelhams. He was rector of two separate parishes in Lewes, but these livings were not very lucrative. He was, therefore, constantly in financial straits, and required frequent help to keep his creditors from accosting him.[15] His financial burden continued to grow and, eventually, he came to feel that his Whig patrons were simply not doing enough. The Tories (especially Thomas Sergison) were promising to help, and he began to listen. Sometime in 1739 it became apparent that he was ready to shift alliances. When that occurred, Walter Barttelot, Rector of Rottingdean (who, it will be recalled, could himself have justifiably harbored some grievance with Newcastle), "got him over to Rottingdean & kept him with me a whole week in hopes of diverting his attention." He argued with him on principle, on the obligation and gratitude Bristed owed the Pelhams, and on the consequences of his actions. But "no Argument of this nature would prevail," and Bristed quit the Duke of Newcastle's interest.[16]

But this change of allegiance did not alter Bristed's Low-Church outlook. He remained a Whig in principle, if not in alliance. Bristed was a tolerant man, and he did not understand or appreciate the High-Church passion for protecting the church through exclusion or persecution. Bristed thought that the church was secure enough as it was, and he counseled forbearance from harassment of Dissenters and even infidels.[17] Thus if there was such a thing as High-Church Whigs at this time, then there was also such a thing as Low-Church Tories, and John Bristed is a good example of the latter.

Bristed's action suggests a couple of things. First of all, it indicates that allegiance to Whiggery or Toryism was no longer determined by principle. Though principle could still be a factor for Tories who were boxing shadows from former times, the parties had in essence divested themselves of their original ideologies. Though the residentiary, John Parke, was incensed when parsons defected from the Tory cause,[18] there was really very little cause left: most incumbents simply did not see a reason to continue opposing Newcastle and his friends. The church was no longer in danger (at least not from Whiggish Latitudinarianism), the Whigs were not the bogeymen they had once appeared to be, and the future of the county and the church lay with the Newcastle organization. So more and more clergymen agreed that opposition was unjustifiable and vain.

Bristed's shift to the Tories was unusual. The Tories were clearly on the decline, and their appeal was not strong enough to generate support except in unusual circumstances. Bristed's reversal did not take place out of principle, but out of pure interest. Bristed thought that he could profit more from the Tory interest than that of the Whigs, and so he made the switch.

Bristed may have gained financially through this change of allegiance, but when he jumped ship he found that he had signed on for a journey in a leaky vessel that was being abandoned hastily, for the Tory party was in sad shape. Only a few clergymen can be shown to have been active in opposition in 1740–41. Whereas in 1733–34 at least four out of ten clergymen opposed the Pelham party, in 1740 the Whigs could name only ten or eleven who still clung to the banner of Toryism.[19] These few constituted a sad remnant of the once powerful High-Church/Tory party. They were those who refused to accept Whig patronage and still felt that the Whigs' values were dangerous to the welfare of the church. But they were very much alone in this. It was not that other clergymen had lost their High-Church ethos—it was just that they no longer feared the Whigs.

So, one by one High Churchmen drifted into the Whig camp. Thomas James, John Starkey, Richard Lawson, Edward Stuart, William Bean, Edward Powell, Edmund Marten, and Charles Lyddell all decided that opposition was unnecessary and futile. They had come "to look upon the attempt as impudent and ridiculous," since there was such little reason for it.[20]

Some of these converts, it is true, were won over on account of interest (that is what the Whig campaigners maintained, anyway). But that is largely because there was little or nothing left in the way of ideology to keep them from going over. Edward Stuart, Rector of Wiggonholt, for instance, was lured into an alliance with the Whigs through interest, but he does not appear to have been truly Tory to begin with, since he voted a mixed ticket in 1734. Sir Cecil Bishopp, the ardent Tory, was his "near Neighbour" and a good friend, and so in deference to Bishopp, Stuart had traditionally reserved one vote for the Tories. But he had no reservation against voting with the Whigs, so he usually cast his other vote for them. In September of 1740, Stuart found himself in a situation in which he needed help. At that time he had been granted the presentation to the vicarage of Goring in addition to his living at Wiggonholt. Stuart wanted to hold Goring, however, without being officially instituted to it, so that he could avoid the expense and inconvenience of a chaplainship and dispensation. Archdeacon Ball thought he could help. Ball suggested that the Duke of Newcastle could simply keep the Crown from appointing anybody when the living lapsed, so that Stuart could hold the living and yet not be officially appointed to it, thus saving him much difficulty and expense. Stuart was delighted, and promised that if Ball could effect this that he would henceforth vote only with the Newcastle interest.[21]

Newcastle moved to assist him, and promised to "interpose" with the Lord Chancellor, in order to keep the living open. Unfortunately, the patron of Goring, Thomas Bridges, would not go along with the plan. He insisted that Stuart be officially inducted into the living, which meant that he was obliged to find a chaplainship and obtain a dispensation. But even here the Whigs assisted: they recommended him as a chaplain to Jemima, Marchioness Grey, and tried to reduce the amount of the fees he had to pay for his dispensation. In gratitude for this assistance, Stuart declared himself "entirely devoted" to Newcastle's interest, "to the great surprize and mortification . . . of his near neighbour Sr Cecil Bishopp," and he promised henceforth to vote exclusively Whig.[22]

William Bean also allowed himself to be wooed by the Whigs. Bean had been a Tory in 1734, and was presented to the living of Arlington in 1738 by Simon Manningham, a resolute Tory. Nevertheless, in 1740 he was declaring for Pelham and Butler, despite the fact that his patron was pressing him to vote for Medley.[23] Bean's motives are unclear, but the events suggest that he was drawn into the Duke of Newcastle's orbit. In May of 1741 he was created chaplain to Spencer Compton, the Earl of Wilmington, and was immediately presented to the vicarage of Willingdon by the dean and chapter of Chichester.[24] If he did not turn Whig for the sake of preferment, then he was rewarded for the turnabout by the Whigs who appreciated his change of heart.

The case of Thomas James is more difficult. James had been presented to the living of Ripe by the Duke of Dorset in 1727. But this patronage did not sway him to vote for the Whigs. In 1734 he voted solidly Tory. He may have been influenced in this direction by his family background. James was related to Sir John Dixon Dyke, baronet, and he considered the gentleman a close friend.[25] The Dyke family was staunchly Tory, if not Jacobite, and James was probably strongly influenced politically by his family ties.

But for some reason, James reversed himself. In July of 1740 Lord Abergavenny asked the Duke of Dorset to "press Thos James . . . to declare on which side he will be."[26] He was undoubtedly successful in his application, for, from this time on, James worked in concert with Dorset, voting in his interest and acting in his favor, and Dorset, for his part, continued to prefer him. In 1742 the duke presented James to the rectory of Waldron, and four years later to the substantial living of East Grinstead. It is quite likely that his friend and relation, Sir John Dyke, approved of these moves, for they remained good friends until James's death in 1757. It is very possible, in fact, that Dyke joined forces with the Whigs even before James did. Not a few Tory gentlemen were going over to Newcastle at this time, and Dyke may have been in their number.[27] This would certainly help to explain why James defied Dorset in 1734, but backed him in 1741.

In any case, the continual migration of clergymen to the Whig forces demonstrates that the walls were down. This kind of switching between camps would have been inconceivable a few decades earlier, because at that time it would have meant betrayal to principle and ideals. But converting from one interest to another was no longer an issue of integrity or churchmanship, but one of family and friends. It is unlikely that many of these men would have switched had they doubted the sincerity and good intentions of the Whigs, or if they feared for the security of the church under their protection. The "friendship" of the Duke of Newcastle and his supporters simply was more valuable than any other alliance.

Though Medley might well have stuck to his word and stood "even if he only had 50 votes," he contracted smallpox a month or so before the election and died.[28] The Tories were thrown into confusion and failed to put up another candidate.[29] Thus the Whigs won by default. In Lewes, Sergison stood the poll, but lost by a narrow margin.[30] Sergison was undaunted, and vowed to fight again another time. Little did he realize that that time would come very soon—in a matter of days.

The Bi-Election of 1741

No sooner had the election taken place, with the Whigs triumphant, than James Butler, the reelected MP, fell ill with smallpox. Just days after the poll, Newcastle received the disagreeable news.[31] Between 13 and 17 May, a vigil was kept at Butler's home, and almost hourly reports were sent to the duke. But Butler was not to recover. On Sunday evening, 17 May, his son wrote a melancholy report to Newcastle: "This morning at half an Hour aft Ten o'clock was my Father's Fatal Minute."[32]

Within a week Newcastle had chosen a candidate to replace Butler, and this candidate would stir the remnant of opposition against Newcastle into action, and would rile many clergymen because of his reputation. Though the Tories had no chance of success, they once again raised their voice against the Pelham oligarchy.

The candidate Newcastle proposed was Charles Sackville, Earl of Middlesex, and son of the Duke of Dorset. Though Middlesex had been an MP for East Grinstead (1734–41), he was objectionable as a Knight of the Shire for two reasons. First of all, he was from Kent, not Sussex.

Many West Sussex freeholders, following the Duke of Somerset, wanted a candidate who was resident in their portion of the county,[33] and were particularly unhappy when the person proposed was not from Sussex at all.

But the second objection was one that must have worried the clergy quite a bit, and that was that Middlesex was a reputed Presbyterian and a rake. The charge stemmed from several different episodes. For one thing, Middlesex was known to be a carouser. He and his friends were notoriously dissolute, and they were frequently sacrilegious, if not blasphemous, on the occasions of their revels. In one episode, while Middlesex was on the Grand Tour in Italy in 1732, his friend Sir Francis Dashwood, undoubtedly inebriated at the time, entered a church and began whipping the worshipers with a bull-whip on the pretense that they needed a better thrashing than they were receiving from their ceremonial scourges (which they had been given as symbols of penitence).[34] These antics were on everyone's tongue. Middlesex, furthermore, was known for his connection with suspect clubs and associations. He was a freemason, and even was responsible for introducing freemasonry into Italy.[35] In 1732, he assisted in the founding of the Society of the Dilettanti, which he brought back and established in London. The society's stated purpose was to promote aesthetic arts such as opera, which they genuinely did, but their meetings were so raucous and debauched that the club earned a reputation for profligacy.[36]

The Society of the Dilettanti, further, came to be viewed by some as merely an extension of the Calf's-Head Club. In the eighteenth century, the Calf's-Head Club was thought to be a nefarious organization of individuals bent on perversion or subversion of established religion and government. It began in 1650, as a republican club. Its members met every year on 30 January to celebrate, in a most irreverent manner, the beheading of King Charles. Because of their republicanism, the clubmen were widely thought to be Presbyterians. Furthermore, they seemed to make a mockery of the established church by perverting solemn sacraments. Their most notorious rite, whence the name of the club derived, was the "sacrament" of drinking wine from the skull of a calf, which "communion" was celebrated after the intoning of their infamous Anniversary Anthem. The Calf's-Head Club had a shadowy history, and their bacchanalias were espied now and again, only to disappear from view for years at a time.

In 1734 Middlesex and several other members of the Society of the

Dilettanti gathered in a session that seemed to onlookers like a meeting of the notorious Calf's-Head Club. The society met at the White Eagle Tavern in London on 30 January, which observers took to be the occasion of their assembly, and proceeded to call attention to themselves through their drunken revelry. Some of the onlookers thought they glimpsed a calf's head on the table, and jumped to the conclusion that this was a gathering of the sinister Calf's-Head Club. A mob quickly materialized, and the members of the Society of the Dilettanti, despite their protests of loyalty, had to fend for themselves in the ensuing melee. The incident was widely reported, and for this reason, Middlesex gained a reputation as a Calf's-Head member.[37]

With such a candidate standing for the Whigs, the Tories thought they had a real chance. Seldom had they opposed a candidate whose character and actions were so vulnerable to criticism. When it became known that Middlesex was to be the nominee, Sergison redoubled his efforts at opposition, because he was well aware of the earl's reputation and was determined to give him a run for his money.

Though data for this campaign are relatively sparse, there are hints that there was more opposition from the clergy than there had been previously. On 23 May (before Middlesex declared, but after it was known that he was to be Newcastle's candidate)[38] there was a "pretty large meeting of all the gentlemen in the opposition at the Starr" in Lewes. Here they announced their firm resolution to "espouse Mr. Sergison's interest at their own expence." This was the most concerted effort the Tories had mounted in years, and one can only assume that it was their dislike of Lord Middlesex that bound them together, when only months earlier they were shivering apart. At least five clergymen attended this meeting[39]—John Davis, Charles Dixon, Lewis Jones, Edward Wilson, and Timothy Burrell—and they agreed to "make what interest they could and to lay out what money they should think fit and charge the expense of it to Mr. Sergison."[40] Though five clergymen may seem a small gathering, it was a larger proportion than the Tories had ever managed to bring together at such a meeting, even during the hotly contested campaign of 1733–34.[41]

The rumor of Middlesex's connection with the Calf's-Head Club must have scared many. Certainly the opposition attempted to capitalize on it. On one occasion in July, John Board had made a treat for the freeholders at which Middlesex himself appeared. "In the morning before his Lordship came," however, "there was an Intention to insult him at Lindfield." Several "fellows" came into town, undoubtedly at Sergison's behest, "wth a Calves head fixt on one end of a long Pole, which they carried in Procession several times up and down the Town huzzaing & crying out as they went . . . no Calves head clubmen, no Presbyterians." Board claimed that they were not able to get up a mob as they had hoped, and that their intended insult resulted only in their own embarrassment, since his servant "immediately attacked them, took their Calves head from them, beat it about their own ears, & broke one of their heads very handsomely." But even though they were unsuccessful in stirring up popular support, they had the minister's sympathy. The parson of the town (probably Timothy Burrell) assisted them and ordered that the keys to the church belfry be hidden so that the bells could not be rung for Lord Middlesex. Even in this the Tories failed, however, since Board managed to get the churchwardens to open the doors, and the bells pealed loud and clear for the Whig candidate.[42]

Sergison attempted several more times to stir up opposition to Middlesex on the basis of the latter's supposed association with the Calf's-Head Club. Henry Pelham noted in late July: "I understand . . . that after we were all gone Sergisons people insulted him by hallooing and crying no Calves head &c."[43] Likewise William Gage observed that after a cricket match "there was a bustle occasioned by the cry of Calves Head." This one was broken up more forcefully than the first: "some hearty blows were given, and our freind[s] had the worse [of] the battle att First: But the Western Cricketters that had left the place heering of it returnd with the Crickett Batts and dealt some heavier Blows which carryed the victory on our side."[44] This evidently ended the anti–Calf's-Head campaign, perhaps because everyone who attempted it received bodily harm. It may even have been that no one would accept Sergison's commission to instigate it again, because of the physical dangers involved.

The Whigs, in any case, were successful in convincing most freeholders that Middlesex's activity in clubs and associations was due only to youthful indiscretion, and that the candidate was now much more discerning. As John Jewkes said, "the story wch is spread abt. Ld. Midd: was now spoke of as a flight of youth, whch was before a crime."[45] An agent of the Duke of Dorset's—Rev. Mr. Unwin[46]—found some who were affected by the "cursed Tale of the Calfs Head." But he believed that he "coverd the Blot tollerably well," and "urg'd many Things in his Ldship's Excuse." Further, he convinced his hearers that Middlesex was not a republican, but that "He has Now as just a Sense of the Constitution, & was zealous for its Continuance, as the Best of us all."[47]

But this explanation did not satisfy everyone. A broadside published in December 1741 repeated some of the continuing objections against Lord Middlesex. It combined country (neo-Harringtonian) ideology with traditional High-Church concerns, which had been revitalized because of the candidate's reputation. The pamphlet said, first of all, that Middlesex was "an improper Object of your Choice" because he was a peer, and therefore a member of a privileged class. If he was returned, "the Power and Privileges of the Commons are in Danger of a Diminution." Second, it grumbled about the fact that he was not a Sussex resident. If he was elected, Sussex would be "the only one [county] in England, which has not one at least of its Representatives residing in it." Lastly, but perhaps most importantly for the clergy, the circular pointed out that Middlesex had been rejected in his own county (he stood and lost in Kent in 1734), due to his tarnished character and defective churchmanship. The people of Kent must have known something about Middlesex's character, the pamphlet argued, because they turned him out even "before He had so eminently distinguish'd Himself, either by his *Actions,* or his *Conduct* in *Parliament,* in voting for the *Convention, Repeal of the Test, &c&c.*"[48] Given the references to his vote to repeal the Test Act, Middlesex's candidacy evidently stirred up much traditional High-Church opposition to Whiggish values.[49]

Middlesex appears to have received very little unflinching support from clergymen. Some sense of this lack of endorsement from parsons can be discerned from the lists of those who attended dinners at Halland and Bishopstone in support of the Whig candidate. There were four separate occasions upon which freeholders were invited to dine with Newcastle, Middlesex, and other Whig dignitaries. Newcastle must have intended these to be a show of solidarity, like the Horsham assizes had been at the beginning of the 1740 campaign. But if so, it revealed a lack of support from the clergy.

The duke had invited freeholders from seventy-five individual parishes in the eastern portion of the county to attend the festivities on one of the successive evenings. Though there was a great showing of gentlemen, a total of only fifteen clergymen appeared. A careful record of attendance according to parish was kept, and parish after parish lacked representation from clergy.[50] It is true that on the evening of the last entertainment at Bishopstone (1 January 1742) the weather was "so bad [that it] Prevented a Great many Gentlemen from Coming,"[51] but the most zealous supporters were there nonetheless, and those ranks included very few clergymen. It is hard to believe that if the clergy were unreservedly in favor of

Middlesex their showing would have been so pitiful. They may not have voted against him, but their lack of endorsement is telling.

Another indication of faltering clerical support is a partial list of free-holders' sympathies drawn up by one of Newcastle's agents. Although the roster is fragmentary, including only ten parishes, the analysis is sugges-tive: out of ten clergymen, there were six who were against Middlesex, one uncertain, and three in favor. It is interesting to note, too, that in a num-ber of these parishes where the parson objected to the Whig candidate, he was virtually alone in opposition. In Beckley, Iden, Rye, Peasmarsh, and Winchelsea, the ministers stood against the majority of freeholders when they opposed Middlesex.[52] This would seem to explain, in part at least, how the Whig reports could keep emphasizing the failures of Sergi-son's campaign, despite the fact that so many clergymen were against Middlesex.

In many cases, the best the Whigs could hope for from the clergy was abstention. Though they might be coaxed into passive resistance, they could not be moved to vote for Middlesex. John Board exulted that he had convinced "Mr. Gratewicke the Chief Parson [curate of West Grinstead], to declare that he will not move or vote against Lord Middlesex," despite the fact that his rector, Thomas Woodward, was violently in opposition and was pressing for Sergison.[53] Board was pleased that, though there was cler-ical opposition, at least he was able to render some of it innocuous.

This is not to say, of course, that Sergison had all of the clergymen with him—it is only to affirm that there was significant opposition among the clergy to the candidacy of Middlesex. A comprehensive assessment is not possible, since in the end there was no poll, but there is enough evidence to indicate that many parsons balked at the Whig choice for Knight of the Shire, despite the fact that they had no objection to the duke and his oth-er allies.

Some clergymen, however, supported the earl assiduously. Thomas James, for instance, who was mentioned earlier in this chapter, actively campaigned for him.[54] This might seem odd, given the fact that James had been a Tory in county elections up until 1741. But in his case there were mitigating circumstances. First of all, he was a client of the Duke of Dor-set. In 1734 he had defied Dorset and voted against him, but he could hardly do so when the candidate was his patron's son. Second, Middle-sex had been the MP from East Grinstead, which was where James had his living since 1734. This must have made him even more deferential to the candidate and less willing to disregard him. After all, he knew Middlesex personally and had probably entertained him in his own lodgings.[55] The earl undoubtedly won James's respect with professions of sincerity and shows of virtue and piety. Given this situation, it is quite understandable that the rector—even if he was a High Churchman—would support Middlesex.

Middlesex's clerical backing evidently came primarily from the older Whig clergy, on the one hand, and the younger, newly installed parsons, on the other. Long-time Whigs, almost without exception, readily supported him. Thomas Hurdis, Walter Barttelot, George Jordan, Thomas Ball, and others, lent all their influence and assistance.[56] Many of the younger clergymen, undoubtedly eager to get established and earn reputations as men on whom the Duke of Newcastle could rely, also allied with Middlesex. The majority of incumbents who appeared at Newcastle's entertainments were from this group.

Thus it would appear that though the earl had enough support to encourage him, he had less approval from clergymen than has hitherto been recognized. Though in the end there was not enough opposition to effectively challenge Middlesex, and though the majority of parsons had by this time accepted Whig patronage and/or governance, the clergy did not blindly follow the bidding of Newcastle and his associates. They may not have stood in his way, but they did not give him carte blanche either. They objected to Middlesex's character, and undoubtedly even counseled him against voting again to repeal the Test and Corporation Acts. They reserved the right to oppose Latitudinarianism even though they had accepted Whig leadership.

Thomas Sergison tried to capitalize on the base of support he had amongst the clergy and other gentlemen, and he was industrious in canvassing. He traversed the county and gave frequent treats and entertainments for the freeholders, some of which were quite elaborate. One of these was witnessed by Richard Downall, who described the event as follows:

The [Tory] Gentlemen were met & introduc'd into the Town by six foot men dress'd in white, & I think eight women bearing a garland; at their landing they were saluted with, I think, twelve small earthen guns prepared by a Pellar of Wadhurst, & then with a Dance by Women before the Royal Oak. . . . About nine a Clock according to order half a hogshead of shiny beer was set out for the Populace; then another set of the same guns were fir'd off, with the six men in white Drinking Health & Success to Mr. Sergeson, which excepting the ringing of the bells & the Hurra's of the Populace finished the rejoicing.[57]

But these displays could not overturn the support that Middlesex was gaining. Sergison was falling behind, even in his own polls.

For this reason, Sergison realized more and more the hopelessness of his cause. It was said that he feared his campaign was futile as early as August, when he lost the support of Sir Thomas Webster, a long-time foe of the Whigs.[58] By November it was common knowledge that for Sergison "it was a lost game."[59] Nevertheless, he continued his opposition, and, in the view of many, he did so out of pure spitefulness. It was reported by the "Vulgar" that Sergison continued to campaign in order "to make New-Castle's Duke throw away his Mony, who, for every Thousand Mr S expends, must lavish away Five or Six Times as much." Others conjectured that his canvassing had the purpose of keeping "the Interest so united, that whenever His Grace or his Friends set up Two, a Third Person may wedge in between," and defeat one of them.[60]

Several things hindered Sergison's effectiveness in the campaign. First of all, Middlesex managed to overturn his reputation as a Calf's-Head Club member. Though he was not a stellar campaigner,[61] he appeared all over the county and persuaded his would-be constituents of his fidelity and honor. Second, there were no burning issues against the government. In fact, if anything, this was a period of relative satisfaction with the administration, largely encouraged because of a victory produced by Admiral Vernon in the war against the Spanish. News of Vernon's conquest at Porto Bello reached England—and Sussex—late in May, and the celebrations coincided with the initiation of Middlesex's campaign. The joy and festiveness surrounding these celebrations helped boost the reputation of the administration, and this boosted Middlesex's popularity. Though the Walpole government was falling apart, and the war effort was beginning to founder, it was the triumph that was foremost in the public's mind.[62] Fallout from the administration's failures would not be felt in Sussex for some time—long after Middlesex's victory was secure.

Given these handicaps, Sergison decided not to stand a poll. On 23 December he wrote to Middlesex, "I have chosen to give you the earliest notice of my having given up the Sussex Election, that I may appear (as I hope I have during the whole contest) to have acted the part of a generous adversary."[63] Though Dorset's agent thought that Sergison would try again some other time, that was not to be. After this election, no one would attempt again to oppose Newcastle for over thirty years, largely because of an event that drove almost all of Newcastle's critics to seek his friendship and his protection: the '45.

The '45

In the Autumn of 1745, the nagging fears of many Englishmen were realized: the Young Pretender attempted to take back the kingdom by force.
On 24 July, Charles Edward Stuart, the son of James Francis Edward
Stuart (the "Old Pretender") and grandson of James II, landed in the high-
lands of Scotland and began to organize support among the highlanders
for a campaign through Scotland and England to win back the Crown from
the Hanoverians. Though "Bonnie Prince Charley" was barely able to field
an army, he surprised the English by defeating experienced troops and
capturing Edinburgh. Then he turned south towards the border, intend-
ing not to halt until he had reached London. His success, more apparent
than real (since his victories were due more to luck than skill and might),
bred panic in England.[64]

Sussex, though it was in the far south, was seriously threatened by the
actions of the Young Pretender. There was widespread fear, for one thing,
that a massive invasion by sea from France was imminent, and since Sussex had a long, exposed coastline, its inhabitants had every reason to think
that they were in jeopardy. There was also the threat of Roman Catholic
despotism should Charles gain his objective, and clergy and parishioners
alike recoiled at this possibility. On 20 September 1745, Matthias Maw-
son, Bishop of Chichester, issued a circular letter to his clergy warning
them of the severe consequences of a Popish rule and establishment of
"Arbitrary Power" in England. He reminded his charges of the oppressive
reign of James II and how the nation had almost lost its "Religion and
Liberties," and he pleaded with them to fan once again the flames of "zeal
against Popery." The "Unnatural Rebellion" at hand, he warned, "threat-
ens Danger to every Thing that is valuable to Englishmen and Protestants."
He therefore implored his clergy to "use all your Credit and Interest with
the People under your Charge, not only that they may continue firm and
unshaken in their Duty to his Majesty and his Government, but likewise
promote zealously in their several stations, all such Measures as shall be
judged most proper for preserving our present happy Constitution in
Church and State."[65]

The bishop's letter was probably unnecessary: parsons and parishioners alike were already keenly aware of the dangers. Prompted by fear of
invasion and dread of Popery, most non-Jacobites rallied together to defend the county. They laid aside all political differences and partisan divisions in order to accomplish the greater good of protecting their way of

life. The clergy, gentry, and nobility all donned a common yoke and pulled together for the defense of Sussex.

Thus on 11 October an "Association" was set up. A large host of gentlemen met at Lewes that day and framed the organization, which was "entered into by the Lord Lieutenant, Nobility, Bishop of the Diocese, Gentry, Clergy, and Freeholders of the County of Sussex for the Defence of his Majesty's sacred Person and Government against the Pretender and his Abettors."[66] To this they subscribed and pledged donations.

As one would expect, the list included the prominent Whigs of the county: the Dukes of Dorset, Richmond, and Newcastle and Henry Pelham, for example, all contributed 500 pounds each for the cause. Somerset, too, pledged his support, though, as always, he found some fault with Newcastle's scheme.[67] But the Association was much more than a Whig organization—the list also reads like a who's who of men who were, up until this time, implacable Tories. Thomas Webster and Nathaniel Garland each gave 100 pounds, John Fuller gave 60, Edward Medley (the late candidate's son) donated 40, Henry Campion contributed 30, William Dobel offered 25, and John Fagg provided 10. Moreover, of the clergy who immediately subscribed, many were the most unrelenting of Newcastle opponents. John Davis, John Latham, George Lewis, Lewis Jones, Richard Nairn, William Hampton, and Robert Hooper had all been staunch Tories, and yet they contributed straightaway.

Obviously, these men were very anxious to distance themselves from Jacobitism, and this may have been a strong motive for their subscribing to the Association. As Henry Campion, a Roman Catholic who was tainted with a reputation for Jacobitism, wrote to the Duke of Newcastle on the same day the Association was formed, "I beg leave to assure your Grace that no person can have a greater dislike to the Rebellion in Scotland than myself: Nor can any person be more firmly determined to behave himself in his Station as a dutyfull subject to his Majesty King George."[68] The duke apparently believed him and responded that "I am so fully convinced of the sincerity of your Declaration that I thought myself obliged in Justice, to acquaint the king with it."[69] Many others were doing exactly as Campion was: assuring the officers of the government that they would act with complete loyalty and fidelity to King George.

In addition, Newcastle must have come to trust those who had so recently opposed him, because a list of deputy lieutenants appointed for the county includes many prominent Tories. Sir Charles Goring, Sir Walter Parker, Sir Thomas Dyke, Sir Thomas Webster, William Dobel, Edward

Medley, John Fuller, and even Thomas Sergison were made deputy lieutenants for the defense of the county.[70]

There were a few holdouts from the Association, but not many. And those that delayed were considered suspect, usually justly. The Carylls of Ladyholt, for example, were conspicuous by their absence on the list. They were known to be Catholics and Jacobites, and their abstention was completely in character.[71]

There is reason to suspect that members of the Frewen family of Northiam—possibly including Thankful Frewen, the rector of that town—were secret Jacobites too. They do not appear on the Association's roster, and it can be demonstrated that they had Jacobite connections in earlier years.[72] But if they were sympathetic to the Pretender's cause, they were passive in their support for it. They delayed their sponsorship of the Association, in any case, until the threat of invasion was all but over.

But these exceptions were few and far between. The vast majority of the clergy and gentry alike subscribed with alacrity. The result of this defensive alliance was a new fellowship and fraternity that issued in lasting political cooperation. The opposition leaders from 1741 were easily—almost effortlessly—co-opted into Newcastle's organization. They not only joined with the Whigs in order to repulse the invasion, they also entered into their political organization. Cecil Bishopp, for instance, attached himself to Newcastle's interest and deprecated his own brother's folly in pursuing a treasonous course.[73]

But the biggest fish netted by the duke during this period was Thomas Sergison himself. In mid-February of 1746, Sergison dined with William Poole, a long-time friend of Newcastle's. On that occasion, Sergison was so complimentary of his erstwhile nemesis that Poole could hardly believe it. Sergison was "mortified" that he had not been able to pay his respects to Newcastle on a recent visit because of a bad attack of the gout, but he wished everyone to know that the Pelhams were to be "doubly congratulated, first on the Glorious Stand . . . [they] made for the Good & Liberty of . . . [their] Country, and secondly on the success thereoff in redeeming her from ruin."

After making this tribute and proposing numerous healths to Newcastle and his friends, Sergison took Poole into another room and made a startling proposal: "He said he had consider'd & thought a good while about bringing his friends and your Grace's together, or att least of some method whereby those that would might have an opportunity of embracing such union, and wished your Grace . . . would think of some method

most agreeable to you." This was the perfect occasion for such a rapprochement, he maintained, since the two formerly hostile groups of gentlemen
(the Whigs and the Tories) had been meeting together to organize the
military affairs of the county, alternately gathering at the White Hart
(the Whig haunt) and the Star (the Tory pub).[74]

Soon after this dinner party, Sergison himself wrote to the duke and
praised him highly. He observed, in sentiments very similar to those he
had voiced to William Poole, that "the glorious Struggle your Grace &
Friends lately made & the success it was attended with, gives me no small
Pleasure." He then noted that he planned to visit London soon and intended upon that occasion "personally to pay my congratulations."[75]

Newcastle was delighted at this turn of events, and he replied to Sergison's communication immediately in very warm and friendly tones. He
considered Sergison's "testimony" "very flattering," and expressed hopes
that by his "future Behaviour" he, the duke, could earn "the continuance"
of his former enemy's "good Opinion." He encouraged Sergison to call
on him when he was in town and expressed an earnest desire to make
common cause.[76]

In this and subsequent meetings that stretched through the fall, a pact
was made between the two men, and they began calling each other "friend."
Moreover, Newcastle, to demonstrate his faith in Sergison, offered him
one of the next Parliamentary seats for the borough of Lewes. This sealed
their alliance, and though Newcastle seems to have been nervous about
giving up one of his Parliamentary posts to so recent a rival (largely because Sergison refused to promise how he would vote), the arrangement
effectively brought all opposition to a halt. Sergison was elected in 1747
and remained a member for Lewes until his death in 1766. Newcastle
had no reason to fear: Sergison's conversion was genuine, and he looked
after the duke's interests—as well as his own—the entire period of his
tenure.[77]

With the Association, political opposition to the Duke of Newcastle
ceased. There may have been dissatisfaction from the clergy on individual issues, but High Churchmen would not again campaign en masse to
unseat the Whigs because the latter were in some way against the church
or because their policies tended to dilute or denigrate it. Sergison was, in
some ways, the last politician in Sussex to rally High-Church support, and
he did so specifically by casting aspersions on the Whig candidates. When
he joined the Whigs, it was a fatal blow to High-Church opposition.

When the alarm over the "Church in Danger" (and the attribution of that danger to the Whigs) in the clerical community began to subside, the ideal of deference and consensus in society began to reassert itself. After 1745 the county slipped back into a consensual/deferential model[78] of governance that minimized contest. This was not because the patronage system had bought loyalties and reduced opposition through graft and corruption, but because of a combination of the waning of partisan issues and the reassertion of deferential modes of societal governance, which had always remained ideals, impractical though they were in times of crisis (which is how High Churchmen perceived the early part of the eighteenth century). Church and state in the early Hanoverian period in some ways realized the Restoration ideal. Society—at least in Sussex—was far more unified in 1746 than it was in 1680 or 1710. Toleration had been granted to Dissenters, but that did not mean clergymen were happy about diversity and voluntarism. In fact, the toleration actually succeeded in achieving what persecution had intended—the crippling of a menace to society. Thus the ecclesiastical establishment in Sussex in the mid-eighteenth century was more uniform than it had been earlier.

The clergy played no small role in this process. For High Churchmen the security of the church was always their first concern. But, when the church was relatively free from danger, it was in their best interest to preserve the hierarchical and deferential nature of society. Parsons frequently preached obedience to the higher powers and subordination to those in lofty stations. If they wanted their parishioners to submit to their authority as pastors, it was in their interest to submit to the governing elite, especially those who were as eminent and powerful as the Pelhams. The hierarchical order of things, which had been divinely ordained, could thus be preserved. Too much opposition would only erode their own authority, since it modeled for their inferiors a pattern that challenged rank and order in society. Thus by deferring and submitting to the Pelhams, the clergy preserved for a while longer the High-Church world view—that society was by nature and right divinely ordered and hierarchical. Paradoxically, in banding together with the Whigs and Low Churchmen in defense against the designs of a Stuart monarch, the clergy of Sussex reaffirmed and reconstituted High-Church societal values. The Stuarts had become challengers of the status quo and, hence, enemies of God. Thus William Brownsword, a lifelong High Churchman and Tory, wrote Latin encomiums at the end of his life to the Duke of Newcastle as a defender of the faith and the English way of life. The '45 had convinced him that the Whigs were the preservers, not detractors, of church and state.[79]

High Churchmen were High Churchmen still, but their attachment was less to the divine-right of any individual king than it was to the divinely ordained structure of all society, and the Whigs had protected that society from destruction. In Sussex, it was esteem for the Duke of Newcastle that won over so many High Churchmen. Newcastle was respected for his nobility, his leadership, his devotion to king and country, and his piety. And so it is fitting that we conclude this chapter with a clergyman's tribute to the duke, which expounded sentiments that filled the hearts of so many parsons at the end of the period under consideration:

> Joy to the Man whom Gratitude defends
> From Opposition to his worthy Friends
> Whose happy Influence through the Country spreads
> To Dash the Hopes of vain aspiring Heads.
> Favours conferr'd engage the Sussex Coast:
> Party still more: Their Country's Welfare most.
> Nor rashly do they fix their Votive Choice:
> Men of known Virtues gain the Publick Voice.
> True to their Prince; & to their Country true:
> Firmly resolv'd her interest to pursue.
> Permit me thus submissive to impart
> The faithfull dictates of a grateful Heart.
> Your bounteous Gift, great Sir, my Thanks avow;
> Such neither wanted, nor expected now.
> Yet ceases not my Muse to call you Great
> In Birth, in Rank, the Cabinet, the State.
> Three Potent Kings, on earth no greater known,
> In lineal succession, on the throne,
> Thy firm support, through a long train of years,
> Has strengthen'd, more perhaps than all thy Peers.
> Their Councils, & their Actions own thy Sway,
> Glorious by Land, more glorious far by Sea
> Amidst these dignities yet pleas'd we find
> The Friend sincere, the Patron gen'rous, kind.
> And as you've been a Friend, still may you be,
> To George, to Britain, Sussex, & to me.[80]

Notes

1. Newcastle to Thomas Pelham, 21 July 1740, BL Add. MS. 32,694, ff. 211–14.

2. Ibid.

3. Thomas Ball to Newcastle, 28 July 1740, BL Add. MS. 32,694, ff. 337–38.

4. Twenty-nine parsons, or 15 percent of the clergymen in Sussex, appeared. Doubtless this was less than the Whigs had hoped, but it was still a considerable number of clergymen to gather at any one occasion.

5. Newcastle to Sir John Peachey, copy, 9 August 1740, BL Add. MS. 32,694, f. 434.

6. The ad read: "Once more to endeavour at the DOWNFAL of *Corruption*, The Gentlemen, Clergy and Freeholders of Sussex . . . are desir'd to meet at the Star in Lewes . . . in order to nominate two Candidates for the said County" (*London Evening Post,* 15–17 July 1740). The allegation of corruption amongst the Whigs, unusual in such announcements, was taken as a personal affront by Newcastle and his allies. As Lord Hardwicke observed to the Duke of Somerset, "Your grace may probably have seen in the *London Evening Post* of Thursday 1st, the indecent and provoking Advertisement of the Meeting of their [the Pelhams'] opponents. It is an undeserved, groundless & scandalous reproach, not only on the Persons, I am speaking of, but also on those, who have supported them, in former Elections" (19 July 1740, BL Add. MS. 32,694, ff. 189–90). Newcastle himself called it an "indecent and impertinent Advertisement." Newcastle to Thomas Pelham, 21 July 1740, BL Add. MS. 32,694, ff. 211–14.

7. Thomas Curteis to Newcastle, 21 June 1740, BL Add. MS. 32,693, f. 406. John Jewkes observed that he did not think Bishopp would stand because he knew firsthand the "Difficultys & Discouragements a man (as things now stand) must meet with in opposition." Jewkes to Newcastle, 1 August 1740, BL Add. MS. 32,694, f. 391.

8. John Pelham to Newcastle, 24 July 1740, BL Add. MS. 32,694, ff. 292–93.

9. William Gage to Newcastle, 4 September 1740, BL Add. MS. 32,694, ff. 575–76.

10. John Board to Newcastle, 30 August 1740, BL Add. MS. 32,694, ff. 530–31.

11. Thomas Pelham to Newcastle, 22 July 1740, BL Add. MS. 32,694, ff. 228–29.

12. William Gage to Newcastle, 9 September 1740, BL Add. MS. 32,695, ff. 26–27.

13. Sergison was "invited . . . to make his application for Steyning, they having offered as I have been informed to chuse him at the ensuing and general election on moderate terms." John Whitfield to Newcastle, 6 October 1740, BL Add. MS. 32,695, f. 213. Those "moderate terms" could be 2,000 pounds or more, as Steyning was a rotten and venal borough. See Sedgwick, ed., *History of Parliament* 1:338.

14. One example of this occurred in Lewes. There a prominent Tory merchant, John Whitfield, defected to the Whigs. Newcastle was delighted at this turn of

events, and he sponsored Whitfield in new campaign efforts. When this occurred, jealousy among long-time Newcastle allies flared up, and these "old Whigs" threatened to become Tories if this support was not withdrawn. The schism was averted only when Newcastle reduced his sponsorship of Whitfield. BL Add. MS. 32,695, ff. 67, 371, 383–84, 393–94, 408; Brent, *Georgian Lewes,* 173–79. There were similar breaches in Chichester and Arundel. For Arundel, see BL Add. MS. 32,695, ff. 294, 298, 301, 305, 334–37, and Sedgwick, ed., *History of Parliament* 2:229–30. For Chichester, see McCann, ed., *Correspondence,* 54–56, and BL Add. MS. 32,696, ff. 23, 31–32, 337–38.

15. William Hay to Newcastle, 10 November 1733, BL Add. MS. 32,689, ff. 15–16. See also chapter 4.

16. Walter Barttelot to Newcastle, 3 September 1739, BL Add. MS. 32,692, ff. 266–67. See also Brent, *Georgian Lewes,* 151, 174.

17. John Bristed to T. Birch, 18 December 1754, BL Add. MS. 4301, f. 306.

18. Sir Cecil Bishopp complained to John Jewkes that "Mr. Park (the prebend) & Peckham had us'd him, in telling him he had deserted their Cause by refusing to stand for the County." Park undoubtedly was lashing out with the frustration of a defeated man. Jewkes to Newcastle, 3 September 1740, BL Add. MS. 32,694, ff. 571–72.

19. These ten were Paul Batchellor, Samuel Meymott, William Crooke, Bell Carleton, Simon Manningham, Richard Nairn, John Alcock, John Davis, John Bristed, and Charles Dixon. Thankful Frewen of Northiam was also in the opposition, though the Whigs seemed to take notice only of his cousin, who owned the estate there.

20. This was the verdict of Charles Lyddel, who had as recently as the last election voted Tory. John Board to Newcastle, 30 August 1740, BL Add. MS. 32,694, ff. 530–31.

21. Ball to Newcastle, 21 September 1740, BL Add. MS. 32,695, ff. 113–14.

22. Ball to Newcastle, 19 October 1740, BL Add. MS. 32,695, f. 292.

23. Thomas Hurdis to Newcastle, 1 September 1740, BL Add. MS. 32,694, ff. 553–55.

24. Bean beat out several long-time Newcastle supporters for this post. Thomas Browne and John Backshell both requested it—the former as if his life depended on it, and the latter with the approbation of the dean. See Hargraves to Newcastle, 7 March 1741, BL 32,696, ff. 200–201, and Browne to Newcastle, 20 January 1741 and 22 March 1741, BL Add. MS. 32,696, ff. 40, 250. Because of this, Bean's success in obtaining the living is surprising, the more so because there is no evidence of his petitioning for it.

25. James included him in his will as his "very worthy friend and relation." PRO Prob. 11/829 126 Herring.

26. Thomas Pelham to Newcastle, 22 July 1740, BL Add. MS. 32,694, ff. 228–29.

27. Anthony Kemp, for instance, was a staunch Tory and Jacobite prior to 1740. But in that year he deferred to Newcastle and joined his interest. This conversion was highly touted by the Whigs. John Whitfield to Newcastle, 15 September 1740, BL Add. MS. 32,695, f. 67. Sir Thomas Dyke persisted as a Tory (Stonestreet to Thomas Pelham, 24 April 1741, BL Add. MS. 32,696, f. 361), but there is no mention of Sir John Dyke in the opposition at this time.

28. Burnett to Andrew Stone, 6 April 1741, BL Add. MS. 32,696, f. 285.

29. The Tory gentlemen met a couple of times at the Starr Inn in Lewes to determine what to do, but they apparently could not decide on a candidate, or could not find a candidate who would stand on such short notice. So the opposition folded. See Gage to Newcastle, 20 April 1741, BL Add. MS. 32,696, f. 340; Stonestreet to Thomas Pelham, 24 April 1741, BL Add. MS. 32,696, f. 361; John Whitfield to Newcastle, 25 April 1741, BL Add. MS. 32,696, f. 373; and John Pelham to Newcastle, 26 April 1741, BL Add. MS. 32,696, f. 381.

30. A pollbook for the election indicates that Thomas Pelham gained 104 votes, Trevor 102, and Sergison 96. BL Add. MS. 33,085, ff. 429–30. Henry Pelham, however, was under the impression that more votes had been cast and that the margin of victory was much greater. He wrote to the Duke of Richmond that the vote was "Mr [Thomas] Pelham 156, Mr Trevor 154, Sergison 117, by which you see our majority was 39 and 37." Pelham to Richmond, 2 May 1741; McCann, ed., *Correspondence,* 60.

31. John Penfold to Newcastle, May 1741, BL Add. MS. 32,696, f. 511.

32. John Butler to Newcastle, 17 May 1741, BL Add. MS. 32,697, f. 3.

33. Somerset to Newcastle, 28 May 1741, BL Add. MS. 32,697, f. 93. Even Sir John Shelley was "of the opinion (as well as many of his friends) that a western Gentlemen ought to succeed Mr. Butler for the county." Margaret Shelley to Newcastle, 28 May 1741, BL Add. MS. 32,697, f. 98.

34. Hess, "Sackville Family," 25.

35. For some of the radical connections of freemasonry, see Jacob, *Radical Enlightenment,* esp. 109–214.

36. Ibid., 24–25.

37. Cust and Colvin, *History of the Society of Dilettanti,* 36–37.

38. Middlesex's candidacy was publicly announced at a gathering of "gentlemen, clergy and freeholders" at Lewes on 2 June (BL Add. MS. 32,697, f. 143), but his intentions were widely known by the twentieth or twenty-first of May. Gage to Newcastle, 21 May 1741, BL Add. MS. 32,697, f. 27.

39. There may have been more, since the spy who took down the names observed that he only noted "the cheifest of the Gentlemen" in his report.

40. John Whitfield to Andrew Stone, 23 May 1741, BL Add. MS. 32,697, f. 52.

41. In one large Tory gathering during that campaign, the clergy numbered three (BL Add. MS. 32,688, f. 461), while other meetings saw even fewer. The

kick-off meeting in 1733 claimed only one clergyman—Charles Dixon of Lewes. BL Add. MS. 33,058, f. 331.

42. John Board to Newcastle, 4 July 1741, BL Add. MS. 32,697, ff. 276–77.

43. Henry Pelham to Newcastle, 26 July 1741, BL Add. MS. 32,697, ff. 355–56.

44. Gage to Newcastle, 2 August 1741, BL Add. MS. 32,697, ff. 388–89.

45. Jewkes to Newcastle, 12 July 1741, BL Add. MS. 32,697, ff. 306–7.

46. Unwin was an outsider in Sussex, and he toured the county on Dorset's behest to ascertain the state of the campaign there. I have been unable to trace him.

47. Unwin to Dorset, 5 August 1741, Kent Archives Office (hereafter KAO), U269/C150/15.

48. *An Address to the Freeholders of the County of Sussex* (n.p., December 1741).

49. This is clear from the information we have from the Frewen family, which was a High-Church clerical dynasty centered in Sussex. After the campaign, Thomas Frewen wrote that "I think the clergy who were such strenuous Advocates for him, can scarce be reckon'd friends to that Rubrick they have subscribed, For if repealing the Test Act, be not undermining our church & its very foundation; I desire them to tell me what is?" Chamberlain, "High Church Clerical Dynasty" 302.

50. BL Add. MS. 33,085, ff. 441, 443–44, 445–46, and BL Add. MS. 32,699, ff. 5–7.

51. BL Add. MS. 32,699, ff. 5–7.

52. List of Voters, 1741, BL Add. MS. 33,085, ff. 437–38.

53. John Board to Newcastle, 29 October 1741, BL Add. MS. 32,698, ff. 229–30.

54. As he wrote to the Duke of Dorset, "I waited on Lord Wilmington on Monday last, who told me, that Lord Middlesex was to be a Candidate for the County. I immediately went over to my parishes in Surrey and engaged all the voters I could meet with in those parts, and I propose to do the same at Ripe in a very short time." James to Dorset, 28 May 1741, KAO, U269/C150/3. I am indebted to Catherine Patterson for all of the information from Dorset's papers in Kent.

55. As he requested of Dorset, "I beg you will present my Respects to Lord Middlesex and assure him, that whenever his Lordship is called to Grinstead upon this or any other Occasion, my House will be very much at His Lordship's Service." KAO, U269/C150/3.

56. Thomas Hurdis to Newcastle, 13 June 1741 and 13 September 1741, BL Add. MS. 32,697, f. 184 and BL Add. MS. 32,698, f. 41; Walter Barttelot to Newcastle, 1 October 1741, BL Add. MS. 32,698, ff. 92–93; Thomas Ball to Newcastle, 13 October 1741, BL Add. MS. 32,698, ff. 132–33; George Jordan to Mr. Burtt, 21 October 1741, BL Add. MS. 32,698, f. 201.

57. Richard Downall to Mr. Atkins at Halland, 30 September 1741, BL Add. MS. 32,698, f. 83.

58. Though at this time he still had a large proportion of the votes. It was estimated that in Chichester he had 80 out of 205 votes.

59. Richmond to Newcastle, 6 November 1741; McCann, ed., *Correspondence*, 77.

60. Mr. Unwin to Dorset, 5 August 1741, KAO, U269/C150/15.

61. Hess maintains that he was "an ineffectual speaker." But fortunately, he did not have to make effective speeches—he simply needed to make appearances and assure those who saw him that he was neither a republican nor a Presbyterian ("Sackville Family," 32).

62. There were festive bonfires all over the county to commemorate the event. These were often used as occasions for canvassing as well. William Gage reported on a couple of instances in which he capitalized on the joviality and goodwill of the freeholders in his efforts to line up support for Middlesex. Gage to Newcastle, 21 May 1741 and 28 May 1741, BL Add. MS. 32,697, ff. 27, 94–95.

63. Sergison to Middlesex, 23 December 1741, KAO, U269/C150/18; see also Thomas Stonestreet's intelligence of this, which was relayed to Newcastle. Stonestreet to Mr. Ward at Halland, 23 December 1741, BL Add. MS. 32,698, f. 415.

64. On the invasion, see Forster, *Rash Adventurer*.

65. Printed Circular Letter of Matt. Chichester to Clergy of the Diocese of Chichester, 20 September 1745, PRO SP 36, vol. 68, ff. 188–89.

66. List of Donations to the Association, 11 October 1745, BL Add. MS. 33,085, f. 458.

67. As he notified Newcastle, "I shall readily concur" in "whatever now may be thought adviseable & proper at the meeting your Grace has appointed to bee of the Lords and cheif Gentlemen of this County on this Emergent Occasion." But he lectured the younger man that it would be better to call up the militia than to appoint Deputy Lieutenants, since the militia could be assembled more quickly and there were already Acts of Parliament to support such a move. Even in this emergency, Somerset reproached Newcastle. Somerset to Newcastle, 4 October 1745, PRO SP 36, vol. 70, ff. 130–31.

68. Henry Campion to Newcastle, 11 October 1745, PRO SP 36, vol. 71, f. 79.

69. Newcastle to Campion, 17 October 1745, PRO SP 36, vol. 71, f. 268.

70. BL Add. MS. 33,085, f. 467.

71. John Caryll was the head of the family at this time. His uncle, also named John, had accompanied James II into exile, and for this was charged with high treason. In 1724, the equally Jacobite nephew petitioned the king to reverse the charge against his late uncle on the basis that he had been a servant of James's queen, rather than James himself. The petition was apparently successful—a Writ of Error was issued and Caryll was exonerated. PRO, SP 35, vol. 76, f. 77; vol. 77, f. 244. But that did not end the family's Jacobitism. John Caryll remained in close

contact with the Pretender, and though he does not appear to have encouraged revolt in Sussex, he undoubtedly favored Charles Stuart's action and supported the invasion in whatever clandestine ways he could. As late as 1769 he was assisting the Pretender's cause: in that year he became Charles's Secretary of State. See Monod, *Jacobitism,* 137.

72. For a description of this activity, see Chamberlain, " High-Church Clerical Dynasty," 305–8.

73. He maintained that he "intirely . . . differ[ed] with those, who are enemies to our Constitution," and distanced himself from his brother by observing that he had "not so much as exchanged one word with him, or my mother (with whom he lives) for these last twelve years." Bishopp to Newcastle, 7 February 1746, BL Add. MS. 32,706, f. 116.

74. William Poole to Newcastle, 19 February 1746, BL Add. MS. 32,706, ff. 182–83.

75. Sergison to Newcastle, 24 February 1746, BL Add. MS. 32,706, f. 211.

76. Newcastle to Sergison, 25 February 1746, BL Add. MS. 32,706, ff. 215–16.

77. William Poole to Newcastle, 7 August 1746, BL Add. MS. 32,708, f. 35; Thomas Sergison to William Poole, 25 November 1746, BL Add. MS. 32,709, f. 267; Sedgwick, ed., *History of Parliament* 2:416–17. The *History of Parliament* notes that there was an attempt in 1743 to join forces. There certainly were rumors in 1742 and 1743 to that effect. But Sergison assured his friends that the rumor was false. Thomas Frewen wrote to Thankful Frewen that he had been with Sergison, and that if Thankful was to hear anyone spreading the rumor, "I beg you'd contradict it whenever you hear it asserted, that he wrote to his Grace of Newcastle that he never shd oppose him more either in Town or county. It being a notorious falsehood, & rais'd by that sect of men with whom lying is a recommendation." Thomas Frewen to Thankful Frewen, 6 February 1742, ESRO FRE 1304.

78. Mark Kishlansky argues that parliamentary elections (or "selections" as he refers to them) moved in the late seventeenth and early eighteenth century from a consensual and deferential model, where voters simply queued up to affirm the choice of the aristocrats (not unlike modern single-party governments), to actual contests between opponents (*Parliamentary Selection*).

79. Brownsword to Newcastle, 13 January 1747, BL Add. MS. 32,710, f. 43.

80. Humphrey Crawley to Newcastle, 6 April 1761, BL Add. MS. 32,921, f. 352.

Conclusion

What happened to High Churchmanship in Sussex? The answer is nothing and everything. There were some significant changes in the county, but those changes did not destroy High Churchmanship. Rather, many of the changes disarmed High Churchmen because they took away the raison d'être for the party's existence. The ethos could still be found in the eighteenth century, however, and clergymen could still act out of High-Church passion when their principles were threatened.

High Churchmen were clearly in the majority in Sussex at the turn of the seventeenth century. They were deeply worried that Latitudinarians, Whigs, and Dissenters were destroying the church. But by 1745—and in many cases long before that—those fears had ebbed away. The vitality and strength of Nonconformity deteriorated rapidly in the early eighteenth century, making zealous reaction against it unnecessary. Though there were some who maintained their vigilance against Dissent, most were satisfied that the church was no longer in danger from Nonconformists. Those who continued to cry "Church in Danger" simply looked foolish.

In addition, the reputation of the Whigs rose in the estimation of most churchmen. Whereas in the Sacheverell era, Whig politicians and clergymen took a drubbing from High Churchmen who derided them as traitors to church and state, in the period after 1720 the Whigs were increasingly respected as sincere and pious churchmen. In Sussex, this was due in no little part to the conscious efforts of the Pelhams and their "friends" to renovate their reputation by being good churchmen and by sponsoring the church and its ministers. Accordingly, the Whigs offered their protection, benefaction, and patronage for the church, and parsons responded with gratitude and respect. The result of this was that High Churchmen came to trust the Whigs politically and began to align with them rather than the Tories. High Churchmen left the Tory party bit by bit and attached themselves to the Whigs. Patronage was, therefore, a significant element in the process of the decline of High Churchmanship, but only because clergymen had lost their fear and distrust for the Whigs.

Another important element that fostered this trend was the decline of the Tory party as a coherent ideological entity. Many of the stalwarts of the Tory party in the early 1740s still visualized it as the "church party," but their need to resort to expedients in order to marshal a viable opposition belied the image they still held. They emphasized neo-Harringtonian rather than High-Church principles and increasingly found themselves courting the Dissenting vote. These practices demonstrated that the party was only a shadow of what it once had been. Though the image of doctrinaire Toryism remained, much of its substance had evaporated.

The support mechanisms of resistance to Whiggery also deteriorated. In the 1730s and early 1740s the main support for the Tory party came from members of High-Church clerical dynasties, which had managed to preserve and reinforce the old values and perceptions with familial networks. Close-knit families perpetuated old ideas and prejudices among their members so that they were much more resistant to change and adaptation. Many of these dynasties also controlled a number of advowsons and rights of presentation of livings, which meant that they were more independent. They were, accordingly, less susceptible to influence from outside. They could reinforce the family tradition of Toryism/High Churchmanship quite effectively and maintain it longer than those without such supports.

But gradually the number of these dynasties diminished and power slipped away from them. The Whigs imported clergymen from outside the county who did not have the kind of reinforcing mechanisms that local clergymen did. Moreover, as time went on, the dynasties themselves could no longer perpetuate their outmoded ideas: more and more individuals defected from the traditions of their families, which constricted the power base even of the strongholds of High-Church Toryism.

The result of all of this was that the Whigs gained more and more support from the clergy, without the clergy having to capitulate in their churchmanship. Parsons accepted Whig patronage and eagerly campaigned for Whig candidates in the elections, not because they had lost their ideals, but because they came to be convinced that the Whigs supported their ideals and values. The Whigs made huge gains among the clergy in just a few decades: they went from being considered the destroyers of the church to being lauded as its protectors and champions.

There were still tussles at times between the High-Church clergy and the Whig politicians, since many of the Whigs wanted to be more accommodating to Dissenters. By and large they were discreet about that goal, and tried to avoid the subject with the clergy of the established church. This did not always work, however, and parsons were frequently able to delay or frustrate Whiggish designs to lighten the burden of Nonconformists. It is certainly the case that the clergy dug in on this issue (despite the fact that the Dissenters could not at this time present much of a challenge to the established church), and the Whigs were therefore hindered in their desires to liberate the Dissenters.

This constraint on the Whigs demonstrates both the continuing High-Church sentiment of the clergy and their ongoing influence on government and society. The Whigs had not bought out High Churchmanship, so much as the clergy had provisionally accepted the support and guidance of the Whigs. The Whigs felt constant pressure from the clergy not to move in any radical direction regarding the church, and the fact that they listened to the clergy and acknowledged the pressure they applied indicates that the clergy still had significant influence in church and society.

It may be true that religious observance of parishioners declined in the eighteenth century, but if so, it was due more to lack of external controls than clerical indolence. The clergy were more concerned about the state of religion than anyone else, and many of them worked assiduously to correct the problem with the limited means available to them. In any case, their expectations do not appear to have been diminished. Rather, their resources for enforcing their expectations had been reduced.

It cannot be said that the church in Sussex in the mid-eighteenth century was unchanged from the church in Sussex in the second half of the seventeenth century. On the contrary, there were some profound changes. The Revolution, the Toleration Act, and the Protestant succession all left indelible marks. The church was more voluntaristic and more tolerant but it also appeared to be more uniform and harmonious because the divisions in it had been reunited, due in large part to the galvanizing effect of new, more virile threats that appeared, such as heterodoxy.

But the clergy were not, in general, progressive or liberal in their values. The ideals of the average parson were not so different in the middle of the eighteenth century than they had been in the late seventeenth. The changes made in the intervening years changed the church, but they only affected the clerical ethos subtly. Even the Whigs and Low Churchmen were quite conservative in their responses when accepted traditional procedures and norms were threatened.[1] The ancien régime may have been all but over, but if so, the clergy of Sussex could not foresee its demise and certainly would not have wished it. Changes there were aplenty in the eighteenth century, but those changes only gradually altered the clerical ethos.

What can be said with certainty is that those Sussex clergymen who seemed, at first sight, to be weathercocks who shifted political and religious alliances for reasons of personal gain, were not such at all. They did not, as a rule, abandon principle for preferment or other advantage; rather, they switched allegiances only when it became clear that there was no impediment to doing so. When the fear of Latitudinarianism and Whiggery proved unfounded, clergymen saw no shame in making common cause.

The first half of the eighteenth century, then, was a period of accommodation for High Churchmen: as the Whig/Low-Church establishment accommodated them, they accommodated the Whig/Low-Church establishment. It was a marriage conceived out of mutual interest and compromise, and a marriage out of which issued peace and security in the church the like of which had not been seen for decades. Accommodation clearly had its virtues.

Note

1. See my "Limits of Moderation in a Latitudinarian Parson," 195–215.

Selected Bibliography

Manuscript Sources

Christ Church, Oxford
    Archiepiscopal Papers of William Wake

Bristol Central Library, Bristol
    Papers of Alexander Catcott, Jeffries Collection, B 26063, SR 43

British Library
    Caryll Papers, Additional Manuscripts 28,227–28,229
    Duncan Manuscripts of notes on Sussex Clergy, Additional Manuscripts 32,326, vols. 1–109
    Newcastle Papers, Additional Manuscripts 32,687–32,740
    Poll Book for Lewes Borough Election, 1721, Newcastle Papers, Additional Manuscript 33,058, ff. 258–66
    Sloane Manuscripts, Additional Manuscript 4301
    Sussex Poll 1713, Newcastle Papers, Additional Manuscript 32,290
    Manuscript copy of Thomas Curteis's "An Appeal to the Reason and Consciences of all True Englishmen, Concerning their Unhappy Prejudices and the Fomenters of Them," Newcastle Papers, Additional Manuscript 33,344, ff. 86–87

Dr. William's Library, Gordon Square, London
    The John Evans List of Dissenting Congregations and Ministers, 1715–29

East Sussex Record Office
    1710 Pollbook, Danny Papers, 2188
    Ashburnham Papers, 846, 931–33, 975
    Day Book of William Bird, Vicar of Bodiam, AMS 5641/3–6

Frewen Papers
Probate Records for the Archdeaconry of Lewes
Register of Thomas Barnard's Dissenting Congregation in Lewes 1695–1717,
    NU 1/1/1
Kent Archives Office
Sackville of Knole Papers, U269/C148–50
Lambeth Archives, Minet Library, Brixton
Letters of William Simmonds, in Theobald Papers IV/35/27/1–9
Lambeth Palace Library
Archiepiscopal Records of Thomas Secker
Papers of the Society for the Propagation of the Gospel in Foreign Parts
Public Record Office, Chancery Lane, London
Probate Records
State Papers of George I and George II, SP 35–38
Society for the Promotion of Christian Knowledge, Archives, Marylebone Rd.,
    London
Abstract Letter Books, 1707–40
Sussex Archaeological Society, Lewes
Poll Book of 1705 Sussex Election, nineteenth-century copy
West Sussex Record Office
Parish Records
1727 Election Record, Arundel Borough Archives
Tithe Book of Bolney Vicarage, by Drury Bird and William Hopkins, Par
    252/6/7
Chichester Diocesan Records (for catalog, see Francis Steer, *A Catalogue of
    the Records of the Bishop, Archdeacons and Former Exempt Jurisdictions*
    (Chichester: West Sussex County Council, 1966)
Probate Records for the Archdeaconry of Chichester

Published Primary Sources

An Address to the Freeholders of the County of Sussex. N.p., 1741.
Bettesworth, Charles. *A Sermon Preach'd at Petworth in Sussex . . . at a Confirma-
tion held there by Thomas Lord Bishop of Chichester.* London, 1712.
Blennerhaysett, Thomas. *Legal Obedience, in Opposition to Unlimited; the Subjects
Necessary Duty, and a Prince's Best Security. A Sermon Preached January the
30th. . . .* London, 1716.
Bridgen, William. *The Duty and Power of a Magistrate in Matters of Religion Vindicated.
In a Sermon Preach'd at East-Grinsted in the County of Sussex. . . .* London, n.d.
Bristed, Ezekiel. *Religion and Loyalty Recommended; From the History of Pious Princes
Ministring to the Church, as foretold by Isaiah. . . .* London, n.d.

Burrell, William. *A Sermon Preach'd at Horsham in Sussex, at the Assizes held there July 28, 1712*. London, 1712.

The Constitutions and Canons Ecclesiastical. London: SPCK, 1961.

The Criterion; or, TOUCHSTONE, by which to judge the Principles of High and Low-Church. In a Letter to a Friend. London, 1710.

Curteis, Thomas. *Advice to a Son at the University, Design'd for Holy Orders. By a Clergyman*. London, 1725.

———. *Religious Princes the Greatest Blessing and Safety to the Church and State. A Sermon Preach'd in the Parish Church.* . . . London, 1716.

———. *Thankfulness and Unanimity the Proper Return of National Blessings. A Sermon Preach'd on* . . . *the day of Thanksgiving for his Majesty's Accession.* . . . Second ed. London, 1715.

The Distinction of High-Church and Low-Church. Distinctly Consider'd and Fairly Stated. With Some Reflections upon the Popular Plea of MODERATION. London, 1705.

Evans, John. *Moderation Stated*. London, 1682.

An Exact State of the Poll Taken . . . *on the 27th Day of April, 1734. For the Election of Members to Serve in the present Parliament*. London, 1734.

Filmer, Robert. *Patriarcha; or, The Natural Power of Kings*. London, 1680.

Gentlemen's Magazine. London, 1736–71.

Grove, Robert. *A Perswasive to Communion with the Church of England*. London, 1683.

Hammond, Humphrey. *The Duty of God's Ministers. A Sermon Preach'd at the Visitation, Holden at Hastings, April 17, 1714*. London, 1714.

———. *God Save the King. A Sermon Preach'd at East-Guildford in Sussex, January 20, 1714/15. Being the Day of Thanksgiving for Bringing his MAJESTY to* . . . *the throne*. London, 1715.

Hargraves, James. *A Sermon Preached in LAMBETH-CHAPEL at the Consecration of the Right Reverend Fathers in God, EDWARD Lord Bishop of Chichester and WILLIAM Lord Bishop of Bristol*. London, 1724.

Harris, John. *The True State of the Case Between John Harris, D.D., Rector of St. Mildreds Bread-street, London, and Charles Humphreys LLD, Late Lecturer of that Parish*. London, n.d.

Heald, Peter. *A Sermon Preached before the Right Honourable, the Lord Chief Justice TREBY, at the Assizes held at Horsham in the County of Sussex, on the 23rd Day of March 1697*. London, 1697.

Heylin, Peter. *Cyprianus Anglicus; or, the History of the Life and Death of the Most Reverend Prelate WILLIAM by Divine Providence, Lord Archbishop of Canterbury*. London, 1668.

Hopkins, William. *The Liturgy of the Church of England* . . . *Reduced Nearer to the Standard of Scripture*. London, 1763.

Johnson, John. *The Case of Occasional Days and Prayers: Containing a Defence for *not Solemnizing the Accession-Day . . . and for not using Occasional Prayers.* London, 1721.

———. *The Clergyman's Vade-Mecum: or, an Account of the Ancient and Present Church of England; the Duties and the Rights of the Clergy.* London, 1709.

———. *The Unbloody Sacrifice, and Altar Unveil'd and Supported; in which the Nature of the Eucharist is explain'd. . . .* London, 1714.

Lafite, Daniel. *No Lawful Ministry Without a Divine Mission, asserted in a Sermon Preach'd at a Visitation of the Clergy Held at Chichester, June the 8th, 1712.* London, 1713.

Latham, John. *A Short View of the Difficulties and Discouragements Attending Those who Enter into Holy Orders.* London, 1736.

A Letter Written to a Gentleman in the Country About the LATE Northern Invasion, and the Lawfulness of Taking Oaths to the Present Government. London, 1708.

Littleton, Edward. *Sermons upon Several Practical Subjects.* 2 Vols. London, 1735.

Lord, George deF., ed. *Poems on the Affairs of State: Augustan Satirical Verse, 1660–1714.* Vol. 1. New Haven: Yale University Press, 1963.

McCann, Timothy, ed. *The Correspondence of the Dukes of Richmond and Newcastle, 1724–1750.* Lewes: Sussex Record Society, 1984.

Moore, Giles. *The Journal of Giles Moore.* Ed. Ruth Bird. Lewes: Sussex Record Society, 1971.

The Names of Those who Gave There [sic] Votes att at a Pole Taken att the Citty of Chichester Before Allen Wallis, Esq. N.p., 1708.

Needham, John. *Considerations Concerning the Origine and Cure of our Church Divisions. In Two Sermons. The First Preach'd at Petersfield, May 26, 1709. The Second at Wamford [i.e., Warnford], May 11, 1710 in Hampshire. Before the Worshipful and Reverend R. Brideoake, B.D., Archdeacon of Winchester, and the Reverend the CLERGY of the Deanery of Droxford. Published at the Request of the Reverend the CLERGY.* London, 1710.

Nichols, William. *A Defence of the Doctrine and Discipline of the Church of England.* London, 1715.

Nicholson, William. *The London Diaries of William Nicholson, Bishop of Carlisle 1702–1718.* Ed. Clive Jones and Geoffrey Holmes. Oxford: Clarendon Press, 1985.

Patrick, Simon. *A Brief Account of the New Sect of Latitude-Men.* London, 1662; repr. Los Angeles: University of California Press, 1963.

Pearse, Edward. *The Conformists Plea for the Nonconformists. Or a Just and Compassionate Representation of the Present State and Condition of Nonconformists.* London, 1681.

Pelling, Edward. *The Good Old Way, or, a Discourse offer'd to all True-hearted Protestants Concerning the Ancient Way of the Church and the Conformity of the Church of England thereunto: As to its Government, Manner of Worship, Rites and Customes.* London, 1680.

Pleydell, Josias. *Loyalty and Conformity Asserted; in Two Sermons. . . .* London, 1682.

A Poll Taken by Henry Montague, Esq., (Sheriff of the County of Sussex) at the City of Chichester. London, 1734.

Puller, Timothy. *The Moderation of the Church of England. Considered as Useful for Allaying the Present Distempers which the Indisposition of the Time hath Contracted.* London, 1679.

Russel, Richard. *The New Testament, with Moral Reflections upon every Verse, in Order to make the Reading of it more Profitable.* 4 Vols. London, 1719.

———. *The Obligation of Acting According to Conscience, especially as to Oaths. A Farewel Sermon. Jan. 22, 1715/16.* London, 1716.

Sacheverell, Henry. *The Perils of False Brethren, both in Church and State: Set Forth in a Sermon Preach'd before the Right Honourable, the Lord Mayor . . . the 5th of November 1709.* London, 1709.

Secker, Thomas. "Bishop Secker's Diocese Book." Edited by Elizabeth Ralph. In *A Bristol Miscellany,* ed. Patrick McGrath, *Bristol Record Society* 37 (1985):23–69.

Seller, Abednego. *The History of Passive Obedience Since the Reformation.* Amsterdam, 1689.

Sherlock, William. *A Resolution of Some Cases of Conscience which Respect Church-Communion.* London, 1683.

———. *Vindication of the Doctrine of the Holy and Ever Blessed Trinity and the Incarnation of the Son of God.* London, 1691.

Shore, John. *The Threnody of the Bow; or the Country's Lamentation. A Funeral Sermon Preach'd at All Saints Church at Lewes in Sussex, March the 5th 1695/96.* London, 1696.

Stillingfleet, Edward. *Irenicum, A Weapon-Salve for the Churches Wounds. Or the Divine Right of Particular Forms of Church Government . . . Discussed and Examined.* London, 1662.

Taylor, Jeremy. *The Golden Grove; or a Manuall of Daily Prayers and Letanies, Fitted to the Dayes of the Week.* London, 1655.

———. *The Measures and Offices of Friendship: With Rules Conducing it.* London, 1662.

Turner, Thomas. *The Diary of Thomas Turner, 1754–1760.* Ed. David Vaisey. Oxford: Oxford University Press, 1984.

Wake, Robert. *Courage and Sincerity the Main Proof of a Faithful Shepherd: A Sermon Preached at the Triennial Visitation of the Dean of Sarum. . . .* London, 1704.

———. *A Rationale upon Some Texts of Scripture.* London, 1701.

Whitear, William. *An Apology for the Church of England against the Defamations of Deists, with an Address to the Dissenters. . . .* London, 1710.

Willett, John. *The Nature and Mischiefs of Hypocrisy. A Sermon Preach'd at the Assizes, before Mr. Justice Blencowe, and Mr. Justice Gould, at St. Mary's Church in Oxford, July the Fifteenth 1708. Publish'd at the Request of the High-Sheriff, and Grand Jury.* Oxford, 1708.

Wilson, Edward. *A Sermon Preach'd in the Parish Church of Rye in Sussex, on Wednesday, Jan. 30th, 1711/12. . . .* London, 1712.

Wright, John. *Righteousness the Establishment of the Throne: A Sermon Preached at Westminster Abbey . . . Being the Day of His Majesty's Accession to the Throne.* London, 1716.

———. *The Rights of the Christian Priesthood Asserted: In an Ordination Sermon Preach'd before the Right Reverend Father in God, John Lord Bishop of London. . . .* London, 1717.

Secondary Works

Abbey, Charles, and John H. Overton. *The English Church in the Eighteenth Century.* 2 Vols. London: Longmans, Green, 1878.

Addison, William. *The English County Parson.* London: J. M. Dent, 1947.

Addleshaw, G. W. O. *The High-Church Tradition: A Study of Liturgical Thought in the Seventeenth Century.* London: Faber and Faber, n.d.

Albers, Jan Maria. "Seeds of Contention: Society, Politics and the Church of England in Lancashire, 1689–1790." Ph.D. diss., Yale University, 1988.

Andrews, J. H. "The Port of Chichester and the Grain Trade, 1650–1750." *Sussex Archaeological Collections* 92 (1954):93–105.

Baskerville, Stephen W. "The Political Behaviour of the Cheshire Clergy, 1705–1752." *Northern History* 23 (1987):74–97.

Bateson, Mary. "Clerical Preferment under the Duke of Newcastle." *English Historical Review* 7 (1892):685–96.

Beaver, Daniel. "Symbol and Boundary: Religion, Family and Community in Northern Gloucestershire, 1590–1690." Ph.D. diss., University of Chicago, 1991.

Beddard, Robert. "The Sussex General Election of 1695: A Contemporary Account by Robert Middleton, Vicar of Cuckfield." *Sussex Archaeological Collections* 106 (1968):145–57.

———, ed. *The Revolutions of 1688. The Andrew Browning Lectures, 1988.* Oxford: Clarendon Press, 1991.

Bennett, G. V. *The Tory Crisis in Church and State, 1688–1730: The Career of Francis Atterbury, Bishop of Rochester.* London: Oxford University Press, 1975.

———. *White Kennett 1660–1728, Bishop of Peterborough: A Study in the Political and Ecclesiastical History of the Early Eighteenth Century.* London: SPCK, 1957.

Blythe, Ronald. Introduction to *A Country Parson, James Woodforde's Diary 1759–1802.* Ed. Ronald Blythe. Oxford: Oxford University Press, 1985.

Bredvold, Louis I. *The Intellectual Milieu of John Dryden.* Ann Arbor: University of Michigan Press, 1934.

Brent, Colin. *Georgian Lewes, 1714–1830: The Heyday of a County Town.* Lewes: Colin Brent Books, 1993.

———. "Lewes Dissenters Outside the Law, 1663–86." *Sussex Archaeological Collections* 123 (1985):195–214.

———. "The Neutering of the Fellowship and the Emergence of a Tory Party in Lewes 1663–1688." *Sussex Archaeological Collections* 121 (1983):95–107.

Brent, Judith. "The Pooles of Chailey and Lewes: The Establishment and Influence of a Gentry Family, 1732–1779." *Sussex Archaeological Collections* 114 (1976):69–80.

Brewer, John. *Party Ideology and Popular Politics at the Accession of George III.* Cambridge: Cambridge University Press, 1976.

———. *The Sinews of Power; War, Money and the English State, 1688–1783.* New York: Alfred A. Knopf, 1989.

Brooke, C. N. L., J. M. Horn, and N. L. Ramsay. "A Canon's Residence in the Eighteenth Century: The Case of Thomas Gooch." *Journal of Ecclesiastical History* 39 (1988):545–56.

Browning, Reed. *The Duke of Newcastle.* New Haven: Yale University Press, 1975.

Caplan, Neil. "An Outline of the Origins and Development of Nonconformity in Sussex: 1603–1803." Unpublished typescript in library of Sussex Archaeological Society (Lewes), Dr. William's Library, and British Library, 1961.

———. "The Sussex Catholics ca. 1660–1800." *Sussex Archaeological Collections* 116 (1978):19–29.

———. "Visitation of the Diocese of Chichester in 1724." *Sussex Notes and Queries* 15, no. 9 (May 1962):289–95.

Chamberlain, Jeffrey S. "The Limits of Moderation in a Latitudinarian Parson, Or, High-Church Zeal in a Low Churchman Discovered." In *The Margins of Orthodoxy: Heterodox Writing and Orthodox Response.* Ed. Roger Lund, 195–215. Cambridge: Cambridge University Press, 1995.

———. "Portrait of a High Church Clerical Dynasty in Georgian England: The Frewens and Their World." In *The Church of England ca. 1689–ca. 1833: From Toleration to Tractarianism.* Ed. John Walsh, Colin Haydon, and Stephen Taylor, 299–316. Cambridge: Cambridge University Press, 1993.

Clark, J. C. D. *English Society 1688–1832: Ideology, Social Structure and Political Practice during the Ancien Regime.* Cambridge: Cambridge University Press, 1985.

Colley, Linda. *In Defiance of Oligarchy: The Tory Party 1714–60.* Cambridge: Cambridge University Press, 1982.

———. "The Loyal Brotherhood of the Cocoa Tree: The London Organization of the Tory Party, 1727–1760." *Historical Journal* 20 (1977):77–96.

Cooper, William Durrant. "Parliamentary History." Appendix in *The History, Antiquities and Topography of the County of Sussex.* By Thomas Walker Horsfield. Vol. 2. Lewes: Sussex Press, 1835.

Couchman, J. E. "Sussex Church Plate." *Sussex Archaeological Collections* 55 (1912):126–219.

Cragg, Gerald. *The Church and the Age of Reason, 1648–1789.* Harmondsworth: Penguin Books, 1960.

———. *Reason and Authority in Eighteenth-Century England.* Cambridge: Cambridge University Press, 1966.

Curtis, L. P. *Anglican Moods of the Eighteenth Century.* New Haven: Yale University Press, 1966.

———. *Chichester Towers.* New Haven: Yale University Press, 1966.

Cust, Lionel, and Sidney Colvin. *History of the Society of Dilettanti.* London: Macmillan and Co., 1914.

Davies, C. Evan. "The Enforcement of Religious Uniformity in England 1668–1700, with Special Reference to the Diocese of Chichester and Worcester." D.Phil. thesis, Oxford University, 1982.

Davies, Horton. *Worship and Theology in England.* Vol. 3 *From Watts and Wesley to Maurice, 1690–1850.* Princeton: Princeton University Press, 1965.

De Krey, Gary. "The First Restoration Crisis: Conscience and Coercion in London, 1667–73." *Albion* 25, no. 4 (Winter 1993):565–80.

Dickinson, H. T. *Liberty and Property: Political Ideology in Eighteenth-Century Britain.* New York: Holmes and Meier, 1977.

Disney, John. *A Short Memoir of the Late William Hopkins B.A., Vicar of Bolney, Sussex.* Leeds: n.p., 1815.

Eisenstadt, S. N., and Louis Roniger. "Patron-Client Relations as a Model of Structuring Social Exchange." *Comparative Studies in Society and History* 22 (January 1980):42–47.

———. *Patrons, Clients and Friends: Interpersonal Relations and the Structure of Trust in Society.* Cambridge: Cambridge University Press, 1984.

Evans, Eric J. "The Anglican Clergy of Northern England." In *Britain in the First Age of Party, 1680–1750.* Ed. Clive Jones, 221–40. London: Hambledon Press, 1987.

Every, George. *The High Church Party, 1688–1718.* London: SPCK, 1956.

Farrant, John H. "The Evolution of Newhaven Harbour and the Lower Ouse before 1800." *Sussex Archaeological Collections* 110 (1972):44–60.

Feiling, Keith. *A History of the Tory Party, 1640–1714.* Oxford: Clarendon Press, 1924.

Fletcher, Anthony. *A County Community in Peace and War: Sussex 1600–1660.* London: Longman, 1975.

Forster, Margaret. *The Rash Adventurer: The Rise and Fall of Charles Edward Stuart.* New York: Stein and Day, 1973.

Fritz, Paul S. "The Anti-Jacobite Intelligence System of the English Ministers, 1715–1745." *Historical Journal* 16 (1973):265–90.

Gascoigne, John. *Cambridge in the Age of Enlightenment: Science, Religion and Politics from the Restoration to the French Revolution.* Cambridge: Cambridge University Press, 1989.

Gilbert, Alan D. *Religion and Society in Industrial England: Church, Chapel and Social Change, 1740–1914.* London: Longman, 1976.

Goldie, Mark. "Danby, the Bishops and the Whigs." In *The Politics of Religion in Restoration England.* Ed. Tim Harris, Paul Seaward, and Mark Goldie, 75–108. Oxford: Basil Blackwell, 1990.

———. "The Nonjurors, Episcopacy, and the Origins of the Convocation Controversy." In *Ideology and Conspiracy: Aspects of Jacobitism.* Ed. Eveline Cruickshanks. Edinburgh: John Donald, 1982.

———. "The Political Thought of the Anglican Revolution of 1688." In *The Revolutions of 1688.* Ed. Robert Beddard, 102–36. Oxford: Clarendon Press, 1991.

———. "Theory of Religious Intolerance in Restoration England." In *From Persecution to Toleration: The Glorious Revolution and Religion in England.* Ed. Ole Peter Grell, Jonathan I. Israel, and Nicholas Tyacke, 331–68. Oxford: Clarendon Press, 1991.

Greaves, Richard L. "Great Scott! The Restoration in Turmoil, or, Restoration Crises and the Emergence of Party." *Albion* 25, no. 4 (Winter 1993):605–18.

Hampson, Norman. *The Enlightenment.* Harmondsworth: Penguin, 1968.

Harris, Tim. "Party Turns? Or, Whigs and Tories Get Off Scott Free." *Albion* 25, no. 4 (Winter 1993):581–90.

———. *Politics under the Later Stuarts: Party Conflict in a Divided Society, 1660–1715.* London: Longman, 1993.

Hennessy, George. *Chichester Diocese Clergy Lists.* London: St. Peter's Press, 1900.

Hess, Robert L. "The Sackville Family and Sussex Politics: The Campaign for the By-Election, 1741." *Sussex Archaeological Collections* 99 (1961):20–37.

Hirschberg, D. R. "The Government and Church Patronage in England, 1660–1760." *Journal of British Studies* 20 (1980):109–39.

Holmes, Geoffrey. *Politics, Religion and Society in England, 1679–1742.* London: Hambledon Press, 1986.

———. *The Trial of Doctor Sacheverell.* London: Eyre Methuen, 1973.

Hudson, T. P., ed. *The Victoria History of the County of Sussex.* Vol. 6, parts 1–3. London: University of London Institute of Historical Research and Oxford University Press, 1980.

Hudson, William. "The Ancient Deaneries of the Diocese of Chichester." *Sussex Archaeological Collections* 55 (1912):108–22.

Hutter, Horst. *Politics as Friendship: The Origins of Classical Notions of Politics in the Theory and Practice of Friendship.* Waterloo, Ont.: Wilfrid Laurier University Press, 1978.

Hylson-Smith, Kenneth. *High Churchmanship in the Church of England: From the Sixteenth Century to the late Twentieth Century.* Edinburgh: T & T Clarke, 1993.

"Index to Non-Conformist Meeting Houses in Sussex." Unpublished typescript, Lewes and Chichester, ca. 1958. Housed in collections of East and West Sussex Record Offices.

Israel, Jonathan I. "William III and Toleration." In *From Persecution to Toleration: The Glorious Revolution and Religion in England*. Ed. Ole Peter Grell, Jonathan I. Israel, and Nicholas Tyacke, 129–70. Oxford: Clarendon Press, 1991.

Jacob, Margaret. *The Radical Enlightenment: Pantheists, Freemasons and Republicans*. London: George Allen and Unwin, 1981.

Jones, J. R. *Country and Court: England 1658–1714*. Cambridge: Harvard University Press, 1978.

———, ed. *The Restored Monarchy, 1660–1688*. Totowa, N.J.: Rowman and Littlefield, 1979.

Kendrick, T. F. J. "Sir Robert Walpole, the Old Whigs and the Bishops, 1733–1736: A Study in Eighteenth-Century Parliamentary Politics." *Historical Journal* 11, no. 3 (1968):421–45.

Kenyon, J. P. *The Popish Plot*. London: Heinemann, 1972.

———. *Revolution Principles: The Politics of Party, 1689–1720*. Cambridge: Cambridge University Press, 1977.

Kettering, Sharon. *Patrons, Brokers and Clients in Seventeenth-Century France*. Oxford: Oxford University Press, 1986.

Kishlansky, Mark. *Parliamentary Selection: Social and Political Change in Early Modern England*. Cambridge: Cambridge University Press, 1986.

Landau, Norma. "Independence, Deference, and Voter Participation: The Behaviour of the Electorate in Early Eighteenth-Century Kent." *Historical Journal* 22 (1979):561–83.

Langford, Paul. "Convocation and the Tory Clergy, 1717–61." In *The Jacobite Challenge*. Ed. Eveline Cruickshanks, 107–22. Edinburgh: John Donald, 1988.

Lathbury, Thomas. *A History of the Convocation of the Church of England from the Earliest Period to the Year 1742*. London: J. Leslie, 1853.

———. *A History of the Nonjurors*. London: W. Pickering, 1845.

Le Fevre, Peter Joseph. "Justices and Administration: The Political Development of Sussex, 1660–1714." Ph.D. diss., Brighton Polytechnic University, 1989.

Le Neve, John, and Joyce Horn. *Fasti Ecclesiae Anglicanae 1541–1857*. Vol. 2, *Chichester Diocese*. London: University of London Institute of Historical Research, 1971.

Lower, Mark Antony. *The Worthies of Sussex: Biographical Sketches of the Most Eminent Natives or Inhabitants of the County*. Lewes: G. P. Bacon, 1865.

Lowerson, John. *A Short History of Sussex*. Folkestone, Kent: William Dawson and Son, 1980.

Luttrell, Narcissus. *A Brief Historical Relation of State Affairs from September 1678 to April 1714*. 6 Vols. Oxford: Oxford University Press, 1857.

Marshall, John. "The Ecclesiology of the Latitude-Men 1660–1689: Stillingfleet, Tillotson and 'Hobbism.'" *Journal of Ecclesiastical History* 36 (July 1985):407–27.

Mather, F. C. "Georgian Churchmanship Reconsidered: Some Variations in Anglican Public Worship, 1714–1830." *Journal of Ecclesiastical History* 36 (April 1985):255–83.

———. *High Church Prophet: Bishop Samuel Horsley (1733–1806) and the Caroline Tradition in the Later Georgian Church.* Oxford: Clarendon Press, 1992.

McCann, Timothy. "Cricket and the Sussex County By-Election of 1741." *Sussex Archaeological Collections* 114 (1976):121–25.

McClatchey, Diana. *Oxfordshire Clergy, 1777–1869; A Study of the Established Church and the Role of its Clergy in Local Society.* Oxford: Clarendon Press, 1960.

Mingay, G. E. *English Landed Society in the Eighteenth Century.* London: Routledge and Kegan Paul, 1963.

Monod, Paul Kleber. "Dangerous Merchandise: Smuggling, Jacobitism, and Commercial Culture in Southeast England, 1690–1760." *Journal of British History* 30 (April 1991):150–82.

———. *Jacobitism and the English People, 1688–1788.* Cambridge: Cambridge University Press, 1989.

Nadel, G. H. "The Sussex Election of 1741." *Sussex Archaeological Collections* 91 (1953):84–124.

Namier, Lewis. *England in the Age of the American Revolution.* London: Macmillan & Co., 1930.

———. *The Structure of Politics at the Accession of George III.* London: Macmillan & Co., 1929.

O'Gorman, Frank. *Voters, Patrons and Parties: The Unreformed Electoral System of Hanoverian England, 1734–1832.* Oxford: Clarendon Press, 1989.

Overton, J. H. *The Nonjurors: Their Lives, Principles and Writings.* London: Smith, Elder & Co., 1902.

Owen, Dorothy. *The Records of the Established Church in England.* Cambridge: British Record Society, 1970.

Owen, J. B. "Political Patronage in 18th Century England." In *The Triumph of Culture: Eighteenth-Century Perspectives.* Ed. Paul Fritz and David Williams, 369–87. Toronto: A. M. Hakkert, 1972.

———. *The Rise of the Pelhams.* London: Methuen and Co., 1957.

Packer, John William. *The Transformation of Anglicanism, 1643–1660.* Manchester: University of Manchester Press, 1969.

Page, William, ed. *The Victoria History of the County of Sussex.* Vols. 1 and 2. London: Archibald Constable & Co., 1905.

Peck, Linda Levy. *Court Patronage and Corruption in Early Stuart England.* Boston: Unwin Hyman, 1990.

Peckham, W. D. "Chichester Institutions." Unpublished typescript, n.d., West Sussex Record Office.

———. "Non-jurors in Chichester Diocese." Unpublished paper, n.d., West Sussex Record Office, MP 900.

———. "Two Dukes and the Chichester Chapter." *Sussex Notes and Queries* 17, no. 5 (May 1970):146–52.

Phillips, John A. *Electoral Behavior in Unreformed England: Plumpers, Splitters and Straights.* Princeton: Princeton University Press, 1982.

Plumb, J. H. *The Origins of Political Stability: England, 1675–1725.* Boston: Houghton Mifflin, 1967.

Porter, Roy. *English Society in the Eighteenth Century.* Harmondsworth: Penguin, 1982.

Pruett, John H. *The Parish Clergy under the Later Stuarts: The Leicestershire Experience.* Urbana: University of Illinois Press, 1970.

Rector, W. K. "Lewes Quakers in the Seventeenth and Eighteenth Centuries." *Sussex Archaeological Collections* 116 (1978):31–40.

Redwood, John. *Reason, Ridicule and Religion: The Age of Enlightenment in England, 1660–1750.* Cambridge: Harvard University Press, 1976.

Renshaw, Walter C. "Some Clergy of the Archdeaconry of Lewes and South Malling Deanery." *Sussex Archaeological Collections* 55 (1912):220–77.

Roberts, S. K. *Recovery and Restoration in an English County: Devon Local Administration, 1646–1670.* Exeter: University of Exeter Press, 1985.

Rose, Craig. "Seminarys of Faction and Rebellion: Jacobites, Whigs and the London Charity Schools, 1716–1724." *Historical Journal* 34, no. 4 (Dec. 1991): 831–56.

Rupp, Gordon. *Religion in England, 1688–1791.* Oxford: Oxford University Press, 1986.

Sack, James J. *From Jacobite to Conservative: Reaction and Orthodoxy in Britain, ca. 1760–1832.* Cambridge: Cambridge University Press, 1993.

Salmon, John. "Stoicism and Roman Example: Seneca and Tacitus in Jacobean England." *Journal of the History of Ideas* 50 (1989):199–225.

Salzman, L. F., ed. *The Victoria History of the County of Sussex.* Vols. 3, 4, 7, and 9. London: University of London Institute of Historical Research, 1935, 1953, 1940, 1937.

Saville, R. V. "Gentry Wealth on the Weald in the Eighteenth Century: The Fullers of Brightling Park." *Sussex Archaeological Collections* 121 (1983):129–47.

Scott, Jonathan. *Algernon Sidney and the Restoration Crisis, 1677–1683.* Cambridge: Cambridge University Press, 1991.

———. "Restoration Process. Or, If This Isn't a Party We're Not Having a Good Time." *Albion* 25, no. 4 (Winter 1993):619–38.

Seaward, Paul. *The Cavalier Parliament and the Reconstruction of the Old Regime, 1661–1667.* Cambridge: Cambridge University Press, 1989.

Sedgwick, Romney, ed. *History of Parliament: The House of Commons, 1715–1754.* 2 Vols. New York: Oxford University Press, 1970.

Sharp, Richard. "New Perspectives on the High Church Tradition: Historical Background, 1730–1780." In *Tradition Renewed: The Oxford Movement Con-*

ference Papers. Ed. Geoffrey Rowell, 4–23. Allison Park, Penn.: Pickwick Publications, 1986.

———. "100 Years of a Lost Cause: Nonjuring Principles in Newcastle from the Revolution to the Death of Prince Charles Edward Stuart." *Archaeologia Aeliana* 5, no. 8 (1980):35–55.

Silverman, Sydel. "Patronage as Myth." In *Patrons and Clients in Mediterranean Societies.* Ed. Ernest Gellner and John Waterbury, 7–19. London: Duckworth, 1977.

Smith, E. A. "The Election Agent in English Politics, 1734–1832." *English Historical Review* 84 (1969):12–35.

Spaeth, Donald. "Parsons and Parishioners: Lay-Clerical Conflict and Popular Piety in Wiltshire Villages, 1660–1740." Ph.D. diss., Brown University, 1985.

Speck, W. A. *Stability and Strife.* Cambridge: Harvard University Press, 1977.

———. *Tory and Whig: The Struggle in the Constituencies, 1701–1715.* London: St. Martin's Press, 1970.

Spellman, William. *The Latitudinarians and the Church of England, 1660–1695.* Athens, Ga.: University of Georgia Press, 1993.

Spurr, John. "'Latitudinarianism' and the Restoration Church." *Historical Journal* 31 (1988):61–82.

———. *The Restoration Church of England, 1646–1689.* New Haven: Yale University Press, 1991.

———. "Schism and the Restoration Church." *Journal of Ecclesiastical History* 41 (1990):408–24.

———. "'Virtue, Religion and Government': The Anglican Uses of Providence." In *The Politics of Religion in Restoration England.* Ed. Tim Harris, Paul Seaward, and Mark Goldie, 29–48. Oxford: Basil Blackwell, 1990.

Steer, Francis W. *Diocese of Chichester. A Catalogue of the Records of the Bishop, Archdeacons and Former Exempt Jurisdictions.* Chichester: West Sussex County Council, 1966.

Stephens, W. R. W. *Diocesan Histories: The South Saxon Diocese, Selsey-Chichester.* London: SPCK, 1881.

Stieg, Margaret. *Laud's Laboratory: The Diocese of Bath and Wells in the Early Seventeenth Century.* Lewisburg, Pa.: Bucknell University Press, 1982.

Straka, Gerald M. *Anglican Reactions to the Revolution of 1688.* Madison: State Historical Association of Wisconsin, 1962.

Stromberg, R. L. *English Religious Liberalism in the 18th Century.* Oxford: Oxford University Press, 1954.

Sykes, Norman. *Church and State in England in the XVIIIth Century.* Cambridge: Cambridge University Press, 1934.

———. "The Duke of Newcastle as Ecclesiastical Minister." *English Historical Review* 57 (1942):59–84.

———. *From Sheldon to Secker: Aspects of English Church History, 1660–1768.* Cambridge: Cambridge University Press, 1959.

Taylor, Stephen. "Church and State in England in the Mid-Eighteenth Century: The Newcastle Years, 1742–1762." Ph.D. diss., Cambridge University, 1987.

———. "The Government and the Episcopate in the Mid-Eighteeenth Century: The Uses of Patronage." In *Patronages et Clientelismes 1550–1750 (France, Angleterre, Espagne, Italie)*. Ed. Charles Giry-Deloison and Roger Mettam, 191–205. Centre d'Histoire de la Région du Nord et de L'Europe du Nordouest, 1995.

———. "Sir Robert Walpole, the Church of England, and the Quaker Tithe Bill of 1736." *Historical Journal* 28 (1985):51–77.

Tibble, Ronald. "Rev. Henry Snooke, M.A. (ca. 1657–1727), Vicar of Ringmer, Sussex 1690–1727." Unpublished paper in library of the Sussex Archaeological Society, Lewes, March 1987.

Tindal-Hart, Arthur. *The Country Counting House: The Story of Two Eighteenth-Century Clerical Account Books.* London: Phoenix House, 1962.

———. *The Curate's Lot: The Story of the Unbeneficed English Clergy.* London: J. Baker, 1970.

———. *The Eighteenth-Century Country Parson (circa 1689 to 1830).* Shrewsbury: Wilding, 1955.

Trevor-Roper, Hugh. "Toleration and Religion after 1688." In *From Persecution to Toleration: The Glorious Revolution in England.* Ed. Ole Peter Grell, Jonathan I. Israel, and Nicholas Tyacke, 389–408. Oxford: Clarendon Press, 1991.

Triffitt, John. "Believing and Belonging: Church Behaviour in Plymouth and Dartmouth, 1710–1730." In *Parish, Church and People: Local Studies in Lay Religion.* Ed. S. M. Wright, 179–202. London: Hutchinson, 1988.

Virgin, Peter. *The Church in an Age of Negligence: Ecclesiastical Structure and Problems of Church Reform, 1700–1840.* Cambridge: James Clark and Co., 1989.

von den Steinen, Karl. "The Fabric of an Interest: The First Duke of Dorset and Kentish and Sussex Politics, 1705–1765." Ph.D. diss., University of California at Los Angeles, 1969.

Walsh, John, and Stephen Taylor. "Introduction: The Church and Anglicanism in the 'Long' Eighteenth Century." In *The Church of England, ca. 1689–ca. 1833: From Toleration to Tractarianism.* Ed. John Walsh, Colin Haydon, and Stephen Taylor, 1–66. Cambridge: Cambridge University Press, 1993.

———, Colin Haydon, and Stephen Taylor, eds. *The Church of England, ca. 1689–ca. 1833: From Toleration to Tractarianism.* Cambridge: Cambridge University Press, 1993.

Wand, John W. C. *The High Church Schism: Four Lectures on the Nonjurors.* London: Faith Press, 1951.

Ward, W. R. *Georgian Oxford: University Politics in the Eighteenth Century.* Oxford: Oxford University Press, 1958.

Warne, Arthur. *Church and Society in Eighteenth-Century Devon.* New York: A. M. Kelley, 1969.

Warne, Heather M. *A Catalogue of the Frewen Archives*. Lewes: East Sussex Record Office Handbook Number 5, 1972.

Watson, William C. "The Late Stuart Reformation: Church and State in 'The First Age of Party.'" Ph.D. diss., University of California at Riverside, 1994.

Watts, Michael. *The Dissenters from the Reformation to the French Revolution*. Oxford: Clarendon Press, 1978.

Williams, Basil. "The Duke of Newcastle and the Election of 1734." *English Historical Review* 12 (1897):448–88.

———. *The Whig Supremacy, 1714–1760*. Oxford: Clarendon Press, 1939.

Willman, Robert. "The Origins of 'Whig' and 'Tory' in English Political Language." *Historical Journal* 12 (1974):247–64.

Winstanley, D. A. *The University of Cambridge in the Eighteenth Century*. Cambridge: Cambridge University Press, 1922.

Yates, Nigel. "A Kentish Clerical Dynasty: Curteis of Sevenoaks." *Archaeologia Cantiana* 108 (1990):1–9.

Jeffrey S. Chamberlain is an assistant professor of history and chair of the Department of History and Political Science at the College of St. Francis, Joliet, Illinois. He has published articles on social, intellectual, and political aspects of Anglicanism, including "Moralism, Justification, and the Controversy over Methodism," in the *Journal of Ecclesiastical History.* See also his homepage on the World Wide Web (http://www.stfrancis.edu/hi/chamberl.htm).